making

ESSAYS ON THE REVISED
LEAVING CERTIFICATE
ENGLISH SYLLABUS

making it new

ESSAYS ON THE REVISED LEAVING CERTIFICATE ENGLISH SYLLABUS

Edited by Margaret Kelleher

THE LILLIPUT PRESS
DUBLIN

First published 2000 by
THE LILLIPUT PRESS LTD
62-63 Sitric Road, Arbour Hill, Dublin 7, Ireland.
www.lilliputpress.ie

1 3 5 7 9 10 8 6 4 2

A CIP record for this title
is available from The British Library.

ISBN 1 901866 46 7

*The Lilliput Press gratefully acknowledges
the Association of Teachers of English (ATE),
whose generous support made this publication possible.*

Set in Adobe Garamond
Printed in Ireland by Betaprint of Clonshaugh, Dublin

Contents

Foreword

Great literature is simply language charged with meaning to the utmost possible degree.

Ezra Pound, *How to Read*

The essays in *Making It New* are directly focused on texts now being taught in second-level schools. Their publication in the first year of the *Leaving Certificate English 2001* programme is supported and welcomed by the Association of Teachers of English (ATE).

Change is evident in the cultural and economic life of Ireland, and education, which connects with both, is being recast. English as a subject was never ring-fenced—sometimes people read and write seriously only after leaving school—so for this book a broad readership beyond teachers and students can be envisaged. Parents and friends may find themselves reading *Making It New* for its essays on poetry, fiction, drama and film—works which are sure to become the currency of their children's lives.

Making It New is an important collaborative initiative for ATE and we are glad to have this occasion for co-operation between schools and universities. A largely unchanging and unchangeable syllabus tended to reduce curiosity—'dried the marrow from the bone'?—and restrict contact between learning institutions. But with more of our students becoming undergraduates, and with teachers encountering new texts and revisiting old ones in new contexts, we can look forward to a more enterprising, productive relationship.

KATE BATEMAN
Chairperson, Association of Teachers of English

Preface

The last major revision of the Leaving Certificate syllabus took place in the late 1960s. In the years that followed, countless students encountered Shakespearean plays, the nineteenth-century novel, the modern novel and, the most well-thumbed text of all, *Soundings*, Professor Augustine Martin's landmark poetry anthology—subtitled, as the discerning reader may remember, an 'interim anthology'. Thirty years would elapse, however, before a new revised Leaving Certificate English syllabus was introduced. In June 2001 the first students of the new curriculum will sit examinations on this course.

The revised curriculum comprises a wise combination of new and old: Shakespeare is still with us, as are novels by Charlotte Brontë, Charles Dickens and Thomas Hardy, and the poetry of Shakespeare, Keats, Dickinson and many others. But students will now also have the opportunity to encounter more recent writers—three decades *is* a long time to wait—with selections from the poetry of Seamus Heaney, Eavan Boland, Michael Longley, Elizabeth Bishop and Philip Larkin. In an ambitious development, namely the comparative study of texts, teachers may select from a long list of works: novels by Seamus Deane, Chinua Achebe and Jennifer Johnston; plays by Sophocles, Frank McGuinness and Arthur Miller; and, in one of the syllabus's most important innovations, films such as *The Third Man*, Kenneth Branagh's *Much Ado About Nothing* and Jim Sheridan's *My Left Foot*.

The opportunities extended by the new curriculum are manifold, but so also, especially in the early years of its introduction, are the challenges. These essays, written by members of English or Film departments in a range of third-level institutions, are therefore intended to aid teachers and students in their engagement with the prescribed texts, by identifying the contexts of specific works, suggesting new interpretations and opening up questions for debate. With such a choice available, the essays in this collection can cover only a selection of the texts featured in the new syllabus. Each of the four genres—poetry, fiction, drama and film—is featured, and lesser-known works are scrutinized alongside more familiar ones.

The essays in the poetry section feature the five poets (Bishop, Boland, Heaney, Larkin and Longley) introduced by the 2001 programme; each essay pays close attention to a number of the prescribed poems while also offering a suggestive overview of the poet's work. The fiction section provides new readings of two celebrated texts: Charlotte Brontë's *Jane Eyre* and Dickens's *Great Expectations*. These classic examples of the *bildungsroman* are accompanied by Seamus Deane's *Reading in the Dark*, a very recent variation on the theme of coming of age, and Chinua Achebe's *Things Fall Apart*, which presents a markedly different treatment of the individual's relationship with his community. The playwrights chosen for discussion, Shakespeare and Friel, are already well known to teachers and theatre audiences. The two Shakespeare essays included here invite readers to look again at the tragic vision; both are key interventions in seeking to restore an openness of interpretation to familiar texts. The essay on Brian Friel similarly provides a welcome opportunity to look afresh at recurring themes across the breadth of Friel's work.

Concluding the volume are three essays on film. Each of these essays emphasizes the importance of analyzing this medium in its own terms and each is an important guide for teachers and students towards such an analysis. Yet, given film's inclusion as part of a comparative study of texts, these essays also signal many such comparisons: the competing values of 'Shakespeare' and 'film' in adapting Shakespeare for the screen, the concepts of 'narrative' and 'genre' in relation to film and literary texts, and the development and mutation of film genres. This interplay between visual and written forms of communication is for students and teachers one of the most exciting areas of the new syllabus, and most expressive of the changing climate within which we teach and learn.

PREFACE

*

Sincere thanks are due to many people who have helped in envisaging and realizing this project. Above all, my thanks to the contributors to the volume, who responded generously to the initial invitation and graciously to pressing deadlines. All of my colleagues in the English department, NUI Maynooth, extended warm support; my thanks in particular to Professor Brian Cosgrove, Isabelle Cartwright and Karen Donovan, and also to Chris Morash for devising the glossary which accompanies the film section.

This volume was published with the generous support of the Association of Teachers of English; my thanks to chairperson Kate Bateman and to all of the members of the ATE Committee, in particular John Devitt and Kate O'Carroll, for key encouragement in the early stages of the project. In recent years, I have been most fortunate to encounter teachers' groups throughout the country and the idea for this collection stems from conversations with them; many thanks then to Colette Murphy (Cork), Clare Campion (Athlone), and Don Devine and Frank Farrelly (Waterford).

Finally, I wish to acknowledge, with gratitude, the role of Lilliput Press—publisher Antony Farrell and editor Brendan Barrington—in bringing this volume to fruition.

DR MARGARET KELLEHER
English Department, National University of Ireland, Maynooth

Cynicism, Idealism and 'The Importance of Elsewhere': The Poetry of Philip Larkin

CONRAD BRUNSTRÖM

The Man, the Myth, the Misanthrope

In his own lifetime, Philip Larkin achieved enough fame to be turned into an adjective. Even people who rarely read twentieth-century poetry have a sense of what is meant by the 'Larkinesque'. The 'Larkinesque' is not always a pleasant label, and it attracts at least as many hostile critics as it does sincere admirers. Often it seems to stand for a parochial, prejudiced and defeatist point of view. Of course, Larkin was not always Larkinesque himself, but then, Larkin had a strangely deliberate and theatrical attitude towards the poetic persona he chose to display to the world.

Philip Larkin was born in Coventry in 1922. After a rather dull and mildly repressive middle-class childhood, Larkin proceeded to Oxford, where he first discovered a distinctive literary milieu and cemented his sense of literary vocation. An early volume of poems, *The North Ship*, was published in 1945 and was almost totally ignored by the critics. Larkin eventually became a librarian, a vocation which he often mocked, but which he pursued with a strange assiduity and dedication. He spent a number of formative years in Belfast, working at the library at Queens University Belfast, writing some of his finest early poetry. In the mid-fifties Larkin arrived at the University of Hull, where he would continue to work (in a senior administrative capacity) for the remainder of his life. His second volume of poems, *The Less Deceived* (1955), brought him literary fame; his third, *The Whitsun Weddings* (1964), considerably consolidated and enhanced his reputation; and his fourth, *High Windows* (1974), turned him into something of a legend. When he died, in 1985, he was the most famous poet in England.

In many ways Larkin was the very antithesis of the 'famous man of letters'. He did not spend his days giving readings and lectures, and he never lived in London. Instead, Larkin was happy to associate himself with Hull, taking a defiant pride in the unfashionable awkwardness of the place. Hull is a long way from Leeds, without being anywhere near Nottingham. Until the bridge over the Humber was built in the early 1980s, the city was inaccessible from the south (except by ferry) and was therefore extremely difficult to get to from London. About the only claim to distinction Hull enjoys is the fact that it is the largest English city never to have had a soccer team in the premier league.

Much controversy was generated in 1993 with the publication of Larkin's correspondence around the same time as a lengthy biography by Andrew Motion (recently appointed British poet laureate). These two publications appeared to reveal Larkin not only as a grumpy reactionary but as (periodically) a racist, a misogynist, a foul-mouthed lover of pornography—all in all, an unsavoury misanthrope.

The *Real* Larkin?

Why then should anyone read Larkin today? Why especially should anyone who is not English, not male, and not a miserable old cynic make time to absorb such an unsympathetically narrow world view? His status for the Irish reader is especially problematic. It is true that he wrote many of his most important poems while in Belfast, but far too often he appears to endorse a version of 'Little Englandism' that many readers find tiresome and off-putting.

One of Larkin's most unexpected champions is Seamus Heaney, whose profile is about as opposed to Larkin's as can be imagined. Without Heaney's backing, it is hard to imagine how Larkin could appear on the Irish Leaving Certificate syllabus. In several key critical essays, Heaney explains that Larkin's poetry is worth reading because it is full of 'epiphanies'—surprising and beautiful moments of sudden revelation. Describing Larkin in one of his own poems as 'A nine-to-five man who had seen poetry'[1] (although Larkin worked much longer hours than that), Heaney attempted to represent Larkin as someone whose truest instincts were romantic and transcendent, whose petty-bourgeois miserliness was nothing more than a foil, a way of casting 'epiphanies' in sharper relief. In many ways, Heaney's Larkin has proved a valuable corrective vision, since many English critics have been too happy to view 'the Hermit of Hull' as a plodding interpreter of the mundane and depressive.

The poems chosen for the Leaving Certificate syllabus serve to bolster the Heaney view of Larkin as an essentially romantic poet, interested in transient but compelling beauties. Many of these poems are discussed in Heaney's influential essay 'The Main of Light' (1988). Heaney there speaks admiringly of another of Larkin's poems, 'High Windows', which concludes with the lines:

... And immediately

Rather than words comes the thought of high windows:
The sun-comprehending glass,
And beyond it, the deep blue air, that shows
Nothing, and is nowhere, and is endless.[2]

Heaney decides that 'such poems spring from the deepest strata of Larkin's poetic self'.[3] For Heaney, the most 'authentic' Larkin poems start from somewhere very commonplace, and build towards a sense of the immense and infinite.[4] 'High Windows' is a 'romantic' poem in a very specific sense: it seeks to indicate the inexpressible, to appeal to that which cannot be described but which can be (imperfectly) apprehended. Characteristically, Larkin begins this poem with some very blunt and apparently unromantic observations on the sexual freedoms enjoyed by a younger generation. From a specific form of sexual liberation, Larkin moves to a far more abstract version of freedom, a 'deep blue' airy freedom from the defining shapes of knowable existence.

Larkin, in the same year, treated the same theme of sexual liberation in far more comic and rhythmic terms in his poem 'Annus Mirabilis', in which he makes fun of the whole idea of 'the sixties' as a distinct era and arena of uninhibited freedoms. It is worthwhile reading poems such as 'Annus Mirabilis simply for the sake of 'balance', since the poet I am calling the 'Leaving Cert. Larkin' offers little of Larkin the comic role-player or the bleak existentialist. The Leaving Certificate selection does not offer such famously cynical and/or bleak pieces as 'This Be the Verse' or 'A Study of Reading Habits' or 'Aubade'. In fact, what is on offer for the Leaving Certificate emerges as something of a 'corrective' Larkin. I shall be looking briefly at some of the poems chosen for the Leaving Certificate, as well as suggesting other poems, not on the syllabus, that offer illuminating points of comparison.

The Poetry of Philip Larkin

Many of Larkin's earliest poems have a rural setting. Stylistically these verses owe much to the influence of W.B. Yeats, Dylan Thomas and Vernon Watkins (a disciple of Yeats, briefly popular in the 1940s). Looking at the first stanza of the early 'Wedding-Wind' we can see an expression of imprecise energies, a blending of human and elemental forces. This is a poem about sex, sex as breathless anticipation and as rush of affirmative energy. Larkin would often write about sex in later decades, but usually in terms of privation, disappointment, and resignation. 'Wedding-Wind' on the other hand describes the merging sexual energies within larger cosmic forces in a far more affirmative way:

> The wind blew all my wedding-day,
> And my wedding-night was the night of the high wind;
> And a stable door was banging, again and again,
> That he must go and shut it, leaving me
> Stupid in candlelight, hearing rain, ...

This early poem attempts certain things that the 'mature' Larkin would never undertake. For one thing, the poem is 'narrated' by a female voice. Whereas Larkin would often write compassionately and sensitivity *about* women, he would not in later poems attempt to speak in their voices. This is also a poem that seems to be set in the past—or in a present that would have seemed archaic to the poem's contemporary readers.

The poem also illustrates Larkin's abiding facility with rhyme. Most of Larkin's poems employ rhyme to some extent, although many of his poems do not always seem to rhyme unless read out loud. Larkin was a master of assonance and consonance, half rhymes, juxtaposed 'chimes' that create echoes of association in ways that are experienced only half-consciously by most readers. He experimented throughout his career with varied rhyme schemes, elaborating surprising ways in which end-words can correspond to create a fertile variety of belated and unexpected connections between key ideas and images.

The nostalgic aspect of Larkin's muse is especially well represented in the Leaving Certificate selection. 'MCMXIV' is a poem about the outbreak of the First World War. Presenting the title of the poem in roman numerals gives the impression of chiselled lettering on a war memorial. This poem is not, however, a war memorial but a 'pre-war' memorial. What is being memorialized in this poem is a *society* on the verge of being destroyed by the greatest conflict the world had ever seen. Larkin describes long queues of volunteers, totally unaware of the industrial scale of the slaughter that awaits them. This is an elegy to an England blissfully innocent of twentieth-century nightmares, although typically the poem's seriousness is gently undercut by Larkin's wistful reference to the pubs being 'wide open all day'—a reference to the fact that the First World War (among other horrors) saw the imposition of Britain's draconian licensing laws.

> Never such innocence,
> Never before or since,
> As changed itself to past
> Without a word — the men
> Leaving the gardens tidy,
> The thousands of marriages
> Lasting a little while longer:
> Never such innocence again.

The effect of this poem is to freeze a moment, to find strange beauty in the passing of that moment and then to look back with a sense of pity and wonderment. There is no main verb in this poem—all four stanzas add up to one incomplete sentence. Without a main verb there can be no sense of development or progression. The poem's grammatical incompletion registers a sense of the incompletion of these young volunteers: their lives will lack the shape or logic of a complete or coherent sentence.

'MCMXIV' also, inevitably, reminds the reader of the long decline of British imperial power. Larkin is an important post-imperial (if not post-colonial) poet. Just as those interested in the crises of British imperialism often turn to the work of Rudyard Kipling (an avid but traumatized imperialist), so anyone interested in narratives of British decline and uncertainty in the decades following the Second World War (an issue of political concern to anyone in Ireland) should find instructive reading in Larkin. Larkin's relationship with England may well have been crucially defined *by* Ireland, specifically by his time in Belfast. A poem such as 'The Importance of Elsewhere' makes Larkin's Irish sojourn seem very formative. Larkin claims to have needed an 'elsewhere' to 'underwrite' his existence. Without Ireland, Larkin's England could not have existed. The idea of exile as an indispensable phase of constructed Irishness is so familiar that it is perhaps startling to read of someone treating Ireland itself as a place of exile. Perhaps the poem is a reminder of the constructed 'oppositional' nature of all national identities.

However 'constructed' Larkin's Englishness may have been, it was of urgent concern to him. Without a sense of commitment to place, Larkin believed, selfish rootless arrogance takes hold. One of his most scornful poems on this theme is called 'Naturally the Foundation will Bear Your Expenses'. This poem is written from the intentionally unsympathetic perspective of an academic, flying off to give a paper in Bombay, despising ordinary people for being moved by the Remembrance Commemorations. Literally above it all, the academic believes that he belongs to an international élite and that he is entitled to despise all local affections. One does not have to be appreciative of specifically 'English' nationalism to become suspicious, after reading this poem, of attempts by intellectuals to denigrate 'national identity' (whatever that national identity may be).

In the context of his published poetry, Larkin's conservatism is never smug or triumphalist; it is invariably either bitter or elegaic. Indeed, despite Larkin's stated right-wing political views, there is even something (accidentally) Marxist about many of his reflections on contemporary industrial capitalism (an idea briefly explored by Stephen Regan[5]). Larkin's poetry is distressed by a world in which commodities have replaced relationships, in which the acquisition of *things* takes on an urgency that distracts people from other relationships. Poems such as 'Here', 'The Large Cool Store', 'Afternoons', 'Going Going' and 'Money' are worth reading in terms of the ways in which Larkin shows how the modern world fuels misplaced or misdirected desire. Larkin could not or would not imagine any trajectory of development that would heal society in the future, so he sought an uncertain refuge in the past. He is at his most optimistic therefore when most nostalgic, specifically when treating 'popular rituals', comings together that have survived the individualizing and estranging effects of an industrialized modernity. 'To the Sea' and 'Show Saturday' are important poems from this perspective.

At the same time, Larkin is painfully aware of the distortions of nostalgia, the way in which easy emotion smudges and confuses the past to suit the emotional needs of succeeding generations. 'An Arundel Tomb' describes the spectacle of a medieval monument inside Chichester Cathedral in the south of England. The tomb is capped by statues of the Earl of Arundel and his lady wife, hands touchingly clasped.

Time has transfigured them into
Untruth. The stone fidelity
They hardly meant has come to be
Their final blazon, and to prove
Our almost-instinct almost true:
What will survive of us is love.

This final stanza of 'The Arundel Tomb' is often misread, even by literary critics. The 'almost-instinct almost true' does not demonstrate that love lasts for all eternity, but only that love can *seem* to last. The fact 'love' does not quite rhyme with 'prove' is illustrative of this deceptive seeming. (Always, when reading Larkin, we must consider the strength or weakness of rhyming words: whether they rhyme exactly, or whether assonance or consonance is used to evoke a fainter echo. The strength of the rhyme always affects the sense of the poem.) The poem remarks on how the 'altered' people (a pun on 'altar') have long since been ignorant of the meaning of the Latin inscription on the tomb, and are increasingly reading their own meanings anachronistically into the spectacle. 'They would not think to lie so long' (another pun) says the poem, describing how meaning has become detached from either the artist or the occupants of the tomb. Time has told a lie on behalf of this couple and it has told it very well. The poem is full of images of blurring and of vagueness; we can imagine the contours of meaning becoming smoothed over time, just as the edges and the details of the sculpture have become smooth and imprecise. In the meantime, form is that which survives content—form meaning a certain 'attitude' that suggests (broadly) an inspirational relationship. In time, perhaps, this very form will have become so anachronistic and distant that observers will not be able to interpret it at all. Perhaps the form of poetry similarly survives whatever content it may hope to convey.

Reading more widely in Larkin, we discover an aggressively secular poet who was nonetheless fascinated by the forms and rituals of religious belief. A poem such as 'Water' imagines a religion that is all form and no content: a faith in reflections and refractions, a delight in the polymorphic possibilities of faith, as opposed to faith in any one stable thing. 'Church Going', on the other hand, is about a single irreligious visitor looking into an abandoned church and surveying the interior with a mixture of embarrassment and fascination, drawn to the place but unable to account for exactly what it is he wants from it. The visitor will only enter a church if he is sure it is absolutely empty and he is certain that he will not be asked to 'join in' anything or contribute to anything (or, for that matter have anything 'explained' to him). This poem seems determined to believe that religion as we know it is dying a slow death and already belongs to 'the past'. The poem concludes, however, with an attempt to understand the persistence of faith, and the needs to which religions speak:

> A serious house on serious earth it is,
> In whose blent air all our compulsions meet,
> Are recognised, and robed as destinies.
> And that much never can be obsolete,
> Since someone will forever be surprising
> A hunger in himself to be more serious,
> And gravitating with it to this ground,
> Which, he once heard, was proper to grow wise in,
> If only that so many dead lie round.

The sombre resonance of this closing stanza is reinforced by its very slowness. Punctuation forces the reader to pause at the end of almost every line. An irreligious narrator has become 'liturgical' almost in spite of himself. The 'hunger' to be 'more serious' indicates that Larkin's rejection of religion is a troubled rather than a libertarian position. Larkin's attitude to God is sometimes reminiscent of that of Samuel Beckett, who when asked what he thought about God is supposed to have replied: 'He doesn't exist—the bastard!' God may be absent from Larkin's cosmos, but has left behind a God-shaped hole.

Poems like 'Church Going', read in isolation, can give us the inaccurate idea that Larkin believed that some form of religion was desirable and necessary. It is instructive to compare such a poem with his late masterpiece 'Aubade'—published as a sort of gloomy Christmas card in the *Times Literary Supplement* in December 1977. 'Aubade' describes religion as a 'vast moth-eaten musical brocade', offering nothing ennobling whatsoever about the facts of dying and declaring that 'Death is no different whined at than withstood'. It is also significant that although Heaney admired the power of this poem, he disapproved of its sentiment, saying:

The poem does not hold the lyre up in the face of the gods of the under-world; it does not make the Orphic effort to haul life back up the slope against all the odds. For all its heart-breaking truths and beauties, 'Aubade' reneges on what Yeats called the 'spiritual intellect's great work'.[6]

Heaney admits that 'Aubade' defies death in the rhythmic reso-nance of its construction, but clearly he believes that poetry has a responsibility to be affirmative at the level of content as well as form. You will not find 'Aubade' on the Leaving Certificate shortlist, but for a full appreciation of the logical extremity of Larkin's most persistent obsession it is, in a far more important sense, required reading.

Larkin is admired and blamed in roughly equal measure for his fascination with death. A brooding on mortality is in evi-dence even in his earliest poems. A 'middle-period' poem like 'Ambulances' makes some obvious points about the ubiquity (some would say 'democracy') of our impending annihilations. In this poem, the dead cannot speak to the living, nor can the living pity the dead. When people shake their heads at the covered stretchers emerging from a house, they pity their *own* mortality, not a lifeless corpse which is now beyond pity of any kind.

> Closed like confessionals, they thread
> Loud noons of cities, giving back
> None of the glances they absorb.
> Light glossy grey, arms on a plaque,
> They come to rest at any kerb:
> All streets in time are visited.

Since medieval times, we have been used to the emblem of a skeletal figure in a black cloak wielding a savage-looking scythe to explain the solemn inevitability and ubiquity of death. Larkin (at least the mature Larkin) resolutely refused to deploy the ready-made imagery of mythological convention (or 'hold the lyre up in the face of the gods of the underworld' as Heaney would say). The ambulance is turned into a far more relevant 'symbol' (or perhaps synecdoche) of death and dying in the modern world. A later poem on a similar theme, 'The Building', which describes hospital visiting, will not even use the word 'ambulances': they are spoken of, euphemistically, as 'not taxis'.

Far less obviously depressive is 'The Trees'. Although the overt claim of this poem is that trees offer a deceptive impression of constant renewal, that they are as mortal as we are, it is the final two lines of the poem that sing in the memory:

> Last year is dead, they seem to say,
> Begin afresh, afresh, afresh.

The 'meaning' (that is, the logic of the narrator's stated views) in the poem and its 'effect' are almost completely at odds. Like 'An

Arundel Tomb', this poem is often and easily read as a celebration of endurance and renewal. The whole poem pivots around the single word 'seem'. If there appears to be some conflict between the belief that trees are no guarantors of immortality and the closing reflection that trees are very good at playing emblems of endless renewal, we should not be forced to attempt to resolve this conflict. Rather than trying to prove that the poem is 'really' idealistic or 'really' cynical, it is more appropriate to keep the conflict between such possibilities alive in the course of our reading.

Like 'Church Going' and 'An Arundel Tomb', this poem contains a concluding stanza that sounds considerably more spiritually affirmative and profound than the preceding stanzas of the poem. The poems on the Leaving Certificate reveal a poet whose instincts seem far more persuasive than his convictions. In his late poem 'The Explosion', Larkin comes to terms with the story of a tragic mining disaster, and the way in which so many sudden casualties affect a community:

> Wives saw men of the explosion
>
> Larger than in life they managed —
> Gold as on a coin, or walking
> Somehow from the sun towards them,
>
> One showing the eggs unbroken.

This strangely affirmative poem is brilliantly discussed by the critic Andrew Swarbrick in terms which show how technical ingenuity can define and yet defamiliarize our experience of an event:

... the manipulation of tenses (from the continuous present of the pastor's quoted words to the past 'It was said' and 'Wives saw men', and forward to the present participles of the momentary vision) creates the syntactical logic by which men walk 'Somehow from the sun' at the very moment it has 'dimmed' for the underground explosion. The effect of this is quite miraculously to annihilate the moment of death not by meekly editing it out of the poem, but by building it in to what survives that moment of death. The men are unbroken like the eggs. They have simply passed 'Through the tall gates standing open'.[7]

What Swarbrick is saying is that Larkin 'defies' death, not by ignoring it but by playing games, grammatically, with time. The moment of extinction seems to resonate in an eternity that disrupts the inexorable flow of life and death. The mixture of present and past tenses in the poem reminds us of the unusual grammar of 'MCMXIV', which is equally about freezing a particular moment. Larkin had something of a fascination with photography, and the blinding flash of the explosion has almost the feel of a camera flash, preserving in the very instant that it destroys.[8]

Despite the hardening of Larkin's public pose of mundane defeatism, his final infrequent poems written from 1970 onwards show an increasing tendency to 'imagism', a delight in the juxtaposition of images for their own sake. Larkin did not always insist on interpreting his experiences—sometimes he was apparently content just to represent a series of impressions. A poem like 'Cut Grass' is admired more for its effect than for its 'meaning'. Larkin himself described this poem (one of Heaney's favourites) as 'pointless crap', arguing that it was just 'a succession of images'.[9] Needless to say, we do not have to take Larkin's savage self-criticism too seriously. It is well worth arguing that poems develop a self-sustaining existence that is more important than whatever their creators think of them. However, Larkin's own unhappiness with the poem probably indicates that he felt that the poem was lacking in critical intelligence, that it failed to offer any thoughtful commentary on an experience.

Perhaps Larkin's most celebrated poem is 'The Whitsun Weddings', which describes a train journey from North to South, arriving finally in London. In the 1950s, when the poem was written, many English weddings tended to cluster around the Whitsun weekend, and many honeymoons still took off by train. Larkin was especially drawn to train travel as a way of developing a poetic perspective. 'The Whitsun Weddings' is his most famous 'train' poem, but also important are 'Here', 'Dockery and Son' and 'Not the Place's Fault'. These poems (most urgently 'Dockery and Son') use train travel to evoke a sense of destiny. Railway lines are fixed—the traveller is powerless to alter his or her destination. There may be 'points' in one's life where it might appear that life-defining choices have been made, but the impression that we get from Larkin's life on the rails is that the ticket has been purchased well in advance, certainly long before the journey began and the destination is non-exchangeable.

'The Whitsun Weddings' provides a collection of several of Larkin's most persistent themes: solitude, destiny and ritual. Like a train journey, its pace is variable. It pauses to register stations, and it leaps ahead for certain stretches of the journey. The Larkin persona that governs this poem is an observer, not a participant. People appear to him in neat progression, are summed up, simplified and then discarded. This Larkin persona is amused by the vulgarity of the rituals of these weddings, but as the train fills up with happy couples, his mood changes. Initially, Larkin appears to be making fun of the wedding parties, denying them any individuality and sketching them impressionistically in terms of their common salient features. Fathers, mothers, uncles, bridesmaids, all seem to be of the same type, repeating the same lines and gestures from station to station. The Larkin persona makes his observations from behind thick protective glass, and he is not apparently forced to interact with any of the couples once they have boarded the train. Eventually, the train reaches London, and as it does so, a sense of imaginative possibility accelerates with it:

> There we were aimed. And as we raced across
>   Bright knots of rail
> Past standing Pullmans, walls of blackened moss
> Came close, and it was nearly done, this frail
> Travelling coincidence; and what it held
> Stood ready to be loosed with all the power
> That being changed can give. We slowed again,
> And as the tightened brakes took hold, there swelled
> A sense of falling, like an arrow-shower
> Sent out of sight, somewhere becoming rain.

All these weddings are about to be 'released' into a large railway station (King's Cross). The effect of the ending of the poem is of energy, gathered, stored and then expressed—set free. Larkin was fascinated by marriage as an institution which he chose not personally to endorse. As a commitment it appeared to him to be nothing less than super-human. This is not to say that Larkin was anti-romantic, and he was certainly not under-sexed. (A number of his poems give the mistaken impression that Larkin lived in a state of frustrated celibacy.) However, he was fascinated by *other* people's enduring and persistent desire to be changed. It is also interesting that Larkin could be idealistic about a strange sort of 'mass' wedding ceremony (in 'The Whitsun Weddings') but was invariably cynical about individual marriages (for example, in a poem such as 'Self's the Man').

Conclusion
The choice of poems for the Irish Leaving Certificate, together with (and probably inspired by) Heaney's influential interpreta-

tion of Larkin, has produced a Larkin radically different from the figure popularly imagined in England. In England Larkin is imagined as a misanthropic realist; in Ireland he is more likely to be constructed as a brilliant romanticist. Both of these Larkins are one-sided and inadequate. The 'Irish' Larkin at least admits the mundane, downbeat aspects of Larkin's work, only arguing that his idealism ultimately 'transcends' his depressive environment.

However, the complex reality of Larkin's achievement is not ultimately about 'transcendence' but about the quality of the conflict between hope and despair. The tension between cynicism and idealism is never resolved in Larkin's poems. The cynicism sharpens the idealism, and the idealism sharpens the cynicism: beauty is all the more poignant for emerging from unpromising circumstances, and cynicism is all the more bitter for persisting in a world in which visions are possible. Larkin is a poet who sees sudden beauties in dreary situations, and who sees the sordid and the embarrassing in the midst of the most solemn and serious occasions. It is this moving back and forth, this 'oscillation', that makes Larkin of such enduring interest as a poet.

Bibliography

Philip Larkin, *Collected Poems*, ed. Anthony Thwaite (London: Faber & Faber, 1988).

Philip Larkin, *Selected Letters*, ed. Anthony Thwaite (London: Faber & Faber, 1993).

Seamus Heaney, 'Englands of the Mind', in *Preoccupations: Selected Prose, 1968-78* (London: Faber & Faber, 1980).

Seamus Heaney, 'Joy or Night', in *The Redress of Poetry* (London: Faber & Faber, 1985).

Seamus Heaney, 'The Main of Light', in *The Government of the Tongue* (London: Faber & Faber, 1988).

Andrew Motion, *Philip Larkin: A Writer's Life* (London: Faber & Faber, 1993).

Stephen Regan, *Philip Larkin* (Houndmills: Macmillan, 1992).

Andrew Swarbick, *Out of Reach: The Poetry of Philip Larkin* (Houndmills: Macmillan, 1995).

Notes

1. 'The Journey Back', in *Seeing Things* (1991).

2. All quotations from Larkin are taken from Philip Larkin, *Collected Poems*, ed. Anthony Thwaite.

3. 'The Main of Light', p. 20.

4. It is unclear whether Heaney was aware that Larkin had seriously considered concluding this poem with the hanging line 'And fucking piss' (Andrew Motion, *Philip Larkin: A Writer's Life*, p. 355). Of course, we are quite justified in treating the final published poem in complete isolation, but it is interesting to consider the implications of Larkin's repeated need to 'vandalize' his own tendencies towards sublime abstraction. Meanwhile, Heaney's poem 'The Mud Vision' (published in *The Haw Lantern*, [1987]) may well have been influenced by his own sense of what Larkin was 'really' about.

5. Stephen Regan, *Philip Larkin*, pp. 137-8.

6. Seamus Heaney, 'Joy or Night', p. 158.

7. Andrew Swarbrick, *Out of Reach: The Poetry of Philip Larkin*, pp. 141-51.

8. In an earlier poem, 'Lines on a Young Lady's Photograph Album', Larkin seems to cherish the very imperfection of photography, the elements that elude control and composition:

> ... o, photography! as no art is,
> Faithful and disappointing! that records
> Dull days as dull, and hold-it smiles as frauds,
> And will not censor blemishes.

9. Andrew Motion, *Philip Larkin: A Writer's Life*, p. 411.

'My Mother's Tongue':
The Poetry of Eavan Boland

LUCY COLLINS

The poetry of Eavan Boland has acquired a significant readership and considerable critical attention since the publication of her first collection in 1967. Her work occupies a pivotal position in contemporary Irish women's writing. It is remarkable not only for its own particular qualities but also for the questions that it raises about the writing and reception of poetry in this country. Boland draws the private and the public into close proximity and explores the complex and often controversial relationship between them. The poems chosen for the new Leaving Certificate syllabus cover the most enduring of the poet's themes and concerns and display her acknowledged formal talents. It is important, therefore, to consider some of the points of intersection between these poems while also exploring the developments they may suggest in her work as a whole.

An important factor in placing Boland among the most prominent of Irish poets now writing is the way in which she herself has framed her poetry. Her willingness to discuss the background to her work helps to make it accessible to the reader. Likewise, by developing an explicit stance on matters of literary and cultural importance, she has ensured that her poetry is read widely and attentively. Boland is particularly interested in the role of the female poet and the representation of female experience in poetry, and in the history of the Irish poetic tradition. These concerns are evident in the title of her prose work *Object Lessons: The Life of the Woman and the Poet in Our Time* (1995), which provides a number of insights into the particular situation out of which Boland writes. In combining criticism with autobiography she affirms the public importance of these questions and explores their relation to her own personal experience. She also blurs the boundary between collective and individual experience.

Despite the usefulness of Boland's critical writings to serious readers of her poetry, some questioning of the ideas and interpretations which the poet herself puts forward is also necessary. In addition, it is important to assess the changes that have taken place in Irish society and in Boland's own thinking in recent years. Over-reliance on the poet's own commentary may blind us to the highly specific nature of many of its assumptions. In constructing a critical frame for her poetry, Boland risks dominating independent responses and guiding interpretation too closely. Although prose offers her a more direct way of addressing complex issues than poetry would normally allow, the interaction between these two forms of writing alters our perception of each significantly.

Changing cultural contexts play a role in our evaluation of the range of poems offered by the new syllabus. Three of Boland's eight collections are represented here, and seven of the ten poems were first published in book form between 1990 and 1994.[1] Broadly speaking, then, these poems are the product of a mature intellect and a tested experience. A number of them also re-examine or build upon earlier themes, suggesting a degree of continuity in Boland's work and a persistent political and social engagement. A dominant feature is the situating of the personal in a wider context, not simply in fulfilment of a search for satisfying parallels to one's own life, but because of a desire to close the gap between private and public. This gap will have particular relevance when examining the issue of gender in relation to this poet's work, since it is a gap often characterized by the tensions between the detailed stories of everyday life and the larger historical narratives with their emphasis on political or national concerns.

'Broken Images': Early Developments in Theme and Form

Private and public contexts combine in especially direct ways in Boland's first two collections. Some critics have found fault with the precocious achievement of her first book, *New Territory* (1967)—much of which was written during her undergraduate years—because of its conformity and the poet herself has virtually repudiated it for its over-emphasis on form and for its lack of warmth.[2] 'Athene's Song', the opening poem of *New Territory*, begins with a powerful evocation of Athene springing fully armed from the head of her father, and the young Boland's relationship to the tradition from which she herself sprung is clearly an uncritical one. Her interest in Yeats is evident at this early stage in her career, as are her formal skills. Less clear is any sense of originality or relaxed authority.

Her second collection, *The War Horse* (1975), is more subtle in tone and flexible in syntax, and its poems are attentive to Ireland's political climate. In 1974, the year before this volume was published, the crisis in Northern Ireland reached a climax with the workers' strike and the bombing of Dublin. The poem 'Child of Our Time' refers to a photograph of the body of a young child being lifted from the wreckage of a bomb-blast and indicts the adult world that produces such shocking violence. The 'discord' which the poet registers here is not between participants in the political conflict but instead reflects an adult world that has failed in its responsibility towards society's most vulnerable members.

31

For Boland the process of writing is an important part of the attempt to draw meaning from this atrocity. Her poem becomes the site where creation and destruction meet:

> Yesterday I knew no lullaby
> But you have taught me overnight to order
> This song, which takes from your final cry
> Its tune, from your unreasoned end its reason ...

The War Horse is a collection permeated by the violation which this poem records. It inaugurates a new relationship between the poet and her subject-matter, placing the emerging violence of the time against a domestic backdrop through the use of a reflective, personal voice. The title poem exemplifies the subtlety of Boland's political engagement at this point. The poem simultaneously evokes both the volatility of the situation in the north and its remoteness from everyday life south of the border. The oblique reference to the Trojan horse is suggestive of the subtle incursion of violence into an unsuspecting city and sustains the feeling of fear underlying the poem. Likened to a rumour of war, the threat which the horse represents is felt privately by the poet and named by her in the poem. Boland here manages to stress the immediacy of fear alongside a sense of herself as a distant watcher, as one interpreting from within the domestic situation rather than acting in the world outside. Later, she would recognize this distance as a problematic one, writing: 'The poem had drawn me easily into the charm and strength of an apparently public stance.'[3] Nevertheless, this engagement with the political marked a productive change of focus within the constraints of a carefully crafted work. The poem is divided into couplets, but the mimicry of the galloping horse which can be heard here is altered by the slippage of irregular sentences:

I lift the window, watch the ambling feather
Of hock and fetlock, loosed from its daily tether

In the tinker camp on the Enniskerry Road,
Pass, his breath hissing, his snuffling head

Down. He is gone. No great harm is done.

This is an animal out of control, unpredictable; he stumbles twice
and the repetition of that word shows language stumbling with
him. The poem suggests the cyclical nature of violence, that the
threat of it may never truly pass. The Yeatsian cadences of the
conclusion shift economically from present to past '… recalling
days//Of burned countryside, illicit braid:/A cause ruined before,
a world betrayed'.

The invocation of history, as at the climax of this poem,
proves to be of increasing importance for Boland. 'The Famine
Road' employs shifting historical perspectives that operate in
subtle and original ways. The chief narrative strand of the poem
relates to the building of famine roads, a futile task necessitated
by the notion that food must be earned, not simply given away.
Interspersing these stanzas is the story of a woman learning that
she is unable to bear children. The equation of famine with the
feminine is not a new practice but the deftness with which
Boland moves between narratives is remarkable, especially in only
the second collection from a young poet.

The poem enacts the intersection of historical and personal,
of public and private worlds. It also shows the ways in which language can be shaped to impart both descriptive and rhetorical
power. The two narratives have strong male elements, from the
voice of Trevelyan and the letter of Colonel Jones to the insistent
voice of the doctor which at intervals cuts into the account of history. Even within a single historical setting there are crucial shifts
of perspective; the victims of the famine themselves watch one

another, a bleak reminder of the competition for survival. The unnamed woman comes into direct focus at the close:

> *Barren, never to know the load*
> *of his child in you, what is your body*
> *now if not a famine road?*

The childless woman momentarily becomes a thing without meaning, like the road going nowhere without purpose and without future.[4] The poem draws attention to the existence of different perspectives within history and to the silences contained within the official narrative of the past. By examining explicit parallels between private and public here Boland introduces an historical narrative into emotional territory.

Experience and Representation: Towards *Outside History*

Although Boland's third collection, *In Her Own Image* (1980), is not represented on the new syllabus, it is nonetheless worth noting the significance of her move in this volume towards an outspoken and subversive position. As the title suggests, a break with tradition is enacted here and a radical remaking of the female embarked upon, both through new forms of poetic representation and through the evocation of an interior world which had to this point remained hidden in Boland's poetry. For the first and only time in her career, Boland represents the immediacy of female physicality in such poems as 'Anorexic', 'Mastectomy' and 'Menses'. The voice in which they are spoken is resonant with the violence of their themes; their fast pace and angry tones reflect the distortion of the female body in language. Many of the reviews of *In Her Own Image* were hostile and some critics then termed the poems 'unpleasant' and even 'offensive'.

By contrast with *In Her Own Image*, much of Boland's later work virtually ignores the innovative potential of form. Boland explains that this is a conscious strategy: 'The more primitive a

truth gets, the more difficult it gets to formalize, and the real rad-
icalism for me has been to bring the sophisticated apparatus of
poetry nearer to the less easily articulated human experience.'[5] It is
clear, though, that the anger of two decades ago is the sublimated
force behind even the most subdued of the subsequent poems.

The split between the familiar image and the painful reality, a
split bravely explored in Boland's early poems of private grief,
would henceforth remain central to her poetic project. In *Night
Feed* (1982) the domestic interior becomes both the title of a
sequence and central among her themes;[6] in *The Journey*, published the same year, the relationship between this private realm
and the public space of history and tradition begins to be inter-
rogated. Poems such as 'Outside History', from the 1990 collection of the same name, confront the marginalization of the female
implicitly by exploring her distance from events of acknowledged
importance. It is worth noting briefly at this point the way in
which Boland uses ideas and images of space and time in order to
chart this distance. The stars 'whose light happened//thousands
of years before/our pain did' are remote and suggestive of the separation of present and past, of our inability to change what has
already happened ('And we are too late. We are always too late'),
yet the poem also affirms the astonishing proximity of past and
present ('we kneel beside them, whisper in their ear'). 'Outside
History' does not explicitly represent the female, however, and is
more subtle in its use of collective positions and shared assumptions than much of Boland's earlier work.

The past is a recurring preoccupation for Boland. She detects
a moral difference between the male-determined histories and the
kind of history which women will write. Women, as they move
from being objects within poems to being authors of poems themselves, raise, according to Boland, 'questions of identity, issues of
poetic motive and ethical direction'.[7] As the poem 'Outside History' has suggested, the process of connecting with something

beyond the self is crucial. The notion that women stress connection with others as a formative part of their identity is therefore relevant not only to their writing of history but to their creation of accessible imaginative worlds, such as those which the poet herself evokes. This issue has specific personal resonance for Boland. Her decision to turn away from an academic career and to make marriage and motherhood her priority charts a movement to the periphery of artistic society. Boland herself sees this as a physical, as well as an intellectual, transition and in *Object Lessons* dwells on the contrast between suburban and city life for the writer. In this way the margin becomes her centre; her private world the material for public poetry.

Inheriting Women's History: Boland in the 1990s

The private space not only suggests a marginal position in history but also alerts us to the fact that much of the past is ultimately unknowable. 'The Black Lace Fan My Mother Gave Me' depicts a moment in the lives of the poet's parents, and she acknowledges its fugitive nature: 'no way now to know what happened then'. The improvisation she suggests is her own as well as the reader's, as both venture into histories which cannot pretend to certainty. Boland returns to this theme again and again, most memorably perhaps in 'Lava Cameo' from *In a Time of Violence* (1994), where the story 'is not a story,/more a rumour or a folk memory,/something thrown out once in a random conversation'. Her attention to family history signals a concern with consequences and with continuity which is evidenced in more complex ways by her constant doubling back on the past to read and re-read it for new meanings. These concerns are also raised by Boland's use of story, in the form of personal anecdote and especially in the form of myth, where she explores the intersection of factual and imaginative narratives in new ways. She often asks 'what if?', suggesting a different ending or a possible twist in an inevitable tale.

'The Pomegranate' is one poem in which Boland directly explores the predetermined outcome of myth. It centres on the tale of Ceres and Persephone, which is, as the poet herself states bluntly at the outset, 'the only legend I have ever loved'. It is a story that has featured elsewhere in her work, as in the poem 'The Making of an Irish Goddess', which also renders the myth in specifically personal terms:

> Ceres went to hell
> with no sense of time.
> [...]
> But I need time—
> my flesh and that history—
> to make the same descent.

The legend concerns Persephone, the daughter of the Earth goddess Ceres and of Zeus, who as a girl is abducted by Hades, lord of the Underworld, to be his wife. Her grieving mother, searching everywhere for her, refused to allow the earth to flourish; crops failed to grow and no animals reproduced. The earth was dying. Eventually Zeus bowed to the pressure of this catastrophe and sent Hermes to bargain with Hades for the return of Persephone. Hades reluctantly assented to the wishes of the mother, but tricked the girl into eating some pomegranate seeds. Since she had eaten of the food of the dead, Persephone was obliged to return to the Underworld for half the year. On earth, this was the season of winter when no crops would grow.

The myth is often read as evidence of the power of mythological woman. Here Boland calls it 'the story of a daughter lost in hell./And found and rescued there', at first suggesting not separation but recovery as the most memorable aspect of the tale. She identifies with both female figures in this myth—first with the child, exiled in a strange place, but secondly, and more prominently, with the mother:

... Later
I walked out in a summer twilight
searching for my daughter at bed-time.
When she came running I was ready
to make any bargain to keep her.
I carried her past whitebeams
and wasps and honey-scented buddleias.
But I was Ceres then and I knew
winter was in store for every leaf
on every tree on that road.
Was inescapable for each one we passed.
And for me.

Coming near the close of the first stanza the word 'inescapable'
has a special resonance. It is the point around which the poem
turns: the knowledge that the daughter, in growing up, will be
separated from the mother. The flourishing natural world here is
not only suggestive of the power of the Earth Mother but also
hints at the flowers which Hades used to lure Persephone away
from her companions. The mother, therefore, must bear the child
carefully through a world of temptation. The chasm into which
Persephone is swept by Hades occurs at this halfway point, visible in the text of the poem as it pauses between stanzas, and in
the moment of realization which the poet herself experiences.

The importance, even the necessity of the story itself, is clear.
She could have come home safe, the poem argues, but this is
already belied by the inescapable nature of the tale's conclusion.
Boland moves seamlessly here between the imaginative world of
myth and the finely observed realism of the flint-coloured road, of
the suburb with its cars and cable television. The need for the
daughter to inhabit the legend fully is stated, reflecting not only
the inevitability of the split between mother and daughter but the
universal need for the female to live her story completely. Much of

the success of this poem lies in its ability to alert us to the power of myth in unselfconscious ways; the blurring of real and imaginative worlds suggests a narrative that is timeless yet immediate. One of the poem's weaknesses is its failure to acknowledge that the rift between mother and daughter may not be entirely natural and accepted. In her representation of the changing female relationship, Boland omits consideration of the tensions at its centre. Were she to present the sundering of bonds between mother and daughter in all their painful complexity, she would raise crucial questions about the collective nature of female experience and about women's attitude towards the passing on of tradition.

Feminism and Irish Poetry

Myth acquires a positive connotation throughout Boland's work, being validated by her attentive reading and imaginative use of ancient stories. It is never merely a flight from history; there is a conscious attempt to re-address familiar material from a specifically female standpoint. The influence of feminism on Boland's work is strong. Since the publication of *In Her Own Image* (1980), her poetry has reflected a growing interest in feminist thought, though Boland has made the distinction between its importance as a social force and its influence on the direct shaping of the poems themselves. She considers feminism to be a way of seeing, and readers of her poems might use it as such; it is not an interpretive tool to make her poems yield their meanings easily. Boland in interview speaks clearly about this distinction:

Feminism is an enabling perception but it's not an aesthetic one. The poem is a place—at least for me—where all kinds of certainties stop ... a place of experience and not a place of convictions—there is nothing so illuminated and certain as that sort of perspective in the poems I write. My poems have nothing to do with perspective; they have to do with the unfinished business of feeling and obsession. But outside the poem, feminism has been a vital, enabling way of seeing the climate in which I write the poem.[8]

Here Boland, in common with many creative artists, expresses the desire to resist the prescriptive terms of ideology. The poem as 'a place of experience and not a place of convictions' suggests that she is more interested in the life lived than in the life theorized and that her poems are intended to reflect a process rather than an outcome. Feminism informs, but does not dominate, her poetic sensibility yet its perceived presence may restrict her readership nonetheless.

Tradition and the Individual Writer

The relationship between the personal and the political is a complex one, as the following quotation from Boland attests:

I think there are two types of politic in poetry. The first is the private one. It operates somewhere between the experience of the poet—the private, obsessive feeling—and the poet's relation, not just to the poetic tradition, but to his or her own expertise in it ... The second politic ... is more visible and often less influential. It concerns the poet's feeling for the received tradition, for the social environment, for the relation between the artist and society.[9]

Here, Boland is able to work the notion of the political closer to a sense of personal artistic achievement. It is a surprising conflation of what readers are more used to seeing as opposing terms. By problematizing the split between these two realms, the poet affirms the significance of her own particular vision in the tradition as a whole, regardless of whether she seeks to belong to it or to oppose it. Interestingly Boland again uses the word 'obsessive' or 'obsession' to refer to her own poetic process. She is clearly indicating here that the strongest shaping force exerted on her poetry is that of her own private world. Even this private space has broader implications, though, and Boland argues also for the cultural significance of the female poet. The relationship she envisages, then, is not one between women only but between the female writer and the wider literary community. For Boland, the contemporary woman poet is now an 'emblematic figure' because 'in the projects she chooses, must choose perhaps, are internalized some of the central stresses and truths of poetry at this moment'.[10]

Boland's work demands that readers consider the nature of tradition itself, as a disabling as well as enabling force. In *Object Lessons* she identifies the female artist's experiences of exclusion or marginalization, of being constrained by circumstance to work in the borderlands of a tradition that does not accommodate the range—and often the intensity—of female expression. The sense of working creatively without the sustenance which earlier female achievement would bring, of starting from scratch, can increase existing difficulties. As Boland herself writes: 'The way to the past is never smooth. For a woman poet it can be especially tortuous. Every step towards an origin is also an advance towards a silence.'[11] In the Irish context this becomes doubly problematic. Not only has the tradition been shaped largely by men but the symbolic language it uses perpetuates stereotyped versions of woman.

There are other critics who contest this view, however. The Anglo-American poet Anne Stevenson objects to what she describes as Boland's 'claim to be disadvantaged by her national past',[12] citing a medieval Irish tradition of women poets which could provide vibrant and educative models for the modern writer. Boland's argument remains important, though, not because it is definitively 'true' but because it is *felt* to be true. A feeling of exclusion is often sufficient to push a writer even further to the margins of literary society, and in doing so to alter his or her writing in important ways. Boland's poetry may itself be read in the light of this troubled relationship between margin and centre, not only because it is deeply felt by the poet herself but because there is much in the pattern of her developing work which suggests that this is a vital and formative aspect.

We can see, then, that complex readings of history are central to Boland's work. As a key figure among contemporary women poets in Ireland she has been both admired and criticized for her consistent engagement with women's place in history and in literary tradition.[13] Though at times formally unadventurous, Boland challenges us in a variety of ways. By closing the gap between private and public realms she forces us to consider the relationship between them and the implications of this relationship for the act of writing itself. Although the past is a continuous presence in Boland's work and although feelings of loss play a large part in the poetry, we may see her as a poet focused on progression. By addressing and representing the inequalities of history she aims to clear the way for a more inclusive Ireland in the future.

Bibliography

Eavan Boland, *Collected Poems* (Manchester: Carcanet Press, 1995).

Eavan Boland, *A Kind of Scar: The Woman Poet in a National Tradition*, LIP pamphlet (Dublin: Attic Press, 1989); reproduced in Eavan Boland et al., *A Dozen Lips* (Dublin: Attic Press, 1994), pp. 72-92.

Eavan Boland, *Object Lessons: The Life of the Woman and the Poet in Our Time* (London: Vintage, 1996).

Catriona Clutterbuck, 'The Trustworthiness of Treachery', review of *The Lost Land*, *Irish University Review* 29, 2 (1999), pp. 406-9.

Colby Quarterly 35, 4 (December 1999). Edited by Jody Allen-Randolph. Special issue on Eavan Boland.

Deborah McWilliams Consalvo, 'In common usage: Eavan Boland's poetic voice', *Éire-Ireland* 28, 2 (Summer 1983), pp. 100-15.

Gerald Dawe, *Against Piety: Essays in Irish Poetry* (Belfast: Lagan Press, 1995).

Patricia Boyle Haberstroh, *Women Creating Women* (New York: Syracuse University Press, 1996).

Irish University Review 23, 1 (1993). Edited by Anthony Roche and Jody Allen-Randolph. Special issue on Eavan Boland, including Jody Allen-Randolph, 'An Interview with Eavan Boland', pp. 117-30.

Peter McDonald, 'Extreme prejudice', review of Eavan Boland's *The Lost Land*, *Metre* 6 (Summer 1999), pp. 85-9.

Gerardine Meaney, *Sex and Nation: Women in Irish Culture and Politics*, LIP pamphlet (Dublin: Attic Press, 1991); reproduced in Eavan Boland et al., *A Dozen Lips* (Dublin: Attic Press, 1994), pp. 188-204.

Nuala Ní Dhomhnaill, 'What foremothers?', *Poetry Ireland Review* 36 (Fall 1992), pp. 18-31; reprinted in *PN Review* 19, 3 (January–February 1993), pp. 35-9.

Anne Stevenson, 'Inside and outside history', *PN Review* 18, 3 (January–February 1992), pp. 34-8.

Nell Sullivan, 'Righting Irish poetry: Eavan Boland's revisionary struggle', *Colby Quarterly* 33, 4 (December 1997), pp. 334-48.

Deborah Tall, 'Q. & A. with Eavan Boland', *Irish Literary Supplement* 7, 2 (Fall 1988), pp. 39-40.

Rebecca Wilson and Gillean Somerville-Arjat (eds), *Sleeping with Monsters: Conversations with Scottish and Irish Women Poets* (Dublin: Wolfhound Press, 1990).

Notes

1. Boland's most recent collection, *The Lost Land*, appeared in 1998, following *In a Time of Violence* (1994). In addition to her eight collections of new poems she has produced a number of selections of her work both in Britain and America.

2. Of what Gerald Dawe has called its 'strained literariness' (*Against Piety*, p. 174), Boland has commented that 'of course that's ... the flaw in the book. It's written by a poet. That's the lens I used almost all the time' (Jody Allen-Randolph, 'An Interview with Eavan Boland', p. 20).

3. Boland, *Object Lessons*, p. 177.

4. Later in her career Boland would explore this image again and draw different resonances from it: 'When you and I were first in love we drove/to the borders of Connacht/and entered a wood there.//Look down you said: this was once a famine road' ('That the Science of Cartography is Limited' [1994], *Collected Poems*, p. 174). The lovers here acknowledge not only the hardships of history but the ways in which this pain has been disguised by time and by the slanted nature of history's narrative. At one level the poem alerts readers to the dangers of reading history in a two-dimensional way only. At another it mourns the loss of unrecorded history, at the same time as it

acknowledges the inevitability of such a loss.

5. Deborah Tall, 'Q. & A. with Eavan Boland', p. 40.

6. Throughout her career, Boland has used paintings as a source of inspiration. The domestic interior, together with the still life, can be both a realistic rendering of women's experience and a means of interrogating the act of representation itself. Among the chosen poems 'This Moment' draws implicitly on this painterly approach.

7. Boland, *A Kind of Scar*, p. 6.

8. Jody Allen-Randolph, 'Interview', p. 25.

9. Ibid. p. 22.

10. Boland, *Object Lessons*, p. xv.

11. Ibid., pp. 23-4.

12. Anne Stevenson, 'Inside and outside history', pp. 35-7. See also Nuala Ní Dhomhnaill's rebuttal in 'What foremothers?'.

13. Boland continues to attract the attention of scholars and commentators in Britain and Ireland, as well as in the United States where feminist literary theory often provides the framework for examining her poetry. Her recent collection *The Lost Land* has attracted much negative comment, especially from critics who regard the work as repetitive in both theme and form. Peter McDonald's review of *The Lost Land* in *Metre* 6 argues this case particularly strongly; in contrast, Catriona Clutterbuck's review in the *Irish University Review* 29, 2, offers a positive assessment of the volume.

Out of the Water, Down to Earth: The Poetry of Elizabeth Bishop and Michael Longley

PETER DENMAN

I. The Poetry of Elizabeth Bishop

Since her death in 1979, Elizabeth Bishop's reputation has risen steadily, as the admiration in which she is held by fellow poets has percolated through to a more general readership, aided by the publication of her letters, which have given a greater understanding of the background to her poems. Bishop's poems will strike readers in Ireland as remarkably free and liberating. As well as being carefully modulated observations of experience, the poems seem to exist in a world that offers itself at face value. The fish, in her poem of that name, is primarily a fish, not a symbol of something else—of life, say, or of Christ, or of sexuality. Her armadillo is an armadillo, and the can of motor oil in 'Filling Station' is just that. Perhaps her particular achievement is to enable us to see images such as these in a new light, so that we attach imaginative weight to them for themselves, rather than for some representative quality that points to an idea outside them. But this aspect might appeal to any reader of poetry grown slightly wary of the supposition that a poetic statement is necessarily oblique and that, whatever a poem means, it does not mean what it actually says.

An additional quality to be observed in Bishop's poems is the way they float free of their background no matter how meticulously she describes it. This may seem novel to Irish readers, accustomed as we are to poems that carry a weight of history, of inherited values, of tradition. Eavan Boland's 'The Famine Road' is not simply about a road; it is a memory of the Famine and all the racial hurt of that event travels down it. A keynote poem of hers is 'Outside History', which starts from the assumption that validation goes hand in hand with historical presence: if the speaker is outside history, she is devalued by that very fact. Simultaneously to possess and be possessed by history, in one sense or another, is what confers value. The present must be informed by the past. Similarly, Seamus Heaney created his early poetry out of a sense of language imbued with Viking, English and Irish pasts; his bog poems see Ireland as a physical repository of history and symbolic figures that link into a northern European consciousness; and even the luminous and playful poem from 'Lightenings' begins with an appeal to historical sources: 'The annals say'. These poems reflect in different ways the highly developed role of historical awareness in the shaping of Irish consciousness. Bishop's poems carry relatively little such baggage, and the fact that they travel light adds to their effectiveness.

It is useful to bear Bishop's American nationality in mind as an aid to understanding her work. Poems such as 'The Bight' and 'First Death in Nova Scotia' refer specifically to a North American environment. But equally important is the fact that she was a traveller, and she lived in Brazil for a significant part of her life. One of her collections was called *Questions of Travel,* and its title poem asks a series of questions about the traveller's viewpoint, which are answered by an appeal to the immediacy and vitality of incidental experience:

But surely it would have been a pity
not to have seen the trees along this road,
[...]
—Not to have had to stop for gas and heard
the sad, two-noted, wooden tune
of disparate wooden clogs
carelessly clacking over
a grease-stained filling-station floor.

Although the poem attempts to suggest connections between the incidents observed, the tone of this section is rhetorical and emotive rather than logical and conclusive, and the conclusion is a traveller's jotted note about what she has observed. The note is made of further questions, and ends

> '... Should we have stayed at home,
> wherever that may be?'

The fundamental, far-reaching problem concerns not whether the poet should have stayed or strayed, but the nature and whereabouts of 'home'.

'The Prodigal' is based on the parable of the prodigal son told in the gospel of St Luke (ch. 15). Bishop's treatment concentrates on the initial part of the parable; it does not, except in an implicit and anticipatory fashion, deal with the prodigal's return home. The poem is not about the return, but the possibility of a still deferred return. Bishop enters into the consciousness of the prodigal, and speaks for him while simultaneously allowing the prodigal to speak for her. The poem is carefully balanced in its form, with two fourteen-line stanzas which weigh up the misery of the situation and the possibility of getting away from it. Bishop thought of the stanzas as two sonnets while writing the poem, but they clearly constitute a single work. The movement of thought and images starts with stench and rottenness, set out in various

images through the first half-stanza. These have become the condition of the prodigal's life, so that he can no longer appreciate
the full awfulness of his condition ('too close ... / for him to
judge'). The speaker of the poem is observing and slightly
detached, able to evaluate the experience in a way that the prodigal himself is not. The middle section of the poem suggests some
relief, as the dawn sun gives a spurious beauty to the farmyard
muck. But, correspondingly, the first half of the second stanza
centres on a warning star, and the light comes not from the sun
but more faintly from the reflection on pitchforks and the
farmer's lantern which in this instance is 'going away'. Before the
end there is a suggestion that insight is bringing an awareness of
his situation, and this insight is not consolatory but unsettling—
like 'the bats' uncertain staggering flight'. Knowledge brings pain
and difficulty, but this is part of being human, while the animals
have a 'self-righteous' and 'cheerful' stare, and are 'safe and com-
panionable'. In the end the prodigal will make the difficult decision. His progress in the poem has been from an inability to
judge at the outset, moving on to the 'thought he almost might
endure' at the end of the first stanza, and finally arriving at the
'shuddering insights' and resolution to go home.

As we have seen in 'Questions of Travel', the expatriate state is
characteristic of Bishop. There is a certain freedom that goes with
not belonging. This set in early in Bishop's work, as family circumstances meant that she did not have a conventional family
upbringing and she was raised by her maternal grandmother in
Nova Scotia in Canada, and then by members of her father's
family. The poems 'Sestina', 'First Death in Nova Scotia' and 'In
the Waiting Room' draw on her childhood experience.

The sestina is a poem of six six-line stanzas, a form originally
devised during the Renaissance. It does not rhyme; instead, the
words used at the ends of the lines in the first stanza are also used
to end the lines in each of the other five, with the order in which

they occur at line-endings varying according to a fixed pattern. A sestina concludes with a three-line stanza in which the six words must again be used, in the middle and at the end of the lines. The secret of a good sestina lies in the choice of the six end-words. They must be such that they allow for variation and progress, or the poem ends up circling around the repetitions. In Bishop's poem one of the key words, and the word towards which the entire poem moves, is 'house'. The word which this fends off is, of course, 'home' (the final word of both 'The Prodigal' and 'Questions of Travel'). 'Sestina' is a very sad poem about childhood.

At the start of the twentieth century, the influential critical school of Russian Formalism argued that it is the special function of literature to 'defamiliarize' the world it describes, and to make us look with new eyes. The state of being abroad gives a peculiarly fresh awareness. This is most apparent in 'The Armadillo', which gradually contrives a setting in which the components, although described in a matter-of-fact way, become increasingly exotic. Where is this country that regularly launches fire balloons? Fire balloons are something strange, and yet here they are a feature of the calendar, at once expected and exotic. Mention of the Southern Cross locates the poem away from North America and Europe, as the Southern Cross is a constellation seen only south of the equator. The armadillo makes its entrance in the final stages. I stated at the outset that Bishop's poetry resists symbolic weight. However, when she does want to transform an image, it is done knowingly. That is why the final stanza is in italics; it is at once a part of the poem and a comment on what the poem has presented. The 'falling fire' is obviously that of the balloon. The 'piercing cry' comes from the owls, the 'panic' probably from the rabbit, and then the 'weak mailed fist' figures the armadillo. Are they mimicking the human condition, or is that too large a claim to make? The ending of this poem poses questions about itself. It is thus the most uprooted and expatriate of all Bishop's poems, destabilizing its own foundations.

A connection exists between this poem and Seamus Heaney's poem 'The Skunk'. Bishop dedicated 'The Armadillo' to her friend Robert Lowell (1917–1977). Lowell in return dedicated his poem 'Skunk Hour' to Bishop, and in it imitated something of the movement of 'The Armadillo'—a New England summer resort is described, and then in the night-time a family of skunks moves down the street to forage in the rubbish bins. Lowell's disturbing poem, one of his most famous, is rooted in mid-century USA, and the prowling confident skunks stand as emblems of a sick society and a distressed psyche. Later, in the 1970s, the elder Lowell befriended Heaney, and when Lowell died suddenly after flying back to New York from Ireland, the Irish poet wrote a fine elegy. But he also wrote the playfully loving poem 'The Skunk', which derives its effect in part from its intertextual reference, daringly rescuing the image of the skunk from the anguish of Lowell's poem and giving it erotic significance.[1]

'The Fish' is one of Bishop's best-known poems, one of several diving into the underwater world (see also 'At the Fishhouses' and 'The Bight'). It is worth examining in detail how the effects of the poem are created. Unusually for a poet of such precision, Bishop does not specify the type of fish. It is, however, immediately described as 'tremendous'; this is how it appears to the speaker, the starting point and originator of the poem. The detail of the description is remarkable: the colour and thickness of the old scraps of fishing lines, the speckles and sea-lice on his skin. The detail is not just observed but also imagined, as the internal organs—the bones, the swim-bladder—are enumerated. And ten lines are given to the eyes, into which the poet stares and which she compares to her own. This stare seems almost to enact an exchange between poet and fish. As she looks at the battle-worn, venerable fish, she feels a sense of victory filling 'the little rented boat'. It is not clear just who is victorious, the fish, the poet, or both of them in shared recognition. What matters is the transformation, as the mundane details—oily water in the bilges, rust on the engine and bailer, the cracked thwarts—are transformed into something magical in the chant of 'rainbow'. The battered old fish has somehow—through the poet's vision—wrought a change on the battered old environment of the human.

There is a similar achievement in 'Filling Station', although in this poem we start with rust and dirt and grease and find that 'somebody' presides over this detritus and makes a home there. A series of questions is put by the poet, who in this instance speaks from a stance firmly outside the world depicted. She contemplates the filling station, as the recognition of a loving imposition of order allows her to be included intellectually, not emotionally.

> Somebody embroidered the doily.
> Somebody waters the plant,
> or oils it, maybe. Somebody
> arranges the rows of cans
> so that they softly say:
> ESSO—SO—SO—SO
> to high-strung automobiles.
> Somebody loves us all.

The apparent inclusiveness of the last line is belied by the vagueness of 'somebody', and its affirmation is undercut by the ironic detachment of the speaker. The oil can labels spell out 'SO—SO—SO', which, as Bishop herself explained in one of her letters, is 'the phrase people use to calm and soothe horses'[2]; this in turn makes clear where the description of the automobiles as 'high-strung' comes from, a term more readily associated with thoroughbred horses.

A similar situation is apparent in 'At the Fishhouses' and in 'The Bight', in that the underwater world can be known only from the outside. These are typical of Bishop's poems in that they begin in a deceptively discursive and desultory tone. There is a purposeful accumulation of detail and description throughout the poem, and this gathers and builds to an ending that can surprise by its power. In 'At the Fishhouses', after the conversation with the old man, and the survey of the waterside in which there is an undeniable pleasure in the minutiae noticed, the poem moves towards the unknown:

> Cold dark deep and absolutely clear,
> element bearable to no mortal ...

In an ironic twist, the immortal inhabiting the other world here is not an angel but a seal, to whom nevertheless the poet sings hymns to make him follow her. The other world is not divine, it is simply separate from human knowledge. The poem ends with a magnificent speculation on the nature of knowledge. How do we know what we know? How do we hold on to experience? Knowledge is difficult, and bought at a price, paining the wrist and tasting bitter. This is

> ... like what we imagine knowledge to be:
> dark, salt, clear, moving, utterly free,
> drawn from the cold hard mouth
> of the world, derived from the rocky breasts
> forever, flowing and drawn, and since
> our knowledge is historical, flowing, and flown.

This final sentence starts in anticipation, imagining what knowledge is like, and taking its imagery and language from those used to describe the seawater. But knowledge is not something tangible and defined that we can grasp; it flows. We recognize it only after the event as we learn from experience, and we cannot know something until we have experienced it and it is past. 'Flowing, and flown' enact this. The words capture the image of something in flux. 'Flown' is a multiple-levelled word: while it looks like the word 'flowing', positioned close to it in the line, it is usually the past participle of the verb 'to fly'. There is the sense of knowledge as something that has flowed past us and has flown away from us. 'Flown' is also a half-rhyme to 'drawn', used twice earlier in the sentence, and in the previous line placed after the word 'flowing'. The poem has gathered itself together for this statement about what we know and how we can know it.

The endings of Bishop's poems are often powerfully expressed. This is not unusual—most poems move towards a conclusion in the hope that they will leave some reverberation in the mind of the reader. But Bishop's endings come out of the ordinary, the painstaking descriptions of the pedestrian. 'The Bight', a companion poem to 'At The Fishhouses', studies the sea and the shore with its detritus of rubbish. Derelict boats are like old torn-open letters. The idea of letters leads into the more abstract statement of the next line, and the ending of the poem:

> The bight is littered with old correspondences.
> Click. Click. Goes the dredge,
> and brings up a dripping jawful of marl.
> All the untidy activity continues,
> awful but cheerful.

The torn-open letters as correspondence modulate into 'correspondences', or resemblances, which enable Bishop to read her condition in terms of what she sees. And again, in the apparently offhand almost prosy statements, there is an underlying poetic quality to the language—particularly in the rhymes of 'jawful', 'All', 'awful'. If we want to push the application of the poem to Bishop's own life, then perhaps it is not too fanciful to hear in the 'Click. Click.' of the dredger the sound of the poet's typewriter keys; it too has been used in order to haul matter from the deep and hidden submarine world to the light of the surface.

II. The Poetry of Michael Longley

The power of Michael Longley's poems derives from their restraint, and this in turn seems to spring from a recognition that the capacity of action and emotion to influence our lives is limited. But, even as it recognizes such limitations, there is an assertion that some response is both necessary and life-affirming in the face of experience.

'Last Requests' is an example of this. A number of Longley's poems are about his father Peter Longley, a Londoner who had fought in the First World War. Longley's poems about his father are not just about the difficulties of a family relationship across the generations. 'Last Requests' complicates the idea of a relationship that is primarily emotional and familial by overlaying it with small objects and possessions that become images and totems.

The poem is divided into two eight-line sections, balanced against each other; it thus has a structural similarity to Bishop's 'The Prodigal'. Longley juxtaposes himself against a figure from the past, his father's batman, as both of them misread the situation that confronts them ('Your batman thought …', 'I thought …'). The batman saw an opportunity to help himself to possessions no longer needed, whereas the son brings inappropriate offerings and is unable to supply the cigarette that is asked for. The phrase 'long remembered drag' in the first stanza uses the smoking term to describe the deep intake of breath after a brush with death. The oxygen tent, momentarily prolonging the life of the dying man, is a barrier that hangs between father and son and makes the act of smoking impossible. The oxygen tent and the cigarette take on ironic resonances: the life-supporting oxygen becomes an emblem not just of life but of the difficulty of reaching out to another individual's life, while a cigarette with its smoke, normally associated with health warnings and disease, is the longed-for comforter and unattainable cure.

There is a sense that what is out of reach in 'Last Requests' is not just the father figure, but the history that the father represents—the war, a near-death, another life lived and now over. A great many of Longley's poems are about death or wounding; and from such subject matter he constructs poems that rescue the beauty of living. Perhaps the most powerful example of this is the sonnet 'Ceasefire', a poem which is indissolubly bound up with the events surrounding its publication. The poem was published in *The Irish Times* on 3 September 1994, just after the IRA ceasefire brought a halt to a long campaign of killing. But it had been written in advance of the ceasefire, in response to the mood of Ireland as political events moved onwards. A newspaper editor thus placed the poem on the cusp of the events, so that its appearance coincided with the feeling of national relief as the ceasefire was announced. The impact of the poem is a graphic illustration of the fact that poetry—like other arts—exists in history; a poem's power derives not solely from the inspiration, technique and vision of the poet, but also from some interaction with the community of readers for which it is written.

The background to the poem is an episode from the *Iliad*, near the end of the siege of Troy. Achilles, the Greek hero, has slain Hector, son of Priam, king of Troy, in single combat. After killing him, Achilles violates the conventions of war by dragging the body of Hector behind his horse. It was important that a dead body be treated with respect, and be buried with appropriate funeral rites so that its spirit could join the shades of the dead in the underworld. Priam, the proud king now reduced to grieving father, is pitied by the gods. They intervene to soften the heart of Achilles, and tell Priam to cross the battle-lines to visit Achilles in secret and ask for the body of his son. Priam does so, and goes on his knees before Achilles, urging him to think of his own father. It is at this point that the poem commences. Achilles later agrees to a truce of eleven days, to allow Hector's funeral pyre to be made ready.

If 'Ceasefire' derives some of its power from the moment and circumstance of its publication, it nonetheless is a poem that draws on many of Longley's characteristic motifs. Not least of these is the centrality of the father-son relationship. Another feature of this poem is the manner in which the sonnet is split into four numbered sections, each section a separate syntactical unit; such divisions are characteristic of Longley's poems, as if he wants to ensure that we take these short poems slowly. In Homer, Achilles sets aside cloaks and a tunic in which to wrap the body of Hector. In Longley's version, these become a 'uniform', a style of dress which externalizes a code by which one acts and the corps to which one belongs. Uniforms play a similarly prominent part in the earlier poem 'Wounds'.

A factor that is explicit in the Homeric episode but only implicit in Longley's is the gross mistreatment of Hector's corpse, dragged across the ground; the idea of violent death as a violation of the living is at the core of how Longley responds to the killings that have marked his community. The conjunction of individual and earth is a motif that recurs elsewhere. 'Badger' shows an animal hunted and pulled from the earth; in 'Last Requests' the father is nearly buried alive by an unexploded shell; in 'Poteen' the landscape is depicted as burrowed with souterrains and secret hideaways; in 'Detour' the poet imagines himself making his own funeral journey to his grave.

This merging with the landscape is a recurrent motif, found in various forms in Longley's poetry. It is a motif also found in Heaney's poems—for instance in the bog poems such as 'The Tollund Man' where human figures are absorbed and preserved by the earth. But in Heaney's poems these mergings take on a political significance, and carry connotations regarding allegiance and social purpose. For Longley, they are part of a metaphysical transaction in which individual lives are subsumed into the larger impersonal universe.

Negotiation with the simplicities of the landscape is at its most developed in 'Carrigskeewaun'. Carrigskeewaun, on the coast of Mayo to the south of Clew Bay, is a place where Longley has spent a considerable amount of time, and he finds a repertory of material in its topography which has figured in his poetry at least since the early 1970s. The poem 'Carrigskeewaun', like a number of others by Longley, is made up of a sequence of individual pieces. These draw their subjects from the landscape, almost in the manner of a naturalist's sketches, and are related by their subject matter—mountain, path, strand, wall, lake—and by their form (each is made up of one sentence covering six lines). The individual title for each sestet prevents us from seeing them as stanzas, and raises the question of whether the ordering of the five pieces is important. At first sight there appears to be no narrative or logical sequence, but on closer scrutiny a progression becomes evident. The first one shows the poet standing, and in the second he steps out along the path, so that in the third he makes a discovery of tracks on the shore left from yesterday. In this third section the time span has opened out from the closely observed present of the first two to encompass the past—first of all the immediate personal past of yesterday's activity, which is then set against the longer geological time span of erosion. The syntax of this sentence leaves the meaning unclear: is it the feet of the animals and people that crush the shells into sand, or the activity of the waves at 'the water's edge' that does it? The larger reach of the third section is continued in the next, 'The Wall', where the poet imaginatively joins others who have been here before him in the past, and looks towards a domestic interior, indicated by the turf smoke. All four sections of the poem so far have been populated. The figure of the poet ('I') is introduced as a participant and observer, and in three of the four sections other persons are implied—family members, men. In the final section there is no 'I'. The lake is described impersonally, and there is a daring poetic fancy—you cannot tilt the surface of a lake—as it reflects the components of scene. The heron, mare and foal are privileged ('special') here, not the humanity evoked in the earlier sections.

If we pick out significant words and phrases from the successive sections, we can trace another line of progression. In the first the poet 'stand[s] alone', and in the second the suggestion of solitude is continued as birds are dislodged and fly off, disturbed by his approach. (The final line of this section, describing the swan, is the one weak line in the poem; the idea of the swan being pushed to the other side 'of its gradual disdain' introduces an inappropriately abstract conceit into a poem that otherwise relies on observed events.) The remaining three sections bring a counter-movement of a sensed community. On the strand there are traces of others, and the word 'linking' introduces an idea continued in the first verb 'join' in 'The Wall' and in the plural possessive adjective 'our'. This move to plurality from solitude culminates in the final section, which is about duplication and reception; the lake's mirroring of its visitants can be read as a friendly acceptance and greeting. This brings a wholeness which is a radical change from the images of skulls, bones, and rock with which the poem opened. The only query surrounds the figure of the poet, who has now disappeared from his own creation.

'Wreaths' exhibits a similar serial structure; all three poems that make it up are elegies and reflections on people killed in the Northern Ireland troubles. In each case Longley's technique is to juxtapose the hideous enormity of violent death with the routine incidentals of everyday life. Longley insists that death is a brusque interruption, not a transformation. No Yeatsian terrible beauty here, simply the awkwardness of coping with an event that human sensibility and emotion can hardly comprehend. I suggested above that the mix of action and abstraction in the final line of 'The Path' in 'Carrigskeewaun', about the swan, was unsuccessful; here, in 'The Civil Servant', there is a similar device used with devastating effect:

> A bullet entered his mouth and pierced his skull,
> The books he had read, the music he could play.

The brutal physicality of the bullet and the damaged skull impinges on the intellectual and aesthetic sensibilities that constituted the personality of the dead man. As a physical presence he is awkward and uncomfortable, dead in his house, making those around him shuffle. The final images are a reprise of those images of the opening stanza: the bullet hole in the cutlery drawer (the knives and forks for eating his fry that morning) and the music gone out of the life in the house.

Against the background of the poems we have already looked at, the particular qualities of 'Wounds', a relatively early poem by Longley, are more apparent. It is an important poem, both because it shows him moving in on the characteristic modes of treatment that we have already identified, and also because, more generally, it is an Irish poem that is able to encompass areas of historical experience beyond nationalism. The 'Wounds' of the title are a legacy of the First World War, the pain carried for fifty years afterwards, and also the pain and damage of the deaths inflicted in contemporary Ireland.

The poem operates in pairings. In the very first line it sets out to proffer 'two pictures', which are outlined in the first stanza: the Irish soldiers from Ulster at the Battle of the Somme, translating the world war into local terms at their moment of extremity and fear, and the British chaplain suavely preserving minor decencies while surrounded by obscene death. Set against the first stanza and its evocation of the past is a second stanza of equal length, in which memories and remnants of the past are overwritten by the contemporary deaths. These deaths are again paired: the teenage soldiers with the shot bus-conductor. The poem refuses to offer an explicit opinion on its material, but the bathos of the final line, 'I think "Sorry Missus" was what he said', is indicative of the pointlessness of all the deaths. Technically, the poem is remarkable because it moves from a language that suggests energy and noble military endeavour to an episode that is depicted as trite and banal, yet it does this without undercutting the remembered value of any of the deaths. This is achieved in part through the closural balance of the poem. Although the final line is tentative in expression ('I think'), it introduces a final rhyme, 'said', which echoes the word 'head' five lines earlier and rounds off the poem. Once we notice this, we notice that the word 'head' has been used in the first and last lines of the first stanza also. This organizing principle of repetition is further apparent in the use of the words 'bewilderment/bewildered'. In the first instance the bewilderment is the father's attitude, linked to admiration, as he recalls the action of the soldiers whom he survived; in the second instance the bewilderment has descended on the uncomprehending wife who must live through the death of her husband, shot in front of her.

Longley is a poet of great poise, but this is not to say that his poems avoid engagement with the situations they depict. When I wrote of 'Wounds' as the poem in which he developed his characteristic mode of treatment, I was thinking in particular of the third section of 'Wreaths' ('The Linen Workers'), perhaps the most puzzling in its assemblage of effects. The massacre of the ten linen workers risks becoming remote to us because it is already distanced by time, because it is one atrocity among many, and because the scale of that killing is almost too large to comprehend. But read in the context of 'Wounds', it is apparent that Longley makes it meaningful by relating it to the familial death of his father. This is not just a device to give the death a human scale, it also confers intimacy on those deaths and takes them within a personally felt context. In this way, Longley's poise is a means of making his poetry alive to the difficult world he lives in.

III. Conclusion

Both Bishop and Longley suggest that the world has had a recalcitrant history, and one of the virtues of their poems is that they offer an alternative, and salvific, vision. Bishop's poems manage it by downplaying the historical, suggesting that the pressure of the present moment outweighs the past; the accumulation of detail dredged up in her poetry is not simply observation, it is a mode of knowing and of understanding. For Longley, a sense of history is inescapable. Everything mentioned in his poems is brought within its ambit and, as in the phrase from the poem 'Snow' by Louis MacNeice, his world is 'incorrigibly plural'. But, while the two poets differ in their methods, Bishop's speculative metaphysics and Longley's lyrical sensitivities move with reference to their respective elements—out of the water, down to earth.

Bibliography

I. Elizabeth Bishop
Elizabeth Bishop, *Complete Poems* (London: Chatto and Windus, 1983).
Elizabeth Bishop, *The Collected Prose* (London: Chatto and Windus, 1984).
Elizabeth Bishop, *One Art: Letters*, selected and edited by Robert Giroux (London: Chatto and Windus, 1994).

A considerable body of critical writings exists on Bishop, among them the following:
Seamus Heaney, *The Government of the Tongue: The 1986 T. S. Eliot Memorial Lectures and Other Writings* (London: Faber and Faber, 1988). In the title essay in this collection, Heaney discusses 'At The Fishhouses'.
Seamus Heaney, 'Counting to a hundred: on Elizabeth Bishop', in *The Redress of Poetry: Oxford Lectures* (London: Faber and Faber, 1995).
David Kalstone, *Becoming a Poet* (New York: Farrar, Strauss and Giroux, 1989).
Tom Paulin, 'Dwelling without roots', in *Minotaur: Poetry and the Nation State* (London: Faber and Faber, 1992).

Tom Paulin, *Writing to the Moment: Selected Critical Essays 1980-1996* (London: Faber and Faber, 1996). In the title essay of this collection, Paulin discusses Bishop's letters, while a 1992 essay is concerned with Bishop's poetry.

There are several websites relating to Bishop and her work. These are of variable quality, but the following might serve as a starting point: *http://iberia.vassar.edu/vcl/information/special-collections/bishop/. *www.georgetown.edu/bassr/heath/syllabuild/iguide/bishop.html.

II. Michael Longley

Michael Longley, *Poems 1963-1983* (Edinburgh: The Salamander Press; Dublin: The Gallery Press, 1985).

Michael Longley, *Gorse Fires* (London: Secker and Warburg, 1991).

Michael Longley, *Selected Poems* (London: Jonathan Cape, 1998).

Longley can be heard reading his poems on the Leaving Certificate syllabus on the CD accompanying *Explorations I*, ed. John G. Fahy (Dublin: Gill and Macmillan, 1999).

Longley's poetic career is still very much in progress, and his work awaits the full critical evaluation it merits. The following essays might be noted:

Peter McDonald, 'Michael Longley's homes', in *The Chosen Ground: Essays on the Contemporary Poetry of Northern Ireland*, ed. Neil Corcoran (Mid Glamorgan: Seren Books, 1992).

Michael Allen, 'Rhythm and Development in Michael Longley's Earlier Poetry', in *Contemporary Irish Poetry: A Collection of Critical Essays*, ed. Elmer Andrews (London: Macmillan, 1992).

Notes

1. Heaney has written appreciatively of Bishop in the course of the title essay in *The Government of the Tongue*, and devoted one of his lectures as Professor of Poetry at Oxford to her work: 'Counting to a Hundred' in *The Redress of Poetry*.

2. Bishop, *One Art*, p. 638.

Unlocking the Word-Hoard: The Poetry of Seamus Heaney

JOHN DEVITT

And he who was sitting on the throne said, 'Behold, I make all things new!' And he said, 'Write, for these words are trustworthy and true.' (Apocalypse 21:5)

A dozen poems by a major living poet, culled from collections published over a thirty-year period (1966–1996), must constitute a mouth-watering prospect for teachers previously limited to the narrow spectrum of possibilities provided by the slender, supposedly 'interim' anthology, *Soundings*, which has had to satisfy some fifteen or sixteen generations of Leaving Certificate students. Not that all is lost. In teaching the poetry of Seamus Heaney, new readings and new uses of poems grown perhaps too familiar will inevitably suggest themselves. For it is precisely those poets most generously represented in *Soundings* (Wordsworth, Keats, Hopkins, Hardy, Yeats and Kavanagh) who have been most instrumental in forming Heaney's sensibility and determining his poetic bent;[1] he has written judiciously about all of them and responded to them in the very act of composing his own verse; most are given honourable mention in 'Crediting Poetry', the 1995 Nobel

Lecture, while Yeats has emerged as the acknowledged master, admired though not uncritically, and no longer to be feared.

While this essay focuses sharply and more or less exclusively on the prescribed poems, familiarity with Heaney's entire oeuvre is desirable if not indispensable. This is a tall order. Quite apart from *Opened Ground* (1998), which includes almost 450 pages of verse but is still far short of being a collected edition, there are four volumes of criticism, a play (*The Cure at Troy*, 1990), innumerable essays and reviews lodged in journals and newspapers, not to speak of interviews, taped readings, radio broadcasts and television programmes. Nevertheless some sense of Heaney's development, a development which is both surprising and, at least in retrospect, coherent, is necessary for reading any of the poems fruitfully, or teaching any of them with authority. We might take to heart the Fool's advice to Lear: 'Have more than thou showest' (I.iv.28), words which are capable of a wider application than the dramatic occasion requires.

The Mystery of Work
In 'Crediting Poetry' Heaney speaks of his 'temperamental disposition towards an art that was earnest and devoted to things as they are',[2] a disposition reinforced by the culture of his native place with its dour gospel of hard work, its scrupulous preference for realism of the most prosaic kind, and its corresponding suspicion of all imaginative excesses and rhetorical flourishes. While it is true that in *Seeing Things* (1991) Heaney transcended the burden both of nature and of nurture, it would be wrong to suggest that he has escaped it completely. Who has ever done so, who ever can? That which is internalized early, unconsciously and completely, cannot be finally discarded; it constitutes the ground of our being in the world. The very ambiguity of the phrase 'seeing things' has a bearing on this point: it conveys the idea of

seeing what is not present to the senses, as in a vision or a drunken stupor, for instance; but it also insists obstinately on another sense, seeing things precisely as they are.

Be that as it may, three of the prescribed poems celebrate the mystery of work: 'The Forge' (1969), 'Sunlight' (1975) and 'The Harvest Bow' (1979).[3] 'Sunlight', surely the best of them, manages to be both idyllic and exact. We might describe it as nostalgic, provided we allow that the poet's nostalgia does not blur the object that attracts it. (Something similar might be said of Thomas Hardy's poetry and fiction.) The opening line ('There was a sunlit absence') is a complete sentence in itself, radiant and yet puzzling. Absence prompts memory into action, while simultaneously underlining the gap between the present moment and the past which is evoked. The remembered scene in the first two stanzas includes no human figure, though one is implied if only to operate the pump and sling the bucket. When the poem's dedicatee does finally appear she is unnamed, identified first by the work of 'her hands'. Mary Heaney, the poet's aunt, is so much part of the scene and of the poet's inner life that no name is needed.

It is worth attending to the description of the farmyard, though 'description' is a rather limp word for what is going on in lines 2 through 9. The pump, lightly personified in being 'helmeted', magically heats its own iron, repudiating any debt to the sun. In the phrase 'water honeyed', honey, best known for its taste and colour, is converted to musical sound. The faint biblical echo (Joshua 10:13) of 'The sun stood' is just sufficient to lift the scene from ordinary secular time into *illud tempus*, a kind of sacred timelessness. But these imaginative and suggestive details are counterpointed by down-to-earth realism. The simile 'like a griddle' (a griddle is a shallow pan once used to bake bread) domesticates the sun. The remembered afternoon may be as long as memory would like to pretend but it is not endless; it is, after all, one afternoon among many such, as 'each long afternoon' quietly indicates.

Mary Heaney commands the interior scene. We move from outside to inside, from the heat of the farmyard to the more intense heat of the kitchen, between lines 9 and 10; the heat of the kitchen is something solid and palpable, a 'plaque'. The woman's apron is filmed with flour as she sets about baking: 'floury' is perhaps an homophonous pun on 'flowery', suggesting subliminally the pattern on the apron. She is, incidentally, a tidy worker who deserves her moment of repose by the window.

So many of the properties associated with the scene belong to an irrecoverable past, available only to the most tenacious of middle-aged memories. We would not expect to find a pump in a modern farmyard (an outside tap, more likely)—unless as a use-less survivor, mute witness to a remote past. The griddle pan is now rarely used and a goose's wing is definitely an archaic duster. The aunt's working instruments, which must have seemed immemorial and eternal in their time, belong to a world 'in sus-pension between the archaic and the modern',[4] with no intima-tion of its own impending obsolescence.

Still, Heaney will not suffer the scene to be lost, to dwindle to a museum piece or a textbook illustration of the way things once were. The quality of the attention he pays to scene and agent is another name for love. A clear indication of the nature of his response is given in the unobtrusive shift from the past tense of the fourth stanza ('sent', 'stood') to the present tense of the fifth ('now she dusts …', 'now sits') and subsequent stanzas. This slight quickening of intensity finds its perfect correlative in the unfor-gettable image of the final stanza where the speaker names love without claiming anything for himself beyond the ability to rec-ognize it.

And here is love
like a tinsmith's scoop
sunk past its gleam
in the meal-bin.

The scoop is naturally grey and dull, not bright or gleaming; it shines only with use. Furthermore this particular scoop is so far buried in the meal-bin that its 'gleam' has to be surmised or imagined. Such modesty redounds to the credit of the user and is matched by the speaker's restraint; one hesitates to describe the tone as impersonal in spite of the absence of the first person singular, 'I'. What 'Sunlight' does, by purely poetic means and with little overt moralizing, is to attach value to repetitive and usually unregarded work, to those things which, once done, have almost immediately to be done again: household chores, for instance. Poetry rarely dignifies such work, though Heaney may have remembered similar striking occasions in Vergil and Hopkins.[5] But the most arresting fact about the final stanza is that it does not use the word 'work' at all but finds in 'love' a virtual synonym, as if to say that such work as the woman does becomes love.

What has the poem to say of Mary Heaney? She is not characterized except by a species of metonymy, in and through the work she does. We might say that she is not so much anonymous as unnamed for the moral force of her personality is felt. Some details may hint at her age: the 'measling' of her shins may be produced by heat but could refer to the spotting or freckling of the skin in elderly people; 'broad-lapped' may refer to the result of sitting in a relaxed posture but could also refer to middle-aged spread. The tone does not invite such ingenuities of interpretation, though they need not be ruled out. Heaney certainly does not offer a socio-economic analysis of his aunt's predicament; she is not a type or symbolic victim of systematic oppression. Some readers find fault with him for his silence on this point.[6] But others, less willing to obey ideological imperatives, may be permitted to relish without guilt the poem's superb tact, its affection and respect for Mary Heaney, its gratitude.

'The Forge', too, celebrates work. The sonnet is voiced for an outsider who knows only 'a door into the dark' but is fascinated by the sounds emanating from the smithy and the occasional brilliance of the sights he glimpses, 'The unpredictable fantail of sparks'. The speaker, however, can only surmise that the anvil 'must be somewhere in the centre'. The smith himself is a distinctly unprepossessing figure: he is 'leather-aproned' with 'hairs in his nose'. He 'grunts', by no means a genteel sound, as he turns aside from the motorized traffic to resume his work. But in spite of the fact that his ancient trade is ceasing to be economically viable, he continues to prize the work he is doing. The interior of the forge is vested with mystery, a word whose ambiguity is felt throughout the sonnet. The anvil is said to be 'Horned as a unicorn', a fabulous beast, and it serves as 'an altar' where the smith celebrates the rites of his mystery. The celebrant assumes the aspect of a divinity, a Norse god, perhaps, whose time is passing. The word 'real' (usually an otiose expression, a mere filler) in the poem's last line, 'To beat real iron out, to work the bellows', reverberates with the smith's (and the poet's?) contempt for the cars that flash past outside. But the poem certainly reverences what it sees as a dying trade.

Influenced perhaps by Richard Poirier's brilliant treatment of certain self-reflexive lyrics of Robert Frost,[7] critics tend to see in poems like 'The Forge' Heaney's discovery of a dynamic analogue for the work of creation in which he himself is engaged in the act of writing. The ease with which the smith's work is thus translated into purely symbolic terms which have forgotten their initial, more concrete application is dismaying. Still, such a move is tempting, though the later it is made the better. It is in any case more appropriate to the work of the thatcher (in the companion piece of that name) or to fishing as described in 'Casualty' (1979), where the implicit comparison with Yeats's fisherman must alert the reader to Heaney's self-conscious subtext.

'The Harvest Bow' is certainly a self-reflexive lyric, a modest, homely version, one might say, of Keats's 'Ode on a Grecian Urn'. We might begin, however, by considering what else it offers. The 'you' addressed in the first line practises a skill in plaiting the bow which is conventionally feminine; the second stanza identifies the 'you' as male. It is only in the third and subsequent stanzas that we can with confidence recognize the poet's father. The 'mellowed silence' implicated in the bow by a skill so practised as to be 'somnambulant' reminds us of much that was unspoken in the father-son relationship and in the culture of silence ('That original townland/ Still tongue-tied in the straw') in which Heaney was formed. The mere writing of the poem involves the transgression of a cultural imperative, though the tone is neither resentful nor rebellious. On this occasion at least, silence is not impugned; the low-key quality of the poem and its undisturbed serenity communicate a kind of wistful acquiescence.

The setting may be a pastoral one, but it is not prettified; the 'old beds and ploughs in hedges' are not conventional adjuncts. Nor is the sight of the father decapitating weeds and striking hedges in keeping with a Hubbel figure. 'Beats out of time' is a lovely ambiguity which awakens the reader to another frame of reference. On the level of prosaic but reliable realism it suggests discordant and irregular strokes but it simultaneously suggests that this remembered scene, like the farmyard in 'Sunlight', is redeemed from the flux of time, is virtually timeless. Not the least of the poem's merits is that the latter reading is not urged aggressively.

The italicized sentence at the beginning of the last stanza ('*The end of art is peace*') is derived from the Victorian poet Coventry Patmore (1823–96) via an essay of Yeats[8] from which Heaney has frequently quoted. Its emphatic position alerts the reader to its profound ambiguity, hardly intended by Patmore and not registered by Yeats. 'End' may refer to the purpose or intention of art; or it may mean the final state of perfect equilibrium achieved by art in balancing rival claims. But the sentence could also mean that peace removes the very conditions that make art possible or necessary. This last possibility, once registered by the reader, must recall the disturbing questions Yeats raises, not in the essay of 1905, but in the great poems of his middle period which address the relation between art and violence.

The very fragile nature of the harvest bow, which has by this point earned its symbolic equivalence for works of art in general and for poetry in particular, hints at the fragility of all artefacts. Nevertheless the skill needed to make the bow has not been allowed to lapse; the bow pinned up in an honoured place on 'our deal dresser' can only have been made by the poet himself. Unless we want to make that particular harvest bow into the very poem we are reading, a dissolving symbol of 'The Harvest Bow' itself. The final word, 'warm', insists that art, whether modest artefact or equally modest poem, is 'a friend to man' as Keats says of the Grecian urn.

There are some awkward moments in 'The Harvest Bow' as well as some rich delights. The texture of the weaving is both complex and legible: the speaker can read its meaning 'like braille'. But 'gleaning the unsaid off the palpable' is too explicit and tendentious; 'palpable' is a clumsy conversion of adjective into noun. Some phrases are tired, almost clichés: 'fine intent', 'golden loops'. But the final image, in which the bow is likened to a snare from which the elusive 'spirit of the corn' makes good his escape (burnishing the woven bow as it goes), emits a beautiful light.

Digging Deep

Heaney's own account of the genesis of 'Bogland' (1969) is illuminating. As a young lecturer in Queen's University, Belfast, he diligently researched the myth of the American West, whose importance in poetry, fiction and film hardly needs underlining. But he had long been brooding on a very different and more familiar landscape, that of the Irish bog, 'a landscape that has a strange assuaging effect on me, one with associations reaching back into early childhood'.[9] However, his vague desire to write a poem about the bog remained an aspiration until in the course of his research the phrase that was to become the first line of 'Bogland' ('We have no prairies') presented itself to him. The chain of associations thus released finally achieved perfect poetic form. Space, Heaney must have realized, has the same turning moment for the American mind as time has in what he calls 'our national consciousness'.[10]

'Bogland', then, contrasts two landscapes and two modes of perception, sometimes explicitly, more often by implication. The effect is similar to double exposure. While the primary focus of the poem is on the bog which sponsors memory and historical awareness, the diction and imagery evoke American vistas whose peculiar charm is that they do not attest to the passage of time. There is something unmistakably cinematic in the image of the prairies slicing 'a big sun at evening'. Likewise, 'our unfenced country' is evocative not only of bogland but also of the open range, another standard visual motif in westerns, this time one which often assumes thematic importance. Indeed, individual words ('horizon', 'pioneers', 'camped') have essentially the same resonance.

The tone of 'Bogland' is informed by a kind of serene wonder: Heaney is secure and untroubled in his rapt contemplation of whatever the bog throws up, whether the skeleton of an extinct creature or the work of human hands like butter. Only in the reference to the Cyclops or in the cautionary last line, 'The wet centre is bottomless', is there a hint of danger. The same cannot be said of 'The Tollund Man' (1972) or of the famous sequence of 'bog poems' in the first part of *North* (1975). Heaney has recorded his own misgivings about dealing with the radioactive material his reading of P.V. Glob's *The Bog People*[11] provided. 'When I wrote this poem ('The Tollund Man'), I had a completely new sensation, one of fear.'[12] The need for complete seriousness, for a total imaginative commitment, was borne in on him; he became involved in an exploration of the darkest corners of the human psyche, without being able to take refuge in the blandness of condemnation or in sophistical self-excluding generalizations about 'men of violence'.

'Bogland' was written before Heaney read Glob, before the violence of the Northern Troubles reached that point of appalling intensity where it had to be addressed, somehow. There is no need to rehearse here the contents of *The Bog People* beyond commenting on the fact that the remarkable photographs of the victims of barbaric forms of punishment or of human sacrifice in iron-age Denmark are sufficient provocations for all but the most comatose imaginations. And one other point may be made in this connection, if only because it has eluded critics. The archaeological bent of Heaney's imagination, reinforced by his reading of Glob and others, has given him a completely different perspective on European history from that found in the classical, more-or-less imperial narratives of Greek and particularly Roman historians which have determined the outlook of most writers in English since the Renaissance. From a certain point of view the distance between iron-age Denmark and modern Ireland is a very short one.

In Heaney's public reading of 'The Tollund Man', Aarhus sounds very like 'our house' does in the speech of Northern Ireland. The poet's intimacy with the victim exhumed from a cauldron bog in 1950 has a familial closeness. The appositional phrase 'Bridegroom to the goddess' might on first reading identify poet and victim, until the syntax clarifies the ambiguity without quite dispelling it. The second of the poem's three parts suggests a tentative identification not with the victim but with those who observed the rites to the goddess in which the Tollund Man was sacrificed:

> I could risk blasphemy,
> Consecrate the cauldron bog
> Our holy ground and pray him
> To make germinate ...

The lines that follow commemorate the murder of four Catholics by Protestant paramilitaries in the 1920s, an incident still remembered in the folklore or oral history alive in Heaney's youth, and link their deaths with the Tollund Man.

In the final section of the poem, poet and victim are again imaginatively identified as the Tollund Man rides the tumbril towards his terrible death. The word 'tumbril', of course, links his death with those of the victims of rough justice in the French Revolution. There is a kind of hope against hope implicit in this terrible inventory of violent death: surely history has supplied enough victims already to slake the thirst of gods and men? But the final lines do not permit even the most timid hope to flourish; the projected pilgrimage to Aarhus will not bring a healing benediction, only an appalling combination of strangeness and familiarity.

Out there in Jutland
In the old man-killing parishes
I will feel lost,
Unhappy and at home.

The bog poems in *North* (1975) offer, if such a thing is possible, even bleaker recognitions than 'The Tollund Man'. They do not figure on the list of prescribed poems, presumably because their intensities, aggravated by sexual and religious feelings disturbingly compounded with scenes of appalling violence, were deemed by the syllabus committee to be too punishing for youthful sensibilities. It is hard to quarrel with their exclusion. As things stand, 'Sunlight', already dealt with, and 'A Constable Calls' are the only two poems from *North* that require attention here.

In 'A Constable Calls' the account of a policeman's duty call to the Heaney homestead is given from the point of view of the poet's younger self. The young Heaney registers emotionally the latent tensions of the fraught occasion without articulating them; he is silently aware that a row of delinquent turnips is undeclared. But the child's fear is hugely in excess of what the constable's mere policemanship accounts for and can only be explained in terms of the political divisions of the community. There is something obviously incongruous in an armed policeman pursuing routine enquiries about root crops; the child's eye is magnetized by the polished holster in which a revolver reposes. Slightly less obvious is the menace attaching to the bicycle itself: the 'spud' of its dynamo is cocked as if it were ready to fire; when, duty done, the constable pushes off, the same innocent machine ticks insistently like the timer of a bomb. Indeed the very book which records the constable's findings becomes 'the domesday book'.

'A Constable Calls' is an interesting poem and, within its own rather narrow terms, a successful one. One could not reasonably object to its melodramatic air given the recent history of Northern Ireland. But the poem is so completely identified with the child's perspective that the reader cannot gain access to the constable's mind. What did the visit mean to him? What might he have guessed from the monosyllabic answers his questions provoked? The poem gives no warrant for such speculations, which are certainly futile but, equally, inevitable.

Homo Ludens

In 1989 the literary journal *Agenda* marked Heaney's fiftieth birthday with a special issue devoted entirely to his work; it included, amid the customary critical appreciations, a tiny poem beginning 'The annals say' which sounds a new note on a new instrument. While every writer is enmeshed in brutal or banal historical circumstances to which some response must be made, every writer (and every reader) longs to escape, however briefly, from their jurisdiction. Making room for such desires is not an act of irresponsibility or self-deception. In 'Preface to Lyrical Ballads' Wordsworth defended the pleasure of poetry against the misgivings of puritans: 'it is a homage paid to the native and naked dignity of man, to the grand elementary principles of pleasure by which he knows and feels, and lives, and moves'.[13] In *Homo Ludens* Johan Huizinga, a Dutch medieval historian, offers a defence of play in very similar terms.[14]

'The annals say' took its place in *Seeing Things* (1991) as one of the forty-eight poems in the sequence 'Squarings', each twelve lines long and arranged in four tercets. Many of these poems—and others in the same collection—are 'ludic' in precisely Huizinga's sense: they assert imaginative freedom in the very act of voluntarily embracing a severely rule-bound form; they are simultaneously playful and serious; they take delight in excavating 'the ore of longing' and celebrating 'Sweet transience' in a light, glancing fashion.[15] They are composed in eternity's sunrise. The poetry of *Seeing Things* took courage to write, though not the kind of courage involved in walking naked according to the dictates of the confessional mode, the only kind officially certified. There is a certain insouciance, a devil-may-care quality, about many of these poems which is simply ravishing. Some, of course, are made of sterner stuff. 'Shifting brilliancies', the very first poem in 'Squarings', has the same terrible exigency as Yeats's 'The Cold Heaven', to which it is a response. But, as Horace observes, 'it is sweet to act the fool at times'[16] and Heaney claims that licence again and again in *Seeing Things*.

The narrative basis of 'The annals say' is fantastical and, from a certain point of view, frankly incredible. It demands of the reader what Keats called 'negative capability',[17] which might be glossed for present purposes as the ability to relish possibilities and even impossibilities without submitting to the laws of probability and necessity. Poetry, after all, is not to be limited to everything that is the case, for that would exclude everything that is not the case and everything that could not conceivably be the case, an intolerable restriction on the freedom of the imagination. It would certainly be churlish not to credit stories such as this one about the monks of Clonmacnoise, although the ship which sails through the upper air into their oratory is a figment of imagination. But once that much is accepted the poem turns out, with delightful perversity, to have as high a quotient of verisimilitude as the most naturalistic novel. 'Rocked' in the phrase 'the big hull rocked to a standstill' is a stroke of genius: the ship rocks because its movement in the fluid medium of air is arrested; it cannot stop of a sudden, being buoyant. Heaney has seen ships drop anchor and imagined this airship.

The abbot's spontaneous expression of concern for the brave sailor who spins down the rope to release the trapped anchor, thereby risking death by drowning, is perfectly in keeping with his profession of Christianity. The danger of the sailor's drowning in air is logically impeccable, the poem's premise once granted. And the sudden transformation of the familiar oratory into a strange and marvellous place involves a departure to an alien perspective which is imaginatively rewarding: paradoxically, it brings home a sense of the marvellous.

Much of what has been said about 'The annals say' is applicable to 'St Kevin and the Blackbird' (1996). At first sight the opening line, 'And then there was St Kevin and the Blackbird', might suggest a certain weariness, a reluctance to recite yet another fanciful tale from the inexhaustible repertoire of the medieval imagination. On the other hand, returning to it in the light of what the poem as a whole provides, one might read the line very differently: here is another tale worth attending to, worth playing with. Heaney's source for the story is Giraldus Cambrensis, whose *History and Topography of Ireland* he almost certainly read in John O'Meara's translation.[18] The pious tale has the kind of extravagance one finds in medieval hagiography where scrupulous realism does not restrict authorial piety.

There is a formal as well as a thematic connection between the two poems. 'St Kevin and the Blackbird' repeats the twelve-line form of 'The annals say', twice. In the first half of the later poem, the first squaring one might say, we are offered the traditional story of the saint at prayer in his cell, being visited by a blackbird which nests in his outstretched hand and hatches its young. Kevin, with a Franciscan reverence for living things, keeps his hand extended for weeks rather than disturb the mother bird. It is a story once heard, never forgotten. But what use is it? How seriously should one take it?

The same teasing ambiguity of tone audible in the first line of the poem is found also at the beginning of the second part: 'And

since the whole thing's imagined anyhow ...' Does this not anticipate a dismissive gesture? 'Forget about it, it's only a story.' But
this is the very move Heaney does not make. Instead he plunges
unapologetically into highly imaginative speculation about
Kevin's feelings, his bodily condition, his state of mind. In short,
he takes the story and its implications seriously, or playfully, if
you prefer; it is impossible to distinguish the two, just as it is
finally impossible to distinguish the saint's body from his mind.

> Alone and mirrored clear in love's deep river,
> 'To labour and nor to seek reward,' he prays,
>
> A prayer his body makes entirely
> For he has forgotten self, forgotten bird
> And on the riverbank forgotten the river's name.

Kevin's self-forgetfulness, born of love, ends in oblivion, the total
loss of self and world; for which the entrancing music of the
poem's last lines may be recompense or requiem.

If the saint is a figure too extreme to be imitated, the woman
at the heart of 'Field of Vision' is, unambiguously, exemplary. Her
view of the world is severely limited, not by choice or through
some culturally induced astigmatism, but of necessity. She is confined to a wheelchair and the scene she looks at is to all intents
and purposes unchanging:

> The same small calves with their backs to wind and rain,
> The same acre of ragwort, the same mountain.

But the very steadfastness with which she regards the unchanging
scene has its reward: she becomes a seer, a visionary of the mundane, close kin spiritually to Kavanagh's Father Mat who observed
'the undying difference in the corner of a field'. By virtue of her
acceptance of her condition ('She never lamented once') and her
refusal of emotional excess, she becomes the poet's tutor in the art

of looking ('an education'). Although its sentiments are admirable, 'Field of Vision' is a dull performance: it does not achieve poetic lift-off.

Love Lyrics

The best of Heaney's poems of love and marriage, 'The Underground' (1984), is so good that it may be smuggled in here though it is, unfortunately, unprescribed. Perhaps because the imagination is in love with beginnings, this recollection and virtual re-enactment of a honeymoon trip to London is tender, playful, utterly irresistible. Without a hint of self-importance, Heaney figures in rapid succession as Ovid's Pan, the Hansel of folklore and the legendary Orpheus, tragic prototype of poets and lovers. Yet the poem is firmly rooted in the actual world, its geography precise ('Between the Underground and the Albert Hall'), its observation of a deserted railway station detailed and nicely ominous. 'The Underground' may thus owe something to Georges Franju's eerie film 'La Première Nuit' (1958) which relocates the Orpheus story in the Paris Metro.

'The Skunk' (1979) is a recollection of a different kind, of the poet's separation from his wife during the mid-seventies when he was living briefly in California and writing love letters home. The skunk, almost immediately feminized, is a regular nocturnal visitor, parading confidently in her finery. She is described in terms more appropriate to the absent wife.

> And there she was, the intent and glamorous,
> Ordinary, mysterious skunk,
> Mythologized, demythologized ...

Tactfully, no mention is made of the skunk's most notorious property, her smell. She is, after all, a guest and a stand-in for the poet's wife.

In the last stanza the time-frame shifts from the past to the present, or rather to 'last night'. Husband and wife are reunited. She frantically searches in a chest of drawers for a suitably sexy nightdress while he suddenly remembers the skunk.

> It all came back to me last night, stirred
> By the sootfall of your things at bedtime,
> Your head-down, tail-up hunt in a bottom drawer
> For the black plunge-line nightdress.

Perverse? Incongruous? Mischievous? Insulting? Hilarious? The tone is difficult to determine and liable to change with every fresh reading of the poem. But the scene is unforgettable largely because of the magical 'sootfall' which softly connotes the sound of clothes falling on a carpet, in a barely audible prelude to physical love.

The early love poems are slighter things, though they have charm. A stern critic might be tempted to dismiss them as 'adolescent', meaning gauche, embarrassing, ambitious beyond their means, unconsciously derivative, insecure in tone—in short, vulnerable to irony. There is something pedagogically dysfunctional in employing such terms before a class of enthusiastic adolescents as yet unschooled in life's disapppointments. Besides, to pull rank is to confess weakness. It is difficult to see why criticism should repudiate the expression of youthful awkwardness in a poem such as 'Twice Shy' ('We thrilled to the March twilight/ With nervous childish talk') simply because it does not wear a carapace of irony.

Students can surely be allowed to enjoy Heaney's early poems of love for what they are worth. On a good day they may even succeed in teaching their teachers to recover that openness to experience which is the peculiar grace of adolescence.

The Verbal Medium

No poet is more careful of the secret life of language than Heaney. The latent ambiguities of words, their complex histories and etymologies, their cultural resonance and emotional colourations, have occupied him for decades, since 'Digging' confirmed his sense of vocation. He is, among other things, an archaeologist of language. 'Among other things', for his poetry claims our attention by its personal urgencies and its responsiveness to the currents of the times. That he has been affected by scruples of doubt about his chosen medium is clear from the substance and indeed the title of his address to the World Reading Association in 1982, 'Words Alone?'[19] That question-mark, and the vocal inflection it demands, is proof positive of his unease: not for him the certainty with which the young Yeats proclaimed 'Words alone are certain good'.

Yet such misgivings have not paralysed him or kept his tongue from speech. In poems like 'The annals say' he can persuade us that the truest poetry is indeed the most feigning, as Shakespeare's Touchstone puts it.[20] But on occasion, in 'Sunlight' for instance, he has used Cordelia's idiom, 'words trustworthy and true', to honour experience and celebrate its potential. Only a great poet can do justice both to Touchstone's mischievous definition of poetry and Cordelia's prescription for speech.

Bibliography

Seamus Heaney, *Preoccupations: Selected Prose 1968-1978* (London: Faber and Faber, 1980). This is the most useful of Heaney's prose works, for its biographical excursions, its account of the genesis of a number of poems, and its critical responses to Patrick Kavanagh ('From Monaghan to the Grand Canal') and Philip Larkin ('Englands of the Mind').

Seamus Heaney, *The Place of Writing* (Atlanta: Scholars Press, 1989). This work is valuable for Heaney's criticism of Irish predecessors (including Yeats) and contemporaries (Michael Longley, Thomas Kinsella, Derek Mahon).

Seamus Heaney, *Stepping Stones* (London: Penguin Books, 1995). This tape, in which the poet reads more than thirty poems, commenting helpfully on many of them, is unquestionably the best introduction for students coming to Heaney for the first time.

Seamus Heaney, *Opened Ground: Poems 1966-1996* (London: Faber and Faber, 1998). This volume contains most of Heaney's best work, including selections from *Sweeney Astray* (1983) and *The Cure at Troy* (1990).

Patricia Coughlan, '"Bog Queens": The Representation of Women in the Poetry of John Montague and Seamus Heaney', in *Gender in Irish Writing*, ed. Toni O'Brien Johnson and David Kearns (Milton Keynes: Open University Press, 1991), pp. 88-111.

Denis Donoghue, 'The Literature of Trouble', in *We Irish* (Brighton: The Harvester Press, 1986). Here, Donoghue considers the relation between Heaney's poetry and the political violence to which it responds.

Desmond Fennell, *'Whatever You Say, Say Nothing': Why Seamus Heaney is No. 1* (Dublin: ELO Publications, 1991).

David Lloyd, 'Pap for the dispossessed', in *Anomalous States* (Dublin: The Lilliput Press, 1993).

Michael Parker, *Seamus Heaney: The Making of the Poet* (Dublin: Gill and Macmillan, 1993). Of the many books on Heaney's poetry, Parker's remains the most useful. Parker makes intelligent use of biographical and historical information, and offers shrewd, detailed commentaries on virtually all the major poems down to, and including, *Seeing Things*.

Helen Vendler, *Seamus Heaney* (London: Harper Collins, 1998). This work traces Heaney's poetic development. Vendler is more selective than Parker but does offer close readings of 'Bogland', 'The Tollund Man' and 'St Kevin and the Blackbird'.

Notes

1. In all conscience the name of Robert Frost should be added to this list.

2. See 'Crediting Poetry' in *Opened Ground*, p. 451.

3. Heaney's poems are identified in the text by the date of their first appearance in book form.

4. Heaney, 'Crediting Poetry', p. 447.

5. '*Sulco attritus splendescere vomer*' (*Georgics* I, L.46) is virtually translated by Hopkins in 'The Windhover': 'sheer plod makes plough down sillion shine'.

6. See Patricia Coughlan's '"Bog Queens": The representation of women in the poetry of John Montague and Seamus Heaney'. Apart from Coughlan's essay, other hostile accounts of Heaney's poetry which are worth quarrelling with include David Lloyd's 'Pap for the dispossessed' and Desmond Fennell's pamphlet '*Whatever You Say, Say Nothing': Why Seamus Heaney is No. 1.*

7. Richard Poirier, *Robert Frost: The Work of Knowing* (Oxford: Oxford University Press, 1977), see especially pp. 281-313.

8. W.B. Yeats, 'Samhain 1905', in *Explorations* (London: Macmillan, 1962), especially p. 199.

9. Seamus Heaney, 'Feeling into Words', in *Preoccupations*, p. 54.

10. Ibid., p. 55.

11. P.V. Glob, *The Bog People* (London: Faber and Faber, 1969). The photograph facing p. 8 is particularly relevant.

12. Heaney, 'Feeling into Words', p. 58.

13. See 'Preface to Lyrical Ballads' in *Romantic Poetry and Prose*, ed. Harold Bloom and Lionel Trilling (London: Oxford University Press, 1973), p. 603.

14. Johan Huizinga, *Homo Ludens: A Study of the Play Element in Culture* (London: Paladin, 1970).

15. These phrases are from 'Sand-bed, they said', *Opened Ground*, p. 385.

16. Horace, *Odes* iv, 12, line 28. ('*Dulce est desipere in loco.*')

17. *Romantic Poetry and Prose*, p. 768.

18. Cambrensis, *The History and Topography of Ireland* (Harmondsworth: Penguin, 1982), pp. 77-9.

19. An edited version of the lecture 'Words Alone?' appeared in a special supplement to *An Múinteoir Náisiúnta* 26, 3 (Autumn 1982). Unfortunately, it has never been published in book form.

20. *As You Like It*, III.iii.19-20.

'Speak I Must': Charlotte Brontë's Jane Eyre

MARGARET KELLEHER

Introduction

Charlotte Brontë's novel *Jane Eyre* may justly be described as 'a classic', a novel that has stood the test of time because of its fresh appeal to new generations of readers. As the story of a child's coming of age, it belongs to the category of *bildungsroman* or novel of education—though, unusually for the *bildungsroman*, with a *female* protagonist—and bears interesting comparison with other examples of the genre, including Charles Dickens' *Great Expectations*, Mark Twain's *The Adventures of Huckleberry Finn* or Seamus Deane's *Reading in the Dark*.[1] Each of these novels opens with the alienation experienced by their young subject, a character who is marginalized not alone by the strength of economic and social injustices but by virtue of childhood itself. The child gradually learns to negotiate the various codes and hidden rules that function throughout the society in which he or she lives: within the family, among neighbours and friends, at the heart of systems of education and employment, and, in the most painful discovery of all, even in the most private realms of love.

The status achieved by *Jane Eyre* in the hundred and fifty years since its publication was not, however, what was predicted by many of its first reviewers. While the novel was greeted favourably in some of the notices that appeared in English journals in 1847, the reactions of others varied from mild dislike to extreme outrage. For some of its first readers, *Jane Eyre* was an offensive and dangerous book; for example, in the opinion of Elizabeth Rigby, an influential reviewer in her time, Brontë's novel was 'pre-eminently an anti-Christian composition', guilty of 'gross vulgarity' in the frankness of conversation between Jane and Rochester and of spreading 'ungodly discontent' through Jane's complaints against the injustices she encounters.[2] Since then, other critics have come to share Rigby's view of the novel as revolutionary in effect but positively so, a novel that is radical in its emphasis on personal feeling and on the authority and value of one's own desire.[3]

The continuing appeal of *Jane Eyre* for its readers has many different sources: the haunting memory of the terrified ten-year-old locked into the 'red room'; the graphic depiction of the calculated cruelty practised in Lowood Institution; the suspense with which omens gather that all is not right in Thornfield House; or, the ultimate of happy endings in which the wronged woman is finally restored to fortune and union with 'the man of her dreams'. And yet it is important to note from the outset that some readers are annoyed by the priggishness and arrogance of the young Jane and are estranged rather than involved by Jane's telling of her story. The relationship between Jane and Rochester is, for many, unconvincing or problematic—most notably in the novel's ending which is judged as too happy by readers unconvinced by its elements of fantasy and romance, and as not happy enough by readers unimpressed by Jane's choice of partner.

The nineteenth-century realistic novel, of which *Jane Eyre* is now one of the most famous examples, is fundamentally concerned with the individual's relationship with society. It traces the lives of men and women who attempt to reconcile the demands of the world with their own desires. Charlotte Brontë's contribution to this genre is at its most powerful in her depiction of the psychological dimensions of this struggle. Jane's desperate need to express her identity, to assert her very existence, comes into conflict with society's requirements that she silence her voice, repress her opinions, stifle her longings and aspirations. These central themes of expression and repression, of endurance and resistance, will be traced in the following discussion of the novel and offer a means of uncovering both the appealing and less appealing qualities of *Jane Eyre*. Viewed as a whole, the novel emerges as a forceful study of an individual's search for liberation but also as a sobering, even uncomfortable, reminder that such a quest takes place in the context of the many forces that confine and restrict our lives. As in the closing episodes of so many nineteenth-century novels, Jane's ultimate 'happy ending' is achieved only through substantial compromise.

Gateshead and Lowood: Chapters 1–10

The title-page of *Jane Eyre* announces that it is 'an autobiography'—a rubric whose significance extends well beyond the many details that are drawn from the life experience of its creator, Charlotte Brontë. The novel is itself about autobiography, the creation of one's own life-story. In this regard, it is crucial that Jane be the narrator of her tale. '*Speak* I must' declares Jane in chapter 4. Henceforth, her story may be viewed as the search for a sympathetic audience through encounters with various listeners: the doctor and Bessie in the Reads' house; Helen Burns and Miss Temple in Lowood; Rochester, most attentive of all whom Jane encounters; and, ultimately, all of us, Jane's readers.[4]

From the beginning of the novel, Jane is painfully aware of her own insignificance, as poor relation, orphan and dependant: 'heir' to nothing, insubstantial as 'air'. The first chapter locates her physically in a window-seat, largely unnoticed by those indoors, barely 'protected' but 'not separated' from the coldness outside. Significantly, the story begins with Jane's first real resistance, but the consequences of that act of rebellion, in the further worsening of Jane's already vulnerable position, are also immediately apparent. The theme of oppression and resistance will return throughout the narrative, as complex questions are encountered by the young Jane: how much to endure, when to rebel, when to submit? The psychological dilemmas are figured through the recurring images of fire and ice, or red and white, representing the psychological extremes of fiery passion and chill repression. Through resistance at least one knows one exists, and the 'strange little figure' (ch. 2) that Jane glimpses in the mirror can be given form and gain a voice. As one critic astutely notes, 'For someone as socially isolated as Jane, the self is all one has.'[5] Yet the continuing danger Jane faces is that rebellion will eliminate the fragile self which she possesses. Significantly, in these early chapters, Jane's psychological well-being—her very sanity—is threatened by the vehemence of passion released within herself as much as by the ill-treatment she suffers from others. Her first psychic crisis is the breakdown she experiences in the red-room—one too easily forgets that Jane is, at this point in the narrative, only ten years old.

The developing stages of Jane's personal journey are given concrete form through the different houses in which she lives: Gateshead Hall, Lowood Institution, Thornfield Hall, Moor House and Ferndean. Each of these locations brings with it temptations and dangers while the various inhabitants present Jane with alternative models of behaviour. In Lowood, Helen Burns seeks to teach Jane the forbearance, self-control and moderation necessary in order to survive the hardships of this institution. One crucial lesson for Jane to learn is the importance of her own inner resources: 'If all the world hated you, and believed you wicked, while your own conscience approved you, and absolved you from guilt, you would not be without friends' (ch. 8). For Jane, at this point in the story, 'that is not enough; if others don't love me, I would rather die than live'. To Helen's exhortation, 'love your enemies', she counters the vigorous dictum, 'When we are struck at without a reason, we should strike back again very hard; I am sure we should—so hard as to teach the person who struck us never to do it again' (ch. 6).

The words of Helen Burns carry the full weight of Christian tradition and the scene of her death ranks among the most memorable in the novel. Yet the model which she offers, as martyr-heroine, is not unambiguously positive. Helen's fate also exemplifies the dangers of extreme submission, whereby full denial or sacrifice of the self results in death. Similarly, the influence of Miss Temple, the model of temperate rebellion, is at best partial and wanes quickly following her departure. At the end of eight years in Lowood, the restless eighteen-year-old girl still longs for 'liberty' or 'at least a new servitude' (ch. 10).

While this discussion has concentrated on the personal dimensions of Jane's narrative, Brontë's work continually highlights wider economic and social issues arising from the individual life. Thus the Lowood episode, fuelled by Charlotte Brontë's personal experience, also presents a savage critique of the deprivation and hypocrisy fundamental to the school's operations while under the direction of Mr Brocklehurst. The girls housed within its walls do not fit easily into social categories; many, like Jane, are orphans from more genteel families who are no longer welcome among their wealthier relatives. The educational aims of the school carry an explicit agenda: to make the young girls 'humble' and 'useful', to remove any 'worldly sentiment' and to train them 'in conformity' with their position and prospects. One of the few forms of employment open to Lowood graduates is the position of governess. The Victorian governess, as the critic Mary Poovey has shown, occupied a particularly tenuous position in society at the time. Charged with the upholding of firm class divisions, the governess herself was a curiously 'in-between figure'— distinguished from the upper classes because she worked for a living, yet separable from the working class as a 'genteel' and 'well-bred' figure to whom the younger members of the upper class could be entrusted.[6] Many were vulnerable to the sexual advances of their employers though forbidden any opportunities for marriage; transgressions, as Jane is vividly reminded by Blanche Ingram's childhood recollections of the unfortunate Miss Wilson (ch. 17), were speedily punished. Yet, to the horror of some of its first readers, the novel *Jane Eyre* is one in which the crossing of class boundaries—a governess marrying her employer—is both possible and to be applauded.

Thornfield: Chapters 11–27

Jane's progression from place to place is also a movement from chamber to chamber: from the terrifying red-room in Gateshead and the small closet in which Jane lives, to the freezing rooms of Lowood and onward to the galleries and attic of Rochester's home. On her first arrival, Thornfield House offers the 'snug' and 'cheerful' interior of Mrs Fairfax's chamber and, for Jane, a small 'solitary' bedroom—a room of her own, for the first time (ch. 11). The house itself is a gentleman's manor-house; as Jane carefully observes, it is not 'a nobleman's seat' yet it possesses 'the aspect of a home of the past—a shrine of memory' (ch. 11).

The new opportunities which Thornfield offers, however, are not enough to contain Jane's restlessness. In chapter 12, she describes how her sole relief then was 'to walk along the corridor of the third storey, backwards and forwards'. From her own inner rebellion against physical and mental confinement, through tales 'created' and 'narrated continuously' by her imagination, Jane comes to recognize solidarity with the 'silent revolt' of millions. Her protest is the novel's most direct articulation of the desire for liberty and has the quality of a political manifesto. Fuelled by the personal struggles of its author,[7] the implications of this passage extend well beyond the confines of the narrative:

Nobody knows how many rebellions besides political rebellions ferment in the masses of life which people earth. Women are supposed to be very calm generally: but women feel just as men feel; they need exercise for their faculties, and a field for their efforts as much as their brothers do; they suffer from too rigid a restraint, too absolute a stagnation, precisely as men would suffer; and it is narrow-minded in their more privileged fellow-creatures to say that they ought to confine themselves to making puddings and knitting stockings, to playing on the piano and embroidering bags. It is thoughtless to condemn them, or laugh at them, if they seek to do more or learn more than custom has pronounced necessary for their sex. (ch. 12)

Jane's first encounter with Rochester follows quickly on this passage, and, significantly, occurs outside the walls of Thornfield House. The description of their meeting possesses many romantic qualities: a winter's day and rising moon, superstitions in the air, a tall steed and dark rider (ch. 12). A more realistic element enters with Rochester's fall which, in a development heavy with resonance for their later relationship, makes him reliant on Jane's help. Qualities normally termed unattractive render Rochester attractive to Jane. His rude behaviour, haughty demeanour, and an appearance which approaches ugliness, serve to free her from inhibitions. The reader must infer what it is about Jane that draws Rochester to her, since this lies outside the confidences available from narrator to reader: she is honest, frank and a good listener; she lacks the usual affectation of 'raw schoolgirl-governesses'; and, most enviable to Rochester (though the reader knows he is probably mistaken), she appears to possess 'a memory without blot or contamination' (ch. 14). Yet Rochester is also the first person to sense the troubled depths of Jane's interior life, recognizing 'peculiar' and troubled qualities in her water-colour paintings of a 'swollen sea' and 'drowned corpse'. Both remain as yet unaware of the prophetic qualities of her portrait of a 'colossal head' whose features are partially hidden by a 'sable veil' but reveal one eye 'blank of meaning, but for the glassiness of despair' (ch. 13).

Jane and Rochester's developing relationship is most fully conveyed through their dialogues and conversations, with the liveliness of their repartee and frankness of confidences especially expressive of the growing energy between them. The closeness thus established brings, for Jane, an unprecedented sense of intellectual equality and spiritual intimacy: 'I felt at times as if he were my relation rather than my master' (ch. 15). And yet the disparity between their situations is not to be so easily dispelled. Jane castigates herself for dreaming—'he is not of your order' (ch. 17)—and compels herself to draw an 'ivory miniature of an imaginary Blanche Ingram' along with the '"Portrait of a Governess, disconnected, poor, and plain"' (ch. 16). Once again pictures and portraits serve as a guide to Jane's interior life; in this case the paucity of the chalk outline of herself, in comparison with the idealized image of her rival, conveys the painful dimensions of Jane's emerging sexuality and the threat posed to the young woman's fragile sense of self.

The growing intimacy between Rochester and Jane is punctuated by ominous intrusions from Thornfield's uppermost storey. During her first tour of the house, even before Jane meets Rochester, she hears 'a curious laugh—distinct, formal, mirthless' emanating from the rows of black doors 'all shut, like a corridor in some Bluebeard's castle' (ch. 11). Hours after the conversation in which Rochester reveals to Jane many (though evidently not all) of the secrets of his earlier life, Jane is awakened by a 'demoniac laugh' and rescues Rochester from the 'tongues of flame' which encircle his bed (ch. 15). The release of passion evidenced in the gypsy episode, in which Rochester's disguise helps to reveal the truth of his feelings (ch. 19), is immediately halted by Richard Mason's arrival and succeeded by yet another of Bertha's appearances.

While omens gather that all is not well in the Rochester household, the disturbances within Jane's interior life gather force. Brontë's articulation of the depths that lie beneath the conscious self is at its most sophisticated here. A sense of threat gathers not alone from the world outside but also from within the most private realms of the self. Most expressive of this vulnerability and apprehension is Jane's recurring dream: 'scarcely a night had gone over my couch that had not brought with it a dream of an infant, which I sometimes hushed in my arms, sometimes dandled on my knee, sometimes watched playing with daisies on a lawn, or again, dabbling its hands in running water' (ch. 21). The symbolic significance of this infant has been variously interpreted, most persuasively as the burden of the past which Jane cannot yet escape.[8] And, after seven nights of such dreaming, Jane is summoned back to the scene of her childhood nightmares—Gateshead Hall.

The interweaving of past, present and future is especially complex, and occasionally unwieldy, at this point in the narrative. Jane's return to the past brings with it the discovery, of immense future importance, that she possesses an uncle of some substantial fortune. Her visit to the Reeds is also the catalyst for Jane and Rochester's relationship, climaxing in the proposal scene in chapter 23. Jane's earlier negotiations between submission and revolt, the search for independence and liberty within a life of dependence and servitude, return with force here. Given the differences between servant and master, her outcry is a brave assertion of independence: 'I am no bird; and no net ensnares me; I am a free human being with an independent will, which I now exert to leave you.' And Rochester's ensuing proposal to Jane, as 'my equal' and 'my likeness', promises the end of inequity and servitude. Yet can the economic disparity between governess and employer be so swiftly erased? The narrative itself suggests not, even as the chapter ends, through reference to the lightning bolt which splits the great horse-chestnut tree down its centre.

More subtly drawn are the tensions that persist in Rochester and Jane's relationship in the weeks preceding the wedding day. Jane continually resists Rochester's idealization—'I am not an angel ... I will be myself'—and is increasingly uncomfortable with being the object of his affection: 'He smiled; and I thought his smile was such as a sultan might, in a blissful and fond moment, bestow on a slave his gold and gems had enriched' (ch. 24). Once again, her anxieties are revealed through dreams in which images of the past (an 'unknown' little child whom Jane cannot put down) and of the future (Thornfield Hall as a 'dreary ruin') are strangely intermingled with present reality in the form of Bertha's re-appearance (ch. 25).

Two encounters between Jane and Bertha occur here, at the narrative's centre. Two nights before her wedding day, Jane experiences a 'dream' in which a woman 'tall and large' stands before her; her face is 'savage' and 'discoloured', with 'swelled and dark' lips and 'bloodshot eyes', reminding Jane of 'the foul German spectre—the vampire'. This woman places Jane's veil on her 'gaunt head', then removes it and tears it into two parts (ch. 25). Following the interruption of the marriage ceremony, the wedding party visits the third storey and Jane and Bertha come face to face. The contrast between Jane and Bertha is foregrounded, not least by Rochester, as sanity versus insanity: between the 'clear eyes' of his 'good angel' and the 'red balls' of the 'hideous demon', between the cool, rational governess and the 'depraved', 'unchaste' woman (chs. 26 & 27).

Yet Jane and Bertha are linked by the narrative much earlier than this meeting, and not only as opposites. Both suffer forms of confinement; both wander restlessly through the upper floors of Thornfield Hall, 'backwards and forwards'. As noted earlier, Bertha's early appearances in the novel occur at points of crisis in Jane's relationship with Rochester, further establishing a strange kinship between them. Bertha's tearing of the veil, for example, may be read as the expression of Jane's own deep anxieties regarding the forthcoming marriage. On the morning of her wedding day, Jane sees in the mirror 'a robed and veiled figure, so unlike my usual self that it seemed almost the image of a stranger' (ch. 26). For some readers, Bertha, the 'madwoman in the attic', exists as Jane's 'truest and darkest double',[9] the physical embodiment of disturbances within her unconscious self. As an insane and 'fallen' woman she exemplifies the dangers of which Victorian governesses were most acutely aware.[10] More specifically for Jane, she embodies a woman who has passed the limits of what is psychologically bearable. Jane's life-story includes a number of near escapes from madness; one of these immediately follows her meeting with Bertha.

Moor House and Ferndean: Chapters 28–38

Brontë's depiction of psychological trauma anticipates what in Freudian terms would become known as 'the return of the repressed'. Thus crises in the present reawaken memories of past ordeals. The desperate possibilities for resistance envisaged by Jane in the course of her flight from Thornfield echo those contemplated by the suffering child: 'running away ... never eating or drinking more, and letting myself die' (ch. 2). Jane is saved from destitution by her fortuitous meeting with the Rivers family—though the revelation that Diana, Mary and St John Rivers are her first cousins is one of the novel's least convincing plot developments. More importantly, this episode also provides the last challenge to Jane's developing self, through the person of St John Rivers. The following exchange between them, reported in chapter 33 of the novel, highlights the direct contrast between their characters: 'I am cold: no fervour infects me' (St John), 'Whereas I am hot, and fire dissolves ice' (Jane).

St John's offer to Jane to journey with him to India is chilling in its emptiness: 'you are formed for labour, not for love. A missionary's wife you must—shall be' (ch. 34); it involves certain 'premature death' should she accept. Both in his person and in the life-path he has chosen, St John embodies the 'death-principle', itself attractive to Jane: 'I was tempted to cease struggling with him—to rush down the torrent of his will into the gulf of his existence, and there lose my own' (ch. 35). Once again, Jane must choose between 'absolute submission and determined revolt' (ch. 34). Her ultimate decision is to refuse the 'martyrdom' which he proposes, deeming it—with her readers' full approval—to be 'monstrous' (ch. 34).

The novel's ending is facilitated by a number of plot developments whose elements of coincidence and supernatural design sit oddly with the realistic narrative. In one of the novel's supernatural strains, Jane hears the voice of Rochester prompting her to return to Thornfield. By now, she is an heiress in her own right, with a fortune of five thousand pounds remaining to her from her uncle Eyre's bequest. Rochester, she discovers, has been blinded and crippled by the fire which reduced Thornfield to a 'blackened ruin'. In a reversal of earlier imagery, he is the 'wronged and fettered wild beast or bird, dangerous to approach in his sullen woe' (ch. 37). Yet, as Jane famously announces at the beginning of the novel's last chapter, 'reader I married him'. Rochester's attractiveness to Jane is now increased rather than lessened by his dependent status. The narrative ends with Jane as wife and mother, 'supremely blest', in 'perfect concord' with her husband (ch. 38). Strikingly, and perhaps guiltily, the last word in the narrative belongs to St John and to his missionary endeavour.

Divergent opinions regarding Brontë's achievement occur most frequently with regard to the ending of *Jane Eyre*. For the poet and critic Adrienne Rich, the novel's conclusion is positive and persuasive: 'The wind that blows through this novel is the wind of sexual equality—spiritual and practical.'[11] In stark contrast, some readers view Jane's 'happy' marriage as an abominable act of self-sacrifice and loss of identity. For others, the ending is less than satisfactory, if only in the juggling of positions which it seems to require. Rochester is lowered, physically, by injuries that carry clear connotations of punishment,[12] while Jane is raised financially by the bequest received from her uncle in Jamaica. Such details make visible the strain which Brontë encountered in seeking to imagine and portray equality in economic and sexual terms. Thus Gilbert and Gubar argue that while Charlotte Brontë could act out, in her writing, 'a passionate drive toward freedom which offended agents of the status quo', nowhere 'was she able consciously to define the full meaning of achieved freedom'.[13]

Yet another perspective on the novel's ending is possible, however—one that is truer, perhaps, to the language of the novel itself. Freedom *is* found by Jane, but only within servitude, i.e. in serving the needs of another. Thus the novel closes with the reconciliation of forces that had been in tension throughout Jane's story. Contrary to our 'modern' sensibilities which see dependence and independence as clear opposites, Brontë's novel suggests that they are crucially related. Freedom or independence for oneself is to be found within, rather than outside, relations with others. Herein lies one of the most striking differences between Charlotte's vision and that of her sister Emily. The ending of *Wuthering Heights*, for Cathy and Heathcliff's relationship, takes place outside the confines of family, society, geographical space, and time itself. For Charlotte, such a transcendence of the human world is impossible: her heroine must continue to live within, and negotiate, the restrictions which this world demands.[14] The ending of *Jane Eyre* may therefore appeal to or discomfit readers in the relationship which it envisions, finally, between the individual and society. True maturity and self-realization, the novel suggests, involve some degree of conformity and considerable compromise.

Conclusion: The Politics of *Jane Eyre*

For some readers, yet another question troubles the novel's resolution: the fate of the 'madwoman in the attic', at whose expense the happy ending is achieved.[15] The question 'what about Bertha?' has most famously occupied the Dominica-born novelist Jean Rhys, whose 1966 novel *Wide Sargasso Sea* presents a retelling of Brontë's novel from Bertha's perspective. A number of recent studies of *Jane Eyre* examine the novel in the context of nineteenth-century representations of empire; these critics have further emphasized the racialized and racist qualities inherent in Brontë's representation of Bertha.[16] While, as previously discussed, Bertha's significance for the narrative has generally been viewed in psychological terms (Bertha as Jane's 'dark double'), more recent interpretations of the novel emphasize the political aspects both of her character and of her marriage to Rochester.[17]

In contrast to the many characters in Victorian fiction who travel to the colonies (Magwitch in *Great Expectations*, Sir Thomas

Bertram in Jane Austen's *Mansfield Park*, Rochester in *Jane Eyre*), Bertha's journey is from Jamaica to England. As a 'mad' and 'unchaste' woman, she is a threatening figure who brings danger deep into the domestic space of England.[18] Rochester's crime in marrying Bertha is both sexual and economic, prompted by his family's greed at the opportunities provided to their younger, superfluous son by marriage into Jamaican plantation society. His encounter with Jane brings punishment for his immoral and corrupt behaviour, but also offers an opportunity for redemption. Jane's identity, in this reading, is crucially that of reformer. While providing the spur to St John's missionary zeal, she realizes that her primary duty lies at home, in the rehabilitation of Rochester. Significantly, Jane's fortune comes from the same source as that of Rochester—the colonies. Yet the hard work of her uncle, representative of a 'good colonialism', contrasts sharply with the 'bad colonialism' practised by Rochester and ultimately heals the damage it has caused.

Such an analysis clearly extends the significance of Jane's story beyond the individual to the larger political scene. Jane emerges as a much more representative figure, as 'the ideal woman of Empire' and the means through which some of the more troubling ghosts of the colonial experience may be laid to rest.[19] While this reading may not be of interest to every reader, it demonstrates well the range of emphases available within critical studies of the nineteenth-century novel, from psychological and individual-based analyses to more political and social interpretations.

As we have seen, the politics of *Jane Eyre* have been variously interpreted since the novel's publication: as dangerously radical and subversive of class and gender identities, in the opinion of some; as regrettably conservative in its vision of sexual and imperial politics, for others. Common to these differing readings, however, is an emphasis on literature's role in shaping (rather than merely reflecting) cultural identity. That a novel may influence our views on the relationships between men and women, or prompt a rethinking of the treatment of children, or lead us to question the class structures in which we live, is a view shared by readers of *Jane Eyre* from Elizabeth Rigby in 1848 to students meeting the novel for the first time in the early twenty-first century. Not surprisingly, *Jane Eyre* has proved to be a remarkably resilient novel and, some readers' criticisms notwithstanding, seems to have increased in relevance over time. Whether this continues to be the case is a matter that will concern teachers and students for many years to come.

Bibliography

Harold Bloom (ed.), *Jane Eyre: Modern Critical Interpretations* (New York: Chelsea House, 1987). This useful collection of essays reproduces the articles by Bodenheimer, Eagleton, and Gilbert and Gubar that are listed below.

Rosemarie Bodenheimer, 'Jane Eyre in search of her story', *Papers on Language and Literature* 16, 4 (Fall 1980), pp. 387-402.

Charlotte Brontë, *Jane Eyre* ([1847]; Middlesex: Penguin, 1966). All references to the novel are from this edition.

Deirdre David, 'The governess of empire: Jane Eyre takes care of India and Jamaica', in *Rule Britannia: Women, Empire and Victorian Writing* (Ithaca and London: Cornell University Press, 1995), pp. 77-117.

Richard J. Dunn (ed.), *Jane Eyre* (New York: Norton, 1987). This edition provides the text of the novel along with a selection of criticism, including Rigby's 1848 review and extracts from Rich, Gilbert and Gubar, and Eagleton.

Terry Eagleton, 'Jane Eyre', in *Myths of Power: A Marxist Study of the Brontës* ([1975]; London and New York: Macmillan, 1988), pp. 15-32.

Elizabeth Gaskell, *The Life of Charlotte Brontë* ([1857]; London: Penguin, 1975).

Sandra Gilbert and Susan Gubar, 'A dialogue of self and soul: plain Jane's progress', in *The Madwoman in the Attic: The Woman Writer and the Nineteenth-Century Literary Imagination* (New Haven: Yale University Press, 1979), pp. 336-71.

Mary Poovey, 'The anathematized race: the governess and *Jane Eyre*', in *Uneven Developments: The Ideological Work of Gender in Mid-Victorian England* (London and Chicago: University of Chicago Press, 1988), pp. 126-63.

Adrienne Rich, 'Jane Eyre: the temptations of a motherless woman', in *On Lies, Secrets, and Silence: Selected Prose, 1966-1978* (New York: Norton, 1979), pp. 89-106.

Gayatri Spivak, 'Three women's texts and a critique of imperialism', *Critical Inquiry* 12 (1985), pp. 243-61, reproduced in part in Catherine Belsey and Jane Moore (eds), *The Feminist Reader* ([1989]; London: Macmillan, 1997), pp. 175-95.

Raymond Williams, *The English Novel from Dickens to Lawrence* ([1970]; London: Hogarth Press, 1984).

Notes

1. All three of these texts, *Great Expectations*, *The Adventures of Huckleberry Finn* and *Reading in the Dark*, now feature on the Leaving Certificate syllabus.

2. Rigby objected in particular to what she termed the novel's 'proud and perpetual assertion of the rights of man', arguing that the novel contained 'throughout it a murmuring against the comforts of the rich and against the privations of the poor, which, as far as each individual is concerned, is a murmuring against God's appointment'; see Elizabeth Rigby (Lady Eastlake), '*Vanity Fair* and *Jane Eyre*', *Quarterly Review* 84 (1848), pp. 173-4.

3. Thus, for example, Raymond Williams argues that the works of Charlotte and Emily Brontë, while very different, are linked by 'an emphasis on intense feeling, a commitment to what we must directly call passion, that is in itself very new in the English novel'; see Raymond Williams, *The English Novel from Dickens to Lawrence*, p. 60.

4. In her article 'Jane Eyre in search of her story', Rosemarie Bodenheimer emphasizes the importance of Jane's search for an audience as 'essentially a search for love and human connection', p. 394.

5. Terry Eagleton, 'Jane Eyre', p. 24.

6. See Poovey, 'The anathematized race: the governess and *Jane*

Eyre', pp. 126-30. In an observation rich in resonance for the novel, Poovey notes that two of the figures with which the Victorian governess was repeatedly linked were 'the lunatic' and 'the fallen woman'; in the 1840s, 'governesses accounted for the single largest category of women in lunatic asylums' (pp. 129-30).

7. In 1836, the twenty-year-old Charlotte Brontë wrote to the poet Robert Southey, enclosing some poems and confiding in him her ambition to be a writer. Some months later, Southey, then one of England's most famous poets, responded, warning the young woman that 'Literature cannot be the business of a woman's life, and it ought not to be. The more she is engaged in her proper duties, the less leisure she will have for it, even as an accomplishment and a recreation.' See Elizabeth Gaskell, *The Life of Charlotte Brontë*, ch. 8.

8. See Gilbert and Gubar, 'A dialogue of self and soul: plain Jane's progress', p. 358. Poovey reads these dreams as emblems of the enforced helplessness of the governess's position, 'along with the frustration, self-denial, and maddened, thwarted rage that accompanies it' ('The anathematized race', p. 141).

9. Gilbert and Gubar, 'A dialogue of self and soul', p. 360.

10. See Poovey, 'The anathematized race' and note 6 above.

11. Adrienne Rich, 'Jane Eyre: the temptations of a motherless woman', p. 105.

12. Many critics view Rochester's injuries as a symbolic castration, and as punishment for his earlier misdemeanours; see Gilbert and Gubar, 'A dialogue of self and soul', p. 368.

13. Gilbert and Gubar, 'A dialogue of self and soul', pp. 369-70.

14. Similarly, Terry Eagleton argues that Charlotte's 'impulse' is to 'negotiate passionate self-fulfilment on terms which preserve the social and moral conventions intact' ('Jane Eyre', p. 16).

15. This argument receives its most influential, but also most complex, formulation in Gayatri Spivak's article 'Three women's texts and a critique of imperialism'. See also Deirdre David, 'The governess of empire', pp. 77-97.

16. According to the text of the novel, Bertha is the daughter of a Creole woman (ch. 26). The term 'Creole' refers both to descendants of European settlers in the West Indies and to persons of mixed European and Negro descent. Bertha's origins are therefore ambiguous and

her colour is not directly specified. David argues that Bertha is a 'white Creole who behaves like a demented black person' and that the 'horror' of her character (as well as the racism of the text) lies in Brontë's representation of 'a white woman engorged with the rage and sexuality attributed to West Indian black women' ('The governess of empire', pp. 108-9).

17. These readings of the novel by Spivak, David and others belong to the category of 'post-colonial criticism' and provide an important opportunity for comparative readings of *Jane Eyre* alongside other colonial representations such as Doris Lessing's *The Grass is Singing* or in contrast with post-colonial narratives such as Chinua Achebe's *Things Fall Apart.* See Joe Cleary's 'Challenging the Imperialist Narrative: Chinua Achebe's *Things Fall Apart*', in this volume.

18. Similarly, Magwitch's unforgivable crime, in English law, is to have returned from New South Wales to England; his return is dangerous to the social order since his efforts to 'make a gentleman' significantly, though temporarily, disrupt the established class system.

19. See David, 'The governess of empire', p. 77.

'The Return of the Repressed': Charles Dickens's Great Expectations

EMER NOLAN

A Classic Legend of Victorian Britain

Great Expectations was published in weekly instalments in Dickens's own magazine *All the Year Round* between December 1860 and August 1861. It was an immediate success, and remains one of the most popular (and probably the most widely taught) of all his novels. The story opens in the early years of the nineteenth century, the era of Dickens's own childhood and that of his hero Pip. Like Pip, Dickens grew up in the flat marshy country around the Thames estuary in Kent. But despite such autobiographical correspondences, Dickens's life history, as we shall see, bears little obvious resemblance to Pip's in *Great Expectations*.

The world of *Great Expectations*, with its stagecoaches and prison ships (the 'Hulks' of Pip's boyhood nightmares), would have already seemed remote to typical middle-class readers in mid-Victorian Britain (Queen Victoria ascended to the throne in 1837). They inhabited a more technologically advanced, industrialized and urbanized nation—a world of factories and railways.

(In *Great Expectations*, Pip tells us that the education of his brother-in-law, the blacksmith Joe Gargery—himself a powerful image of a pre-industrial craftsman—'like Steam, was yet in its infancy' [ch. 7].) As Janice Carlisle remarks:

Victorian readers would have had little difficulty in recognising that the novel tells a story of social progress and amelioration, however it may comment on that story. For most of Dickens's contemporaries, if not for Dickens himself, and for many historians since, Victorian Britain offers a success story enacted on a national scale; and from some perspectives Dickens's own life may be read as an individualized reflection of that success.[1]

Central to this confident Victorian self-image was the notion of middle-class respectability, 'embodied in Queen Victoria and her consort, Prince Albert'.[2] Both of Dickens's paternal grandparents had been servants. When he was twelve his father, who had achieved at best a precarious middle-class status, fell into debt and was briefly imprisoned, while he himself was put to work in a blacking factory. Although he incorporated the latter experience into the story of *David Copperfield* (1849–50), it humiliated him so deeply that he kept it secret, even from his wife and children. So while Dickens's enormous literary success and considerable wealth served to consolidate his own social position, his relationship to the prevailing ethos of gentlemanly respectability was troubled. Throughout his career, Dickens and his works were dismissed by snobbish contemporaries as common and vulgar. Moreover, at the very time that he was writing *Great Expectations*, this greatest of all Victorian celebrators of home and family had recently separated from his wife, amid various scandalous rumours.[3]

Dickens wrote a number of novels about young men who are at odds with their early environments, and who eventually attain social positions more in keeping with their innate talents and sensitivities. The most famous of these heroes is Oliver Twist. But there is a huge distinction between, say, Oliver Twist or David

Copperfield, and Pip in *Great Expectations*. We recall, for example, that in film and musical versions of *Oliver Twist*, Oliver always speaks and sings in Standard English, while all his companions have broad Cockney accents. He seems to 'remember' his middle-class origins, even though he has no conscious knowledge of them. Oliver's innate gentility is immune to the degrading influences of his environment, and guarantees his eventual return to the comfort and respectability of the middle class. Pip has no such immunity. The adopted son of a village blacksmith, he so desperately wants to be a gentleman that he is easily duped into believing that he will enjoy great property and wealth. But when his fantasy of upward social mobility is destroyed, he is left an exile both from the respectable world of leisured gentlefolk to which he aspired and from the rural community into which he was born.

Pip's good fortune comes in the shape of 'great expectations'—the anticipation of inherited wealth—and so he is not educated for any profession. He is never given the opportunity to achieve social status through his own exertions.[4] Pip's terrible failure may seem to suggest that he is punished for his ambition, and that people like him ought to accept their lowly station in life. But the novel also carries out an important imaginative investigation of 'genteel' life itself. This begins with Pip's encounters in Satis House with the icy Miss Havisham and her adopted daughter, the cruel Estella, the 'toadies and humbugs' that attend on her, and the 'pale young gentleman' who he knocks down in her garden (ch. 11). It is eventually extended into a far-reaching exploration of the idleness, greed and corruption of the ruling class of Victorian Britain.

Above all, the middle-class gentleman is contrasted with Joe, the 'gentle Christian man' (ch. 57), who teaches Pip an honest trade for which Pip, in his artificially genteel world, has no use.

Still, the memory of Joe's warmth and comradeship, forever associated with the heat and light of the forge, and of his refrains, 'What larks!' and 'Ever the best of friends!', haunts Pip throughout his adventures. In the stories of Joe, Pip, and the rest of the characters in *Great Expectations*, Dickens contrasts the idea of a leisured existence with the realities of loss, pain, money and labour. He emphasizes the emotional repression and social injustice on which the bourgeois ideology of progress was based. In the process, he dismantles the entire Victorian notion of the gentleman.

Beginnings (Chapters 1–19)
Pip spends much of his early life attempting to reconcile the identity he has inherited from his family and community with the identity that he wants to create for himself. In the opening lines of the book, he announces:

My father's family name being Pirrip, and my christian name Philip, my infant tongue could make of both names nothing longer or more explicit than Pip. So, I called myself Pip, and came to be called Pip.

Here the child successfully puts his own individual stamp on the name his family has bestowed on him: he 'came to be called' by the name he chose for himself. This is not a totally new name, however, for 'the infant tongue' merely transforms what it cannot reproduce. Similarly, *Great Expectations* will teach us that our freedom to create or re-create ourselves is always circumscribed by our history, and by the decisions that others have already taken on our behalf.

Pip also creates his own images of his dead parents and brothers from the unpromising material of their gravestones and the half-understood inscriptions they bear. Again, the encounter between the individual and his history is played out in language, as Pip struggles to read and interpret the 'texts' he finds in the churchyard. Such reading and interpretation, which ultimately involves examining one's own life as if it were a text to be decoded (with all the attendant dangers of misunderstanding and misinterpretation), will remain central to this novel. But it will take Pip a long time to learn the lessons implicit in his earliest memories.

The encounter with the convict in the graveyard sets in motion one of the key plots in Pip's life—a plot that will remain hidden from him until adulthood. But this scene is also immediately grasped as significant by the child himself. For this is the moment when he achieves self-consciousness: he apprehends the 'identity of things' with a memorable new vividness, and realizes 'that the small bundle of shivers growing afraid of it all and beginning to cry, was Pip' (ch. 1). His accession to this sense of selfhood is based on fear, as the convict turns Pip upside-down and threatens to cut his throat. By forcing him to rob from his sister and to keep a dark secret from the adults around him, the convict helps to create Pip's 'guilty mind' (ch. 3). But as Dickens fills out the details of Pip's home life, we come to understand that the convict has merely confirmed the sense of sinfulness and criminality that has afflicted Pip since infancy. Far from providing a loving surrogate for Pip's absent mother, his sister regards his very existence as an offence:

As to me, I think my sister must have had some general idea that I was a young offender whom an Accoucheur policeman had taken up (on my birthday) and delivered over to her, to be dealt with according to the outraged majesty of the law. (ch. 4)

So Pip comes to believe that he is not just the victim of the terrifying stranger, but his counterpart as well—indeed, his sister predicts that Pip too will end up in the Hulks (ch. 2). The bond between child and criminal is emphasized when the prisoner confesses to the theft of the goods in order to prevent suspicion falling on Pip. Joe (who is for Pip at this stage more of a sibling than a father) also underlines the affinity between those who are marginalized within the family, and those whom society sees as the enemies of law and order. The blacksmith assures the convict that neither he nor Pip begrudged him the stolen food: 'we wouldn't have you starved to death ... poor miserable fellow-creatur' (ch. 5). But as Pip has already remarked, he never regarded anything in the house as Joe's to give away in the first place (ch. 2). Pip's view of Joe as 'a larger species of child, and as no more than my equal' (ch. 2) is based on Joe's complete incapacity to protect Pip from his wife's sharp tongue, her dreaded 'Tickler' and her 'Ram-pages'. We later learn that Joe is haunted by the memory of his own father's maltreatment of his mother, and fears that he too could become an abusive husband. Consequently, both man and boy must suffer Mrs. Joe's tyranny in silence (ch. 7).

The convict and his terrible companion are successfully recaptured. But the incident in the churchyard is recalled, much to Pip's discomfort, when a mysterious stranger appears in the bar at the Three Jolly Bargemen. He gives Pip the two filthy one-pound notes which later trouble his conscience (ch. 10). But the meaning of these events is not to be revealed until the end of the second stage of Pip's expectations.

In this way Dickens manipulates the reader's empathy and curiosity. We can note in particular the generally cliff-hanging conclusions to the original serial instalments of the text; these original breaks in the narrative are usually marked in twentieth-century editions of *Great Expectations*. The first part of the book introduces an array of characters, who inhabit apparently diverse worlds—Satis House, the prison-ships, the forge, London. But the experienced reader of Victorian fiction will herself have 'great expectations' of these characters, knowing that we, as readers of novels, are conditioned to expect the unexpected: the disclosure of secret identities and relationships, the elaboration of plots and sub-plots, sudden reversals of fortune, conspiracies, coincidences. *Great Expectations* will provide all of these in abundance.

But at this early stage, we, like Pip himself, are reading in the dark. We have no more information than he has. Dickens skilfully deploys the double voice of the first-person narrator, registering the confusion and loneliness of the child, but also articulating it in a language that is obviously alien to and more developed than Pip's childhood language. From the narrator's detached and ironic tone we can infer only that Pip's life will not turn out to have the fairytale ending for which the boy longs— but this, for most of the book, remains only an inference. Many of the comic effects in the early chapters in particular are created by the incongruity between the retrospective narrator's mature vocabulary and the intensity of the child's experience that is almost but not quite obscured by the humorous conceit of making him a comic object of exchange in the adult world:

My sister, Mrs. Joe, throwing the door wide open, and finding an obstruction behind it, immediately divined the cause, and applied Tickler to its further investigation. She concluded by throwing me—I often served her as a connubial missile—at Joe, who, glad to get hold of me on any terms, passed me on into the chimney and quietly fenced me there with his great leg. (ch. 2)

Many commentators on Dickens have objected to the elements of caricature and burlesque in his work—as in the depiction of the Gargery marriage cited here. Certainly on a first reading, the verbal tics and extreme personal eccentricities of many of the characters in *Great Expectations* may offend the sensibilities of anyone who expects a novel to provide a sober, realistic and morally serious view of the world. Even the characters' names, with their obvious symbolic resonances—Magwitch, Havisham, Jaggers, Dodge Orlick—seem implausible, like those of a gallery of grotesques from a fairy story. But in this story, as the child struggles to understand and to come to terms with the world around him, these features of Dickens's style seem unusually appropriate. For this is a world perceived through an immature consciousness, for which details like the clicking noise in the convict's throat, the smell of soap on Jaggers's hands, or the strange sounds that sometimes hide in proper names, have not become so familiar as to go unnoticed.

The child's struggle to master the abstract, grown-up world is dramatized in Pip's efforts to learn to read and write. Gaining access to culture is an essential dimension of Pip's social ambitions. A modern man, and a gentleman, unlike an inhabitant of a traditional world, such as Joe, must be literate. Hence Joe cannot teach Pip written language—another illustration of his inadequacy as a parent for this child. But he is nevertheless charmed and delighted when Pip hands him the slate on which he has written his first letter, which of course Joe himself cannot read (ch. 7). (In this he prefigures Magwitch, who asks Pip to read to him in foreign languages which Magwitch himself cannot understand [ch. 40].) Biddy offers more assistance to Pip in his efforts to educate himself. She also seems best placed to counsel Pip about the directions in which his ambition and his passion for Estella are leading him, but she cannot deflect him from his chosen course (ch. 17). During their conversations, we realize that Biddy is the woman whom Pip might have loved and married, had he not become entangled with Miss Havisham.

For Biddy has been displaced by Estella, whom Pip meets in Satis House. In spite of the painful self-consciousness he experiences there, as a 'common' boy, and in spite of Estella's cruelty to him, he persists in loving her. Languishing at the forge after he is officially apprenticed to Joe, he believes that he can never be happy in his inherited role as a blacksmith (ch. 15). Desperate for escape, Pip also maintains his faith in Miss Havisham as a benign, maternal figure in his life, his 'fairy godmother' (ch. 19)—despite all appearances to the contrary. Hence, when Jaggers arrives to announce that Pip has 'Great Expectations', he immediately links this news with Miss Havisham and with Estella (misled also by the coincidence of having first seen Jaggers at Satis House): 'My dream was out; my wild fancy was surpassed by sober reality; Miss Havisham was going to make my fortune on a grand scale' (ch. 18). But Pip has drastically misread his own life story, and he will persist in this misreading during the crucial years ahead.

Returns and Recognitions (Chapters 20–39)
Peter Brooks remarks that the 'middles' of stories are generally harder to analyse than the 'beginnings' or 'ends', and goes on to argue that the 'middle' of *Great Expectations* is

notably characterized by the return. Quite literally: it is Pip's repeated returns from London to his home town that constitute the organizing device of the whole of the London period, the time of the Expectations and their aftermath.[5]

Certainly, after Pip escapes from his labour at the forge, his life does not seem to show much spectacular improvement. Indeed Brooks characterizes it as a 'nightmare of unprogressive repetition'.[6] Although Pip repeatedly resolves to treat Joe more kindly, he fails time and time again to do so. He revisits Satis House, where he learns much more about the unnatural relationship between Estella and Miss Havisham, but he draws no logical conclusions from this, not even after he hears from Herbert the full story of Miss Havisham's abortive wedding. He sees that Estella has grown more beautiful without becoming any more tender towards him, yet he does not cease to hope for her hand in marriage. He hears nothing from his benefactor, and he spends far too much money. He again glimpses the stranger from the Three Jolly Bargemen, and learns that it was 'his' convict who sent him the two one-pound notes, but regards all this as no more than part of a shameful and long-buried history. Pip sees the ugliness of London, the corrupt ways and degrading practices of the law courts and of the whole system of punitive justice. Life in the metropolis, he learns, is so harsh that an individual like Wemmick can only survive by maintaining an absolutely rigid division between his public life and his private life. This automaton of the official world provides an ironic commentary on the Englishman's boast that his house is his castle. His house in Walworth is a castle indeed, equipped with its own moat and drawbridge, but it is a retreat into a realm of feeling that is totally lacking in the public world.

Nothing decisive can happen in Pip's life, it seems, until the secrecy surrounding his legacy is dispelled. His anxiety about this increases as his coming of age approaches. But on his twenty-first birthday, the long-awaited interview with Jaggers is a terrible disappointment. He is to be kept in suspense for even longer (ch. 36). Finally, the disclosure arrives, but from an entirely unsuspected source. The catastrophe is total: 'in an instant the blow was struck, and the roof of my stronghold dropped upon me' (ch. 38). After the anticlimax of his official coming of age, Pip truly comes of age through the shocking revelations of chapter 39.

An old man appears at Pip's door one stormy night, with 'bright and gratified recognition' shining in his face, and an 'air of wondering pleasure, as if he had some part in the things he admired'. Pip is baffled and repelled. But there is worse to come. When he recognizes this man as 'his' convict, Pip tries to discharge his debts and launder the original dirty money he had received, by offering the unwelcome guest two clean, new one-pound notes. But the convict burns the notes before his eyes. He is the source of *all* Pip's money, not just of these two pounds. Pip is facing his mysterious benefactor, his creator, a Doctor Frankenstein (ch. 40) who has made a gentleman out of the poor boy Pip had been, in order to wreak his vengeance on polite society. During these abysmal moments, Pip acquires a new and dreadful genealogy. He has gained a 'second father', as Magwitch calls himself, and he realizes the truth about his surrogate mother, Miss Havisham. He has been no more than a 'convenience' (ch. 39) for her, just as he had been an inconvenience for Mrs Joe. With such a parentage it is no surprise that Pip's sense of who he is should be so troubled.

The Two Endings of *Great Expectations* : Chapters 40–59

Dickens completed *Great Expectations* in 1861, but the final instalment of the novel was not published in the form in which he first wrote it. Instead, on the advice of the novelist Edward Bulwer-Lytton, he changed it to the one which has since been reprinted (with minor variations) in every edition of the text. In the original manuscript, there was no chapter 59. Instead, chapter 58 had three additional paragraphs which describe a further (presumably final) meeting between Pip and Estella. They tell of the death of Estella's abusive husband Drummle, and of her remarriage. Pip meets her in London as he is walking with Joe's son, little Pip. Estella apparently presumes that the child is Pip's. She has been much chastened by sadness and Pip's final remarks are:

I was very glad afterwards to have had the interview; for, in her face and in her voice, and in her touch, she gave me the assurance, that suffering had been stronger than Miss Havisham's teaching, and had given her a heart to understand what my heart used to be.[7]

In the published ending, of course, the pair walk in the grounds of Satis House, which are about to be sold (the house has been demolished). Estella is a widow. They have a longer conversation, during which she stresses that pain has redeemed her moral character: 'I have been bent and broken, but—I hope—into a better shape' (ch. 59). Dickens's famously ambiguous final sentence reads:

I took her hand in mine, and we went out of the ruined place; and as the morning mists had risen long ago when I first left the forge, so the evening mists were rising now, and in all the broad expanse of tranquil light they showed to me, I saw the shadow of no parting from her.

Is Pip merely self-deceived in failing to foresee their final parting? (Dickens rewrote the last clause of this sentence in various ways, initially as 'I saw the shadow of no parting from her but one', and, in the 1862 edition of the novel, as 'I saw no shadow of another parting from her'; none of these variants is entirely unambiguous.) What is the significance of these various endings? Dickens apparently cancelled his first, unhappy ending when he was told that it would be too much for his readers to bear. But yet, even on rewriting, he is evidently unable fully to commit himself to a happy conclusion. Will Pip and Estella continue as 'friends apart', as Estella says, or as husband and wife? The suppressed ending, announcing their separation, lives on in the hesitancy of the revised ending.

What is at stake here is no less than our interpretation of the entire text, but particularly our understanding of Pip's development between the recognition scene of chapter 39 and the end of the book. Pip clearly undergoes an important process of maturation during the last third of the book, as do Miss Havisham, Joe and Estella. But the implications of these changes in the characters are more difficult to assess.

The narrator of *Great Expectations*—the mature Pip—delivers a harsh assessment of the young hero's snobbishness, selfishness and stupidity. In spite of all that we are told about Pip's childhood in the early chapters, Pip never attempts to excuse, for example, his sinful ingratitude to Joe. Pip's badness, we might conclude, flows from his restless, ambitious nature—his original sin—and cannot be blamed on the neglect or the evil of others. Yet Pip achieves moral redemption. He learns to accept his connection with the criminal Magwitch, and is even humbled by Magwitch's misguided generosity and constancy, through which Magwitch had been to him 'a much better man than I had been to Joe' (ch. 54). Pip also forgives Miss Havisham and Estella, who both in turn acknowledge the harm they have done him.

When Joe returns to nurse Pip through the illness which he suffers after Magwitch's death, their early relationship is repeated, but only through the infantilizing of the adult Pip, now once again totally dependent on Joe. However, now there is no Mrs Joe to wreck Joe's good intentions; he successfully restores Pip to health and sanity. But this episode culminates in the false closure which Pip imagines for himself in chapter 58, when he resolves to beg Biddy's forgiveness and ask her to marry him. He contemplates, as it were, a return to the life that was interrupted by Miss Havisham and the 'Great Expectations'. But when Pip arrives 'home', it is on the very day of Biddy's wedding to Joe. The child-like father-figure has grown up and unwittingly stolen away the woman originally destined for Pip, who has still that irresistible urge to be a child again, to go back and start to rewrite the interrupted 'plot' of his life.

We may think that Pip is more than sufficiently punished for his presumption about Biddy by being forever exiled from sexuality, marriage and the possibility of becoming a father. He attends Wemmick's wedding and helps to make Herbert's marriage possible, but is evidently resigned to perpetual celibacy. (After Pip, there will be no more Pirrips.) He is banished not just from his native village but also from England; as a clerk in Cairo he works 'pretty hard for a sufficient living', as he tells Estella (ch. 59). Professionally, he is reduced to being a copyist, a mere transcriber of other people's words. Instead of being a privileged consumer of literature and a gentleman who eagerly anticipated his own life story, he is finally 'cured from plot',[8] that is, reconciled to a life free of drama and suspense.

But the novel raises questions that contest that punitive conclusion, although they never (as we have seen) entirely dispel it. Does Pip, in humbly accepting his fate, in fact render himself worthy of Estella in the end? Having forfeited his destined future in the forge and with Biddy, can he be given a second chance of happiness after all? Perhaps the most obvious response is that he and Estella have been through too much suffering to be deluded into the expectation of romantic happiness. And in the meantime, Estella's very identity has changed in Pip's eyes. Once he understands that both her parents hail from the criminal underworld, and that he himself is Magwitch's spiritual child just as she is his biological child, it seems likely that their relationship might appear more like that of siblings than of lovers. In one light, then, the novel seeks to punish the children, Pip and Estella, who are clearly its central victims for having conformed to the horrible pressures they were subjected to from the start. To point a moral, they must be finally separated. That unhappy ending, which Dickens chose first and then harked after, may seem truer to an official Victorian morality than the happy ending.

But in another light, the novel seeks a more complex but elusive justice. The vision of Pip marrying Estella may seem more congenial to us now than it did to the Victorian reader. For, in spite of Pip's Christian self-criticism, as we assess his life-story we modern readers cannot help but invoke what, in that most crass of twentieth-century phrases, is called 'the abuse excuse'. By locating evil in the social system, in the dysfunctional family, in parents who neglect their actual children (the middle-class Pockets as much as the poor Gargerys) or exploit children they have borrowed and laid claim to (like Magwitch and Miss Havisham), *Great Expectations* shifts the burden of blame away from individuals and certainly away from the child victims. Instead it points the finger at the institution of the Victorian family. Dickens recognized that the family was an institution as much as any of the other more obviously bureaucratic or iniquitous legal or educational systems that he investigates in this novel. Key villains such as Pip himself, Estella and Magwitch are definitely made, not born, bad. Pip indeed is very forgiving towards those who failed him as a child. He seems entirely to repress the memory of Joe's inadequacy as a parent, and feels no resentment towards the new little Pip, safely installed by the fire with his loving parents. This child seems destined to have the life that Pip should have had. Such a Pip would never have fallen prey so easily to a Miss Havisham. In this sense, the possibility of a happy ending may paradoxically seem 'truer' to the more subversive and critical Dickens who believed that men and women are innately good, until deformed by their society.

Even if Pip and Estella are permitted to find solace and maybe even a future together, the power of Dickens's indictment of Victorian Britain remains. *Great Expectations* condemns that world as a place haunted by the spectres of a criminality it would prefer to ignore but upon which it is founded. It is not just Pip's heartless and useless gentility, but middle-class culture in general, that is punished. For, just as Magwitch re-appears after his transportation to 'the land down under', all that polite society has repressed returns within this novel with a vengeance.

Bibliography

Charles Dickens, *Great Expectations*, edited by Janice Carlisle, Case Studies in Contemporary Criticism (London: Macmillan, 1996). This useful volume also contains a number of recent essays on the text, together with introductory essays on contemporary criticism and literary theory.

Peter Brooks, 'Repetition, repression, and return: the plotting of *Great Expectations*', in *Reading for the Plot* (New York: Vintage, 1984).

Reprinted in Carlisle's edition of *Great Expectations*, pp. 481-501. This essay offers a complex psychoanalytical reading of the text.

Michael Cotsell (ed.), *Critical Essays on Charles Dickens's Great Expectations* (Boston: G.K. Hall, 1990).

Dickens Studies Annual 11 (1983). Special issue largely devoted to *Great Expectations*.

Robin Gilmour, *The Idea of the Gentleman in the Victorian Novel* (London: Allen, 1981).

Barbara Hayley, 'The secrecy of terror in *Great Expectations*', *Association of Teachers of English Journal* 11 (Autumn 1986), pp. 7-13.

Franco Moretti, *The Way of the World: The Bildungsroman in European Culture* (London: Verso, 1987). See chapter 4 for an outstanding discussion of Dickens's relationship with other British novelists of the eighteenth and nineteenth centuries, and with the tradition of the *Bildungsroman* (novel of education).

Q.D. Leavis, 'How we must read *Great Expectations*', in *Dickens the Novelist* (New York: Pantheon, 1970), pp. 277-331.

Notes

1. Janice Carlisle (ed.), *Great Expectations*, Case Studies in Contemporary Criticism, p. 6. All quotations from Dickens's text are from this edition.

2. Ibid., p. 5.

3. Robin Gilmour, *The Idea of the Gentleman in the Victorian Novel*, pp. 105-11.

4. Franco Moretti, *The Way of the World: The Bildungsroman in European Culture*, p. 205.

5. Peter Brooks, 'Repetition, repression and return: the plotting of *Great Expectations*', p. 490.

6. Ibid.

7. Carlisle (ed.), *Great Expectations*, p. 440.

8. Brooks, 'Repetition, repression and return', p. 498.

Challenging the Imperialist Narrative: Chinua Achebe's Things Fall Apart

JOE CLEARY

European Colonialism and Western Representations of Africa
At the start of the twentieth century, a number of Western European states—Britain, France, Germany, Italy, Belgium, Portugal and Spain—claimed vast tracts of the African continent as colonial possessions. Much of the history of modern Africa needs to be understood, therefore, as a series of difficult and costly struggles on the part of the native African peoples to shake off European colonial rule. Most of the erstwhile colonies achieved national independence only in the 1960s and 1970s. Several decades after independence, many of these new states still wrestle with staggering political, economic and ethnic problems. Some of these problems are rooted in the exploitative economic systems, autocratic state apparatuses, arbitrary frontiers and consequent ethnic divisions inherited from the colonial era. Others stem from new forms of exploitation visited on poorer regions of the world by a global economic order dictated by the interests of the wealthier states. And some, finally, must be attributed to poor

government and to the internecine wars that have wracked many African states in the post-independence period.

The modern African novel, which is as diverse as the continent itself, has been smithied in this traumatic history of anti-colonial and post-colonial struggle. Some of the major Sub-Saharan African novelists to have emerged over the past several decades include Wole Soyinka, Ngugi wa Thiong'o, Chinua Achebe, Amos Tutuola, Sembène Ousmane, Ayi Kwei Armah, Alex La Guma, Flora Nwapa, Bessie Head, Buchi Emecheta, and one must also include here white South African writers such as Nadine Gordimer, André Brink and J.M. Coetzee. Though their importance is widely acknowledged, many of the major Black African writers still receive comparatively little attention in Europe beyond small, specialized circles. This neglect is neither accidental nor inevitable. It is conditioned by schools and universities, by newspaper arts sections and cultural magazines which do little to encourage interest in Africa, and it is ultimately rooted in the chauvinistic assumption that the continent—usually drawn to European attention only as a site of natural disaster or political calamity—has little of interest to narrate to a supposedly more sophisticated West. More than most, the Nigerian novelist Chinua Achebe has managed to challenge such perceptions. His first novel, *Things Fall Apart*, is now generally accepted as one of the classics of twentieth-century literature. Forty years after its initial publication, it still remains the African novel that Europeans are most likely to read.

Things Fall Apart was published in England in 1958, two years before Nigeria gained its independence. To understand the novel, and to discuss the extent and limits of its achievement, it is necessary to begin by sketching some of the socio-cultural predicaments that confronted writers and intellectuals such as Achebe in the colonial context in which they found themselves. The dominant image of Africa established in the West was of a dark and savage place, one which was both threatening and exotic. Africa was depicted, above all else, as a historically static continent that lacked social development and consequently represented the very antithesis of European progress and civilization. The nineteenth-century German philosopher G.W.F. Hegel famously referred to Africa as 'the land of childhood, which lying beyond the day of self-conscious history, is enveloped in the dark mantle of Night'. Africa, Hegel asserted, 'is no historical part of the World; it has no movement or development to exhibit'.[1]

In a confident and aggressive Europe, which had conducted a massive slave trade in Africans in the eighteenth century and which was expanding its empires across the globe throughout the nineteenth, such views were not in any way peculiar to Hegel. They were, rather, a cultural commonplace, endlessly reiterated in historical and anthropological narratives, missionary tracts, travellers' tales and official reports.[2] Even European liberals who criticized the slave trade or the worst excesses of empire tended to share the belief that native Africans were incapable of making historical progress except under Western tutelage. The denigration of native cultures was a staple feature of imperialism everywhere, but some scholars have argued that European representations of black Africa tended to be exceptionally negative. The Chinese, the Hindus or the Egyptians, it was allowed, had at least achieved impressive civilizations in the distant past, though the peoples now living in these parts were widely believed to have long since degenerated. In contrast, black Africa, it was asserted, had no ancient civilization to its credit; it had remained permanently stuck in a kind of inert historical childhood.[3]

European imaginative writing about Africa tended, on the whole, to uphold such assumptions. In novels set in Africa such as Olive Schreiner's *The Story of an African Farm* (1883), Rider

Haggard's *King Solomon's Mines* (1885) or Joseph Conrad's *Heart of Darkness* (1900), narrative interest is monopolized by white characters whereas the black ones remain remote and marginal. When they appear at all in such novels, Africans tend to be represented as an anonymous savage mass, as decorative picturesques to provide local colour or as passive victims without agency. Edgar Rice Burroughs' *Tarzan* novels, and the many movies that they inspired, demonstrate these qualities in a particularly vivid way. In the Tarzan tales, narrative interest is centred on a white hero of European ancestry who has the capacity to control situations—a capacity that native Africans patently lack. Africa itself is reduced to a landscape of white adventure where Western desires and anxieties are played out. In a variety of ways, the literary conventions that shaped most European fiction about Africa tended to naturalize assumptions about Western superiority and African backwardness, and to confirm the idea that Western rule was ultimately essential to the welfare of the African people.

The Task of the African Writer in the New Nation-State

Writers such as Achebe took up their careers at a moment when African nationalist movements were beginning to challenge European colonial rule and the supremacist ideologies that validated such rule.[4] Hence, for Achebe, a prime duty of the African writer in the new nation is to undo the work of European imperialist denigration, and to restore to Africans a sense of the value and dignity of their indigenous societies. The writer's duty, Achebe has written, is to show his own people 'that their past—with all its imperfections—was not one long night of savagery from which Europeans acting on God's behalf delivered them'.[5] The writer must demonstrate, Achebe writes, that

CHINUA ACHEBE'S *THINGS FALL APART*

African people did not hear of culture for the first time from Europeans; that their societies were not mindless but frequently had a philosophy of great depth and value and beauty, that they had poetry and, above all, they had dignity. It is this dignity that many African people had all but lost during the colonial period and it is this that they must now regain.[6]

As Achebe conceives it, then, the African writer's task is to help his or her people to 'put away the complexes of the years of degeneration and self-abasement'.[7] To do this effectively, litera-ture must challenge the assumption, internalized by many Africans schooled in Western modes of knowledge and percep-tion, that pre-colonial African societies lacked innate value or any independent capacity for internal progress and development. Nevertheless, despite this emphasis on recuperation, Achebe also shows himself vigilant to the dangers inherent in conservative ver-sions of nationalism which tend to idealize the pre-colonial world as a pastoral idyll. Such uncritical glorification of the past is dan-gerous because it is simply a reverse chauvinism which can be used by the new ruling parties to have the people become, in the words of Frantz Fanon, 'drunk on remembrance'.[8] In a new nation, in other words, uncritical idealizations of the past serve only to divert attention from the staggering obstacles still to be overcome if political independence is to mean anything. Hence, for Achebe, while Western denigration of pre-colonial African society must be challenged, 'we cannot pretend that our past was one long technicolour ideal' either.[9] In sum, the challenge con-fronting the African writer is to recover for the present a sense of the innate value and internal dynamism of pre-colonial society, but at the same time to avoid the narcissistic and dead-end seduc-tions of romantic nostalgia.

How well does *Things Fall Apart* measure up to these ambi-tions? To assess this, it is important to consider not only the con-tent but also the form of the novel. Essentially, the novel dramatizes the story of a single Igbo community at the turn of the twentieth century when it first comes into direct contact with the Protestant missionaries and the British agents that were to inaugurate the new colonial regime in the region. The narrative is divided into three parts. The first section, which comprises the first thirteen chapters and more than half the length of the novel, offers a composite account of pre-colonial Igbo society in the period immediately before the coming of the white man. This section of the novel is rich in anthropological detail: the economic and social practices, domestic arrangements, religious beliefs and quotidian customs and values of the Igbo are sketched with skill and economy.

The story is organized around a single protagonist, Okonkwo, but Achebe develops the narrative in ways that compel the reader to engage with Okonkwo not only as a discrete individual but also as a member of the larger social collective that is the Igbo people. In the European classical realist *bildungsroman*, narrative interest is usually centred on the individual psychology of a young hero who chafes against the restrictions of the existing social order. In contrast, Achebe takes on quite a different task. His goal in *Things Fall Apart* is to depict an established individual who already has a respected social position within his community, and who struggles to exemplify in his behaviour the virtues cherished by that community. In contrast to the Western classical realist novel, dialogue in *Things Fall Apart* is mostly restricted and terse.[10] Okonkwo says little in the novel; he has no extended speeches or lengthy conversations with other characters. Nor are there many lengthy interior monologues to allow the reader direct access to his inner thoughts and emotions. Most of what we learn about Okonkwo we learn by inference, by observing his actions, or by means of objective narrative summary. The spare, terse style and this mode of characterization—one which keeps the reader at a distance by restricting direct access to the hero's subconscious—together give *Things Fall Apart* something of the quality of a pre-modern epic or oral folk-narrative. As Michael Valdez Moses has observed, Okonkwo resembles, to some extent at least, the protagonists of pre-modern European heroic literature rather than those of the modern bourgeois novel.[11] In this way, Achebe is able to suggest, at the level of form and not through didactic commentary, that the relationship between individual and community in pre-colonial Igbo society is not the same as in modern Western ones.[12] Unlike the typical heroes in modern European fiction, who struggle against their societies to assert their own personal uniqueness, Okonkwo's goal is to achieve public reputation and recognition by embodying in himself the established values of the community.

Umuofia: Pre-Colonial Igbo Society (Chapters 1–13)

Okonkwo's anxious struggle to exemplify the highest virtues of his community dominates the first section of the novel. The values that the community esteems most are 'masculine' ones: the physical strength and athleticism that warriors require, and the industry and diligence needed for successful farming. Okonkwo's father, Unoko, an improvident man who preferred music and drinking to more strenuous activities, was singularly lacking in these qualities, and died in abject poverty and disgrace. Psychologically scarred by a sense of his father's weakness, Okonkwo over-compensates by aggressive displays of the 'masculine' qualities his father lacked.

When the novel commences, Okonkwo has already—by his skill as a wrestler, warrior, and farmer—won a place of honour in his village. Ironically, his terror that he may somehow betray the 'womanly' weaknesses associated with his father repeatedly causes him to act in ways that undermine the public reputation he values so much. Though we are told that he was not a cruel man, 'the fear of failure and weakness' that dominates his life leads him to rule his household with an unusually heavy hand. 'His wives, especially the youngest, lived in fear of his fiery temper, and so did his children' (ch. 2). The same over-anxious concern to display strength and virility distances him from his eldest son, Nwoye, who displays some of the same sensibilities as his grandfather. His spirited daughter, Ezinma, is the child Okonkwo loves most, but because she is a girl 'his fondness only showed on very rare occasions' (ch. 5).

The major crisis that occupies the first section of the novel is set in motion when a young woman from Umuofia, Okonkwo's village, is killed during a visit to a neighbouring village, Mbaino. In order to avert a bloody feud between the two villages, it is agreed that a young boy from Mbaino, Ikemefuna, should be handed over to Umuofia in compensation for the young woman's death. When he arrives in Umuofia, Ikemefuna is sent to live with Okonkwo and the latter grows fond of him. Some time later, the local Oracle commands that Ikemefuna must die, but Okonkwo is advised to have no part in his killing since the boy loves him.[13] Worried lest the other men in the village think him effeminate if he excludes himself, Okonkwo ignores this advice, however, and insists on being part of the group that is assigned the task and it is he who eventually delivers Ikemefuna the death blow. Okonkwo's friend, Obierika, a more reflective individual than he, declines to take part in the act since the Oracle had not required him to do so, and he censures Okonkwo for his rashness in involving himself. 'What you have done will not please the Earth,' Obierika observes. 'It is the kind of action for which the goddess wipes out whole families' (ch. 8). Obeirika's prediction of disaster soon comes to pass when Okonkwo's old rifle explodes at a funeral ceremony, accidentally killing a boy from his own village. Though Okonkwo is not directly responsible, Igbo law dictates that anyone who inadvertently sheds the blood of another Igbo must spend seven years in exile. The first section concludes on an ironic note, then, with Okonkwo, whose misfortunes can be traced to his unresolved anxieties about his virility, obliged to leave his father's village, Umuofia, and forced to go live with his mother's kin in Mbanta.

Exile in Mbanta and Colonial Contact (Chapters 14–19)
The second section, which comprises chapters 14 to 19, tells the story of Okonkwo's exile. The removal of Okonkwo from Umuofia at this point is a brilliant narrative strategy. It allows Achebe to delineate the initial stage of contact between Igbo and European in Mbanta, and then to return the reader to Umuofia at a later point when the transformation of pre-colonial Igbo society is already well advanced. Okonkwo, who characteristically attributes the disintegration of traditional Igbo society in Mbanta to the 'womanliness' of his maternal kin, expects when his exile is completed to find Umuofia exactly as he had left it. When he returns, however, Umuofia has changed even more than Mbanta. Like all colonized peoples, Okonkwo will have to learn that once one has entered into contact with the world of colonial capitalism there can be no return to some state of pristine pre-colonial innocence.

As Michael Valdez Moses remarks, the chapters set in Mbanta relate how, for the Igbo, 'Christianity leads to a subversion of their most fundamental—that is religious, political, ethical, and cultural—assumptions, and this subversion in turn leads directly to their inability to resist the incursions of British imperialism and preserve their traditional way of life.'[14] Achebe depicts pre-colonial Igbo society in the novel with empathy, but the perspective is never uncritical. He takes pains to establish that the Igbo have their own elaborate conception of justice and value, but he also makes it quite clear that their value-system reflects a patriarchal agrarian society. The inflexible gender roles that structure Igbo society, and the existence of slavery and of a caste of *osu* or untouchables, are clearly indicated. Social practices that inevitably appear repugnant to a modern reader—such as the abandonment of illegitimate children and twins in the forest to die—are also detailed. Had Achebe drawn a veil over such matters and depicted his pre-colonial ancestors in ways less alien to the liberal norms of modern Western or African audiences, readers might more easily identify with them. By refusing this option, Achebe sets himself a more complex task: to challenge the reader to empathize with the Igbo *despite* the gap between pre-colonial norms and values and modern liberal ones.

It is because pre-colonial Igbo society is subject to inner contradictions and divisions that Christianity poses the threat it does. When the missionaries come to Mbanta, the elders allow them to set up a church there because they persuade themselves that since the new religion is absurd it will never win converts. What they fail to appreciate is that Christianity's appeal will not be to the Igbo with power and status like themselves, but rather to the *efulefu* (worthless men without titles), to women, to slaves, to the *osu* and others disempowered by the traditional social order. What unites these otherwise diverse social groups is their common enthusiasm for a religion that preaches their human dignity and spiritual equality. From any wider historical perspective, it must be acknowledged that far from upholding actual (as opposed to spiritual) equality between genders, races and classes, Christianity in Africa, as elsewhere, was often used to legitimate an extremely hierarchical colonial order. To the marginal and the outcast in Mbanta, however, Christianity's immediate appeal is that it offers an alternative ethos to the Igbo one that disempowers them.

While the spiritual appeal of Christianity to some of the Igbo is noted, Achebe's novel makes it clear that material factors are also at play. From the outset, the Igbo are aware that the missionaries have the imperial police at their back. Even before the first missionaries arrive, news has circulated that when the Igbo in Abame killed a white man, the British wiped out the entire village in reprisal. A direct assault on the missionaries, then, risks provoking a similar response. Moreover, once the colonial regime is installed, the missionaries control the education system. When it becomes clear that education is the key to social advancement in the new dispensation, then traditional Igbo concepts of what constitutes social success and personal status are transformed accordingly. At that stage, it is no longer primarily the marginalized Igbo who are attracted to Christianity; many from the upper classes also convert. Achebe's novel suggests, therefore, that for a complex lamination of reasons, both spiritual and material, Christianity prises open existing contradictions in traditional Igbo society, and divides the community against itself.

Return to Umuofia (Chapters 20–25)

The final section of the novel deals with Okonkwo's return to Umuofia, the intensifying divisions and tensions within Igbo society, and Okonkwo's suicide when it becomes apparent to him that the pre-colonial social order is doomed to destruction. As mentioned earlier, when Okonkwo returns to Umuofia, he expects to find things as he had left them, but discovers instead that: 'The clan had undergone such profound change during his exile that it was barely recognizable' (ch. 21). In Umuofia, too, white missionaries have built a church and many Igbo have converted. A new legal system has been installed, and is now administered in courts where officials, who do not even speak the Igbo language, dispense laws that controvert the customs of the community. When conflicts emerge between the old and the new laws, those who abide by the old ways are convicted of wrongdoing and thrown into prison. There they are mistreated by black agents of the new regime, most of whom come from ethnic groups traditionally hostile to the Igbo. New forms of commerce and trading have also emerged, and these too undercut pre-colonial social structures and norms.

Dismayed by all these changes, which are gradually corroding the whole basis of the old social order, Okonkwo wonders in some frustration why the Igbo do not simply drive the missionaries from the land. His friend, Obierika, replies that it is already too late. It would be easy to expel the white missionaries and colonial officials as they are few in number, but reprisals might follow and other whites might simply come in their place. Moreover, he adds, many Umuofians have now converted to the new religion or work in the colonial administration, and Igbo law, which upholds the absolute sanctity of ancestor worship and kinship ties, prohibits the killing of clan members. 'As for [the] converts, no one could kill them without having to flee from the clan, for in spite of their worthlessness they still belonged to the clan' (ch. 18). As a result, the Igbo committed to preserving the traditional order find themselves trapped in an ethical impasse: they cannot destroy the new regime without fighting their own kin, and they cannot fight their own kin without violating a key tenet of the very system they wish to preserve. Either way, the absolute value of kinship, one of the fundamental premises on which the pre-colonial Igbo system rests, threatens to disintegrate.

The smouldering tensions in Umuofia erupt into open conflict when a zealous convert to Christianity publicly unmasks an *egwugwu* (a village elder who impersonates one of the ancestral spirits) during a village ceremony. For the Igbo, this is a shocking act of sacrilege, an act clearly intended to challenge the authority of their tradition. In reprisal, Okonkwo and some of the other elders burn down the Christian church. The British District Commissioner invites the Umuofian elders to a conference to debate the mounting tensions, but when they do so, he has them thrown in prison instead. There they are beaten and humiliated, and released only when their village agrees to pay substantial ransom. Shamed and demoralized by this insult to their authority, the Umuofian elders summon a meeting of all the Igbo villages in the district. At this meeting, Okika, a man of great standing in Umuofia, delivers an impassioned speech in which he suggests that the Igbo have no option but to attack those of their own kin who uphold the colonial order. To do this would have been unthinkable in the past but it has become necessary now, he argues, to meet the exigencies of a situation that their ancestors could never have imagined.

Before the debate can get underway, however, messengers from the District Commissioner arrive to disperse the meeting. Okonkwo, still smarting from the indignities inflicted on him in prison, slays one of the messengers in anger. The elders' horrified response, and the fact that they allow the other messengers to slip away unharmed, convince Okonkwo that his community is too unnerved to wage war against the colonial order, and he turns and walks away. The novel closes with the British Commissioner ordering his servants to remove Okonkwo's corpse from the tree on which he has hanged himself. As he does so, the Commissioner ponders whether this curious incident merits a passage in the book he plans to write about his experiences in Africa. In the final sentence of *Things Fall Apart*, we learn that the Commissioner has already decided on the title for his book: *The Pacification of the Primitive Tribes of the Lower Niger.*

Some Conclusions

The multiple ironies embedded in Achebe's conclusion are suggestive. For the British Commissioner, as the title of his proposed study indicates, Okonkwo is just another exotic African primitive destined to be recorded as a mere footnote in an ethnographic manual designed to instruct other Western imperialists how best to manage their African subjects. But it is this Western imperialist narrative that Achebe's novel is designed to challenge. By subsuming the Commissioner's narrative into its own counter-narrative, *Things Fall Apart* is asserting the Igbo writer's capacity to challenge the imperialist version of events in which civilized Europeans 'pacify' primitive Africans. Despite its apocalyptic Yeatsian title and tragic conclusion, *Things Fall Apart* is not, therefore, simply a story of disintegration and defeat. On the contrary, the novel rescues Okonkwo from the condescension of Western imperialist history, and in doing so offers an alternative perspective on the standard European conception of the colonial encounter. In this way, *Things Fall Apart* can itself be regarded as an act of resistance that overwrites the British Commissioner's imperialist narrative with a new African one.

A question that might be asked, however, is whether Achebe can imagine resistance to the colonial order other than in exclusively cultural terms, whether resistance is reduced to an act of 'writing back' such as he himself is engaged in. Does the denouement in which Okonkwo kills himself in despair, because he knows his people will not wage war against the colonizers, sound a fatalistic note of resignation? Might this conclusion seem to infer that pre-colonial Igbo society was simply not equipped to resist the more advanced West and was inevitably doomed to 'fall apart' once it came into contact with it? Is the attempt to seize control of narrative away from the imperialist West so that the doomed traditional social order can at least be commemorated with some respect the best that can be done in the circumstances?

There is indeed a strong sense of despair at the end of the novel, but it has also to be remembered, as mentioned earlier, that although *Things Fall Apart* is organized around Okonkwo, it is never simply his individual story—it is always that of the larger Igbo community as well. And what the novel shows, it can be argued, is that Okonkwo's conception of things, which reduces everything to a stark choice between absolute war against the new social order or supine surrender to it, is much too simplistic. Okonkwo's perspective throughout the novel is shaped by his position as a prestigious and respected patriarch at the apex of traditional society. What he never grasps is that those who adapt to the colonial regime may have less investment in preserving the traditional order than he, since all do not benefit from it equally. Moreover, adaptation to the new order need not be equated in every instance with submission or surrender. Institutions such as the churches and education system are obviously intended to serve the new colonial order, but they can also be appropriated by the Igbo to advance their struggle against colonialism. Indeed, as the son of Igbo converts to Christianity, and as someone educated under the British colonial system in Nigeria, Achebe himself demonstrates that incorporation into the colonial order is not the same thing as submission to it. What the novel seems to suggest, then, is that while traditional social structures do indeed collapse, the Igbo community is more resilient than those structures. In adapting to the new order, the Igbo are not merely surrendering, as Okonkwo mistakenly imagines, but are also discovering new means to combat the political oppressions inherent in the colonial system.

Achebe depicts a pre-colonial African society in a way that insists on its dignity and inner dynamism, but he also eschews sentimentality and reveals a sophisticated and nuanced understanding of the intricate mesh of historical forces that undermine that society. In the imperialist version of history, pre-colonial African societies collapse because they are stagnant and incapable of historical development. Achebe's novel refutes this racist assumption. Here, pre-colonial society disintegrates due to a complex conjunction of external force and internal contradictions, but the people show themselves to be flexible and resilient. We see in the novel a restlessly energetic people struggling, as circumstances and conditions permit, to overcome the limitations of both the old pre-colonial order and the new colonial one. A sense of the collective and individual trauma involved in the painful dislocations and social transformations that follow in the wake of colonial contact with Western society suffuses the narrative. But so too does a sense of the restless kinetic energy of the community in its struggle for emancipation.[15]

Bibliography

Chinua Achebe, *Things Fall Apart* ([1958]; London: Heinemann, 1986).

Chinua Achebe, *Hopes and Impediments: Selected Essays* ([1988]; New York: Doubleday, 1989).

Elleke Boehmer, *Colonial and Postcolonial Literature* (Oxford: Oxford University Press, 1995).

Philip Curtin, *The Image of Africa* (Madison: University of Wisconsin Press, 1964).

Basil Davidson, *The Black Man's Burden: Africa and the Curse of the Nation-State* (Oxford: James Currey, 1992).

Frantz Fanon, *The Wretched of the Earth*, trans. C. Farrington (New York: Grove Press, 1968).

Simon Gikandi, *Reading the African Novel* (Oxford: James Currey, 1987).

Simon Gikandi, *Reading Chinua Achebe* (Oxford: James Currey, 1991).

G.W.F. Hegel, *The Philosophy of History*, trans. J. Sibree (New York: Dover, 1956).

C.L. Innes, *Chinua Achebe* (Cambridge: Cambridge University Press, 1990).

Abdul Jan Mohamed, *Manichean Aesthetics: The Politics of Literature in Colonial Africa* (Amherst: The University of Massachusetts Press, 1983).

G.D. Killam, *The Novels of Chinua Achebe* (New York: Africana, 1969).

Charles R. Larson, *The Emergence of African Fiction* ([1971]; London: Macmillan, 1978).

Michael Valdez Moses, *The Novel and the Globalization of Culture* (Oxford: Oxford University Press, 1995).

Emmanuel Obiechina, *Culture, Tradition and Society in the West African Novel* (Cambridge: Cambridge University Press, 1975).

Edward Said, *Culture and Imperialism* (London, Vintage, 1993).

Notes

1. G.W.F. Hegel, *The Philosophy of History*, pp. 91, 99.

2. Western representations of Africa and Africans were not fixed and monolithic, but diverse and sometimes contradictory. Nevertheless, the negative conceptions described here were undoubtedly the dominant ones. For more on this topic, see Philip Curtin, *The Image of Africa*. For accessible general accounts of the relationships between literature, imperialism and anti-imperialism, see Edward Said, *Culture and Imperialism*, and Elleke Boehmer, *Colonial and Postcolonial Literature*.

3. For a compelling account of modern African history which critiques Eurocentric conceptions of that continent, see Basil Davidson, *The Black Man's Burden: Africa and the Curse of the Nation-State*.

4. For useful and accessible introductions to the development of the African novel, see Emmanuel Obiechina, *Culture, Tradition and Society in the West African Novel*, and Simon Gikandi, *Reading the African Novel*.

5. Chinua Achebe, *Hopes and Impediments: Selected Essays*, p. 45.

6. Achebe, cited in Abdul Jan Mohamed, *Manichean Aesthetics: The Politics of Literature in Colonial Africa*, p. 154.

7. Achebe, *Hopes and Impediments*, p. 44.

8. Frantz Fanon, *The Wretched of the Earth*, p. 169.

9. Cited in Michael Valdez Moses, *The Novel and the Globalization of Culture*, p. 113.

10. Charles Larson, *The Emergence of African Fiction*, p. 40.

11. Moses, *The Novel and the Globalization of Culture*, pp. 110-12.

12. Achebe's distinction between Western and Igbo conceptions of individualism is elaborated in his essay 'The Writer and His Community', in *Hopes and Impediments*, pp. 47-61.

13. To a modern liberal audience, the Oracle's demand for Ikemefuna's sacrifice has no rational basis and is bound to appear shocking and gratuitous since the boy had no direct role in the Umuofian woman's death and since he is well loved in Umuofia because of his many attractive qualities. In societies that lack a single centralized authority capable of monopolizing legal violence, however, ritual sacrifice is frequently deployed as a means to avoid a potentially damaging cycle of tit-for-tat revenge killings. From this perspective, what is important is not that Ikemefuna is personally innocent, but that someone from Mbaino must be killed to compensate the Umuofians for their loss and in doing so break a potentially destructive cycle of revenge.

14. Moses, *The Novel and the Globalization of Culture*, p. 120.

15. It is possible to argue that Achebe's vision is inflected with a greater sense of nostalgia and loss than this reading suggests. Abdul Jan Mohamed has suggested, for example, that Achebe's novel expresses an unresolved sense of ambivalence about African history. The novel, he contends, is torn by a conflict between recognition of the need to change in order to meet the challenge of the future and a plangent desire to conserve values of the past (*Manichean Aesthetics*, p. 183). It is true that the decision to put Okonkwo, a man with a particularly strong investment in the old order, at the centre of the narrative inevitably moulds the reader's perception in a way that accentuates a sense of loss. Had Achebe centred the novel instead on, say, Ezinma, Okonkwo's spirited daughter, he would undoubtedly have been compelled to tell a rather different tale. In other words, it is possible to imagine a narrative centred on a protagonist as committed to the struggle against colonialism as Okonkwo, but less restrictively tied than he to preserving the pre-colonial social order.

'The Hero of My Own Life': Seamus Deane's Reading in the Dark

RICHARD HAYES

> Whether I shall turn out to be the hero of my own life, or whether that station will be held by anybody else, these pages must show.
> Charles Dickens, *David Copperfield*

The *Bildungsroman*

Reading in the Dark is at once an example of the *bildungsroman* genre and a sort of comment upon it—as befits, perhaps, an autobiographical novel by a distinguished literary scholar. A *bildungsroman* is a 'formation' novel, a novel that describes the creation of the character of one person within a particular social order. Usually the *bildungsroman* ends when the protagonist has reached a point of maturity. In some instances, the hero's maturity allows him to assess critically the society that has formed him and to decide whether to become part of or flee from that world; in other instances, the hero is assimilated unthinkingly into the society in which he finds himself. The 'shape' of the *bildungsroman* plot is usually loosely chronological, is more or less linear, and traces a gradual growth in self-consciousness punctuated by a series of epiphanic moments. The most famous example of the genre is James Joyce's *A Portrait of the Artist as a Young Man* (1916). *Great Expectations* (1861), a very different novel from Joyce's, is also a classic *bildungsroman*.

Reading in the Dark tells the story of the growth of Seamus Greene from youth to maturity. The novel places Seamus within a particular world: the world of the Northern Irish Catholic community in the years between the end of the Second World War and the beginning of the 'Troubles' in the late 1960s. It traces the growth of his consciousness to a point where he can at least assess the society that has formed him—the society of his family, first and foremost, but also his larger society—and decide whether to remain a part of it. The penultimate section of the novel has Seamus returning home from university, while the final section sees him return first for the weekend and then for his father's funeral. These returnings indicate, on the one hand, that he has decided to stay in the society that has formed him; on the other, they indicate that he is returning from somewhere else where, the implication is, his new life is. Whatever way we read the ending, however, *Reading in the Dark* would seem to be a *bildungsroman* in the classic sense.

Portraits of the Artists: Deane and Joyce

Often the *bildungsroman* charts the protagonist's growing sense of vocation. Both Deane's *Reading in the Dark* and Joyce's *Portrait of the Artist as a Young Man* contain key 'vocational' scenes: in Joyce's book Stephen Dedalus famously encounters the Dean of Studies in chapter 5 while in *Reading in the Dark* Seamus encounters the gentle priest who is to tell him about sex (in the fourth chapter, in a section called 'The Facts of Life'). Deane's novel owes a lot to Joyce but also, as we shall see, works in quite a different way. The particular dynamics of Deane's novel can be usefully exposed by mapping some of the similarities and differences between the 'vocational' scenes in *Reading in the Dark* and *Portrait of the Artist.*

There are a number of clear similarities between the two scenes. For a start, the meetings are between young men in the process of forming themselves and older priests with answers to give. The religious landscape of the two moments, in other words, is similar. More important, however, is the encounter with language dramatized in each scene. The priests in both books introduce the younger men to the complexities of language. In *Portrait*, famously, the Dean of Studies marvels at words Stephen uses, words that are not familiar to him as an Englishman—Stephen, for 'funnel', uses the word 'tundish'—and, through the encounter, Stephen becomes aware of his own discomfort in the English language, a language he feels perhaps can never articulate his sense of himself. Joyce writes:

[Stephen] felt with a smart of dejection that the man to whom he was speaking was a countryman of Ben Jonson. He thought:

–The language in which we are speaking is his before it is mine. How different are the words *home, Christ, ale, master*, on his lips and on mine! I cannot speak or write these words without unrest of spirit. His language, so familiar and so foreign, will always be for me an acquired speech.[1]

Stephen realizes here that much is at stake, politically and personally, when we speak. Language appears as a concern also in the vocational scene in *Reading in the Dark*. In 'The Facts of Life', Seamus is called from his classroom to the room of a gentle, elderly priest whose job it is to teach the boys about sex. Seamus is eager to learn but gets confused when the priest starts to use words like 'ejaculation' and to explain these words with reference to their Latin etymological roots. In a moment very similar to that in *Portrait* mentioned above, Seamus, speaking of sex, says:

If there's no Latin involved, that's what makes it a sin. Love is in Latin, lust isn't. I thought of all the words in English I had heard. They surely sounded a lot more savage. (p. 151)

Here he draws explicit attention to the difference between two languages—just as Stephen's attention is drawn to the differences between English as it is spoken in Ireland, and the 'Queen's English', English as it is spoken in England. At the same time, the encounter with language is an occasion of delight for Deane's narrator. He delights in the Latin words, in the sounds they make; and the context within which the whole concern with language is raised quickens that delight. The association between language and sex is an important one as the narrator recognizes that a similar kind of delicious abandon is possible in words as is possible in bed. Words take on another manifestation in Seamus's memory of his Confirmation: here words become something mysterious, holy, peaceful. Seamus recalls being led to the altar along with other children from his school, to be confirmed by the bishop. When asked by the bishop 'What is the nature of God's love for mankind?', however, Seamus's mind went momentarily blank. Then he remembered the answer: 'Unconditional.' The bishop dismissed him, we are told,

But I could not move. I *had* become golden. My whole body was solid: an ingot. They would have to lift me and carry me off the altar and put me kneeling in a niche in the wall of the side chapel. Father Browne touched my shoulder, and I rose at once, the teacher caught my elbow and escorted me to the side where the other four were standing and left me there with them, my skin crawling on my scalp and the word 'unconditional' running in my head, over and over, a word that shone on and off like a lighthouse beam out of my mouth and across the faces of the staring congregation, drowning in the sea of sound as the choir sang.

(pp. 154–5)

The feeling that comes over the narrator following his questioning by the bishop, the feeling of being golden, is a product more of the word 'unconditional' than of the relief at answering the question or of the delight of being at last one of God's army of warriors. Both Seamus and Stephen in these 'vocational' scenes, then, come to see language as a more complex, more problematic medium than first they imagined. However, because of the context in which Seamus's encounter with language appears, Deane's narrator delights in the complexity of language. Stephen, on the other hand, remains suspicious of the words he uses.

Clear differences exist between the two 'vocational' moments as well. We have in Deane's book many of the elements of the moment in Joyce—the priest, the fire, the tense meeting—but, rather than deriving from the encounter some political significance concerning the relationship between Ireland and England, as Joyce does, Deane has the conversation turn to sex, to more personal things. Importantly also the narrative voices are very different; in fact, this is one of the major differences between the two novels. One of the most important questions we can ask of any work of fiction is 'Who is telling the story?' The voice who speaks to us from the pages of a work of fiction may be the voice of an unprejudiced narrator, who speaks from outside the tale, simply reporting on events. On the other hand, the voice who tells the story may be that of a prejudiced narrator, the voice of someone speaking from within the tale, as one of the characters involved in the action. Pip in *Great Expectations* is such a prejudiced narrator: he tells his own story, not always impartially. The narrative voice, also, may take us close to the action or may keep us at a distance from it. The voice in *Reading in the Dark* seems more sympathetic, closer to us; in *Portrait* we are quite distanced by the voice used and think of Stephen as rather cold in his dealings with the world. This has a lot to do with the fact that Joyce's novel is in the third person while Deane's is in the first. Despite the use of the stream of consciousness technique in *Portrait*, Joyce does not take us too close to the character of Stephen Dedalus. He is content to have us consider the man from afar, consider him in the same way in which Stephen considers the rest of the world, in fact. Deane, on the other hand, through the use of the first-person narrative, creates the illusion of closeness.

Of course we are not close to the action in *Reading in the Dark*: the novel's story is, after all, being told in retrospect, from a distance in time many years after the action described. We tend to forget in reading this novel that what we are told, the material presented to us, is shaped, altered, and mediated by the narrator who is older and looking back with prejudiced eyes on his youth. We forget in reading *Reading in the Dark* that we are being manipulated by the narrator as we read. Or perhaps it is more accurate to say that we are aware of the illusion of immediacy perpetrated on us by the narrator, but we choose to ignore it. We ignore the degree to which we are being manipulated by the narrator because we sense that here we have a master-storyteller at work and part of the pleasure of being told a story by a skilled storyteller is experiencing one's own manipulation. We as readers are in a position analogous to the children, including Seamus, who sit at the feet of Aunt Katie early in *Reading in the Dark* to hear a story.

'There was this young woman called Brigid McLaughlin,' she told Eilis and me one afternoon … 'Mind you, this was long before my time. I heard it from your Great-uncle Constantine's mother, God be good to them both.' She fell to brooding for a while. We didn't stir. This was her way of telling a story. If you hurried her up, she cut it short and it lost all its wonder. (p. 61)

The children assent to their own manipulation; part of the pleasure of hearing the story is in its being 'told right', that is, in its hearers being manipulated as the story unwinds.

In the Dark: Fiction or Truth?
Reading in the Dark is full of stories and in a fundamental way is about storytelling. The narrator seeks the truth about his Uncle Eddie through the many stories that he hears told around him. He ends up by bringing all the stories together himself to form

the true story of the life of Eddie. In a sense, he brings the stories together into a story called *Reading in the Dark*, a story which is then related to us. What we could argue happens in the novel then is that the narrator graduates into a storyteller across the course of the novel; the novel we have before us is the first expression of his vocation as storyteller.

The story Seamus wishes to tell in *Reading in the Dark* is gathered together in a section towards the end of the book called 'All of It' (pp. 182–7). The basic components of the story are given to us in this section and this is almost the final point at which the narrator arrives in his tale. Interestingly, many of the places and people of his childhood are implicated in the story. All his relatives appear in the story, relatives who were important in his childhood and influential figures on his life. Various parts of the landscape with which he was familiar as a child surface in the story and are important. In a sense, Seamus's whole childhood seems to be wrapped up in the tale he tells. One place, for instance, that is integral to the story told in 'All of It' is the fort called Grianan with its secret passage. This place appears very early on in the narrative. At one point in his childhood, we are told, the narrator was locked into the fort by his friends (pp. 57–8). We find out later that Eddie had also been locked up in Grianan during his interrogation and possibly murdered there too. It is as if all the events of the narrator's childhood have been leading him to this story.[2]

Importantly, however, the narrator never manages to tell the full tale of Eddie; in this regard it is important to note that the title of that section, 'All of It', is meant ironically, for the narrator has not got hold of all of the story at all. The very next section of chapter 5 begins with Seamus filling in another detail. The section concerns Crazy Joe, another person from around the town with whom the young narrator is acquainted, and opens 'It was Crazy Joe who almost completed the story for me' (p. 188). The story is still not complete and Joe, though he does take it near completion, does not complete it either. There is a sense in which the story, all of it, can never be told.

A powerful image in *Reading in the Dark* is the image of the rat; a section called 'Rats', dated 'November 1950', is to be found in the third chapter of the novel (pp. 77–80). This section of the novel provides us with an interesting metaphor for the powerful story that unfolds at the narrator's hands. First of all, we can see *Reading in the Dark* as a novel intent on bringing something from the darkness into the light, from underground to the surface. The narrator is engaged in flushing out the truth just as the men in this section are engaged in flushing out the rats. Secondly, the narrator is sickened by the rats that emerge from the earth and are burned—so sick, he says, 'that the flesh seemed to tighten on my bones' (p. 80). Similarly, he is sickened and disturbed by the story that emerges from his inquiries into the darkness of his family past. Thirdly, like the great king rat slain at the end of the hunt, the truth emerges for the narrator in fits and starts. The king rat, the narrator tells us, 'seemed to come out in sections, as though it were a snake' (p. 79). The truth emerges likewise for the narrator and the image of the snake is appropriate, for it recalls the image of Satan in the story of Adam and Eve. This is a truth that is evil, disturbing, but also perhaps tempting—it is a truth, the image tells us, best left alone. The truth about his family emerges for the narrator in sections, piece by piece, and it is a terrible, shocking story. Finally, in the last paragraph of the fragment, the narrator tells us that he imagined all the surviving rats planning revenge from beneath the ground. This suggests that some of the truth sought by the narrator cannot be got at—we have already seen how there is a sense in which the stories the narrator wishes to tell in *Reading in the Dark* can never be told. Even more disturbingly, the truth sits there beneath the surface, threatening to reappear to disrupt things in the future just as the rats threaten to reappear. The narrator makes an effort towards the end of the novel to hide the truth, with all the threat it contains, from certain people, his father particularly. Embodying the truth in the image of the rat is an interesting and powerful way of conveying that sense of threat. Of course, finally, the image of the rat is interesting because of the associations between the rat and the informer.

The informer is a presence in much Irish fiction. He is a storyteller, someone who tells a true story—and true stories are often dangerous things in *Reading in the Dark*. In the context of the Northern Ireland pictured in the novel, the truth is something highly politicized: every story, if you like, has a political colour to it. Moreover, the story one has to tell, the truth one relates, reveals in some senses the political standpoint from which one looks in this world. Any truth that is good for one group will be bad for another. Though the truth is highly politicized in this world, however, its effects are more often than not felt personally rather than politically. Even if the informer leads people to their deaths, those deaths are seen as having little political consequence. However, to have an informer in one's family is terribly shameful in the world of *Reading in the Dark* and leaves a permanent stigma. The narrator himself indeed is branded an informer early in the book (and he must use all his ingenuity to rid himself of the name). What all this indicates is that *Reading in the Dark* is in part at least a book that concerns itself with the ways the personal lives of certain people are politicized in certain situations, at great personal cost. Though Seamus has minimal direct involvement with politics, in the fraught situation of Northern Ireland he must carry the burden of politics with him in his life. He himself recognizes that he is trapped in that dark world. He hears voices all around him, accusatory, filled with hate. He has done nothing to merit the political branding he receives; his struggle is in part to shrug off that political burden, to bring light to his own personal darkness.

Deane, in his writings on Joyce, has identified a political context for *Portrait* which in some senses is relevant to *Reading in the Dark* also and worth mentioning at this point. In *A Short History of Irish Literature* Deane writes the following: 'In *Portrait*, the moral history of the development of Stephen Dedalus becomes an example of the liberation which Ireland sorely needed and implacably denied.'[3] This remark is very interesting for it creates a kind of political context for *Portrait*, a context which might, through a little sleight of hand, be transferred to *Reading in the Dark*. What Deane seems to suggest here is that *Portrait* enacts a moment of liberation for Stephen and thus rehearses a moment of liberation for Ireland—the liberation Stephen gains at the end of the book, the liberation particularly into himself which is the liberation that often occurs at the end of the *bildungsroman*, is a liberation sought for by Ireland. The growth of the character and his liberation at the end is, then, a kind of rehearsal for national liberation. The same can perhaps be said of *Reading in the Dark*, particularly given that the novel is set very clearly within the nationalist community in Northern Ireland at a time when that community felt especially marginalized and oppressed.

The narrator's personal life is bound up in the life of his family and their perceived political misdemeanours. Telling Eddie's story becomes a way for Seamus to discover the nature of that personal-political relationship and, in a way, free his personal life from it. Just as the family in the story Katie tells (in the section called 'Katie's Story') is cursed—'And the blight's on that family to this very day', Katie's story concludes (p. 71)—so Seamus wants to tell all of Eddie's story because he feels his family to be cursed. They are cursed because Eddie was known as an informer and the family has had to carry that tag around with them everywhere they go. Seamus's attempt to tell Eddie's story, then, is in part an attempt to tell the truth about Eddie and thus redeem himself and his family. The fact that he cannot tell the full story suggests that such redemption is impossible; political redemption for his family seems always beyond his reach. His own growth, moreover, is dependent on that redemption also; in a sense, his growth is predicated on his telling the story so that he might put it behind him and move on. It is as if the narrator cannot grow up until he has freed himself from the events described in the story, until he has freed himself from his family. There is a strange and sad double edge to this: the narrator, to grow up, has to tell his family's story for, in a sense, it is his own story—his whole childhood is bound up in it—but also, in telling that story, he must leave his family completely behind, must, in effect, sever his links with them. His growing up is predicated, as a result, on moving beyond the circle of his family and leaving them behind.

Whether Seamus succeeds or not in moving beyond his family it is hard to decide—as we have seen, his returning at the end of the novel to the house he grew up in can be taken both as a sign of his liberation from there and his inability to free himself from the pull of his family. Perhaps we can see *Reading in the Dark* itself as a testing of that ambiguity, as if the story pieced together by Seamus in this novel ultimately finds him asking 'Am I free?', 'Have I grown?' In one sense he is entitled to answer these questions in the affirmative. The journey he undergoes in *Reading in the Dark* is like the journey Stephen Dedalus undergoes in *Portrait of the Artist as a Young Man*—it is a journey towards a command of language.[4] The very opening of the book, we can note, displays this mastery of language. The novel begins as follows:

On the stairs, there was a clear, plain silence.

It was a short staircase, fourteen steps in all, covered in lino from which the original patterns had been polished away to the point where it had the look of a faint memory. Eleven steps took you to the turn of the stairs where the cathedral and the sky always hung in the window frame. Three more steps took you on to the landing, about six feet long. (p. 5)

This is not a childish voice. Though the year is 1945 and the child in the story is very young, the story is told by that child grown up and the voice that speaks to us is a voice that has mastered language. However, this mastery over language is not simply a formal achievement—it is an expression of some deeper, moral maturity in life. Seamus's mastery of language is something that equips him to begin his search for the truth, something that makes the past available to him by giving him the tools—the story-telling skills—through which it can be explored, and a sign also of a moral maturity that will allow him to judge carefully and considerately the truth he uncovers.

Conclusion

In Deane's novel, the truth uncovered by the narrator is unpalatable; yet the mastery of language displayed in the way the story is told offers us a sign that he will be able to cope with that unpalatable truth, that he will be able to understand it and acknowledge it and deal with it. His mastery of language therefore is both a sign of moral maturity, a sign of emotional and psychological achievement, as well as a means by which he can explore the past. To put this another way, the reason the novel is told from the point of view of a first person narrator who looks back on his life is that it is only in his later years, looking back, that the narrator has both the linguistic skill and moral strength to reveal the truth fully and to cope with it completely. In a fundamental sense, therefore, we might argue that *Reading in the Dark* is not only a novel about growing up but also a novel about being *grown up*. From this perspective, the novel is itself an expression of freedom. While the story may show the narrator to be guilt-ridden and restricted by his inability to redeem either his family or himself, the act of telling the story allows him to negotiate the darkness and be free.

Bibliography

Seamus Deane, *A Short History of Irish Literature* (London: Hutchinson, 1986).

Seamus Deane, *Reading in the Dark* (London: Jonathan Cape, 1996).

Thomas Flanagan, 'Family secrets', *New York Review of Books* 44. 16 (1997), pp. 54-5.

James Joyce, *A Portrait of the Artist as a Young Man* ([1916]; London: Grafton, 1977).

Michael Wood, review of *Reading in the Dark, London Review of Books*, 5 September 1996, p. 15.

Useful teaching resources include the television programme 'Reading in the Dark' (dir. David Hammond, Flying Fox Films, 1999), first broadcast on RTE in November 1999, and the *Three Modern Novels* series, produced for the National Association for the Teaching of English (Britain) by the English and Media Centre, Sheffield (1997), which includes video and written discussions of Deane's novel along with Toni Morrison's *Beloved* and Romesh Gunesekera's *Reef.*

Notes

1. James Joyce, *A Portrait of the Artist as a Young Man*, p. 172.

2. Grianan also features in Jennifer Johnston's novel *Shadows On Our Skin* (1977), which is also set in Northern Ireland and provides an interesting comparison with *Reading in the Dark*.

3. Seamus Deane, *A Short History of Irish Literature*, p. 182.

4. In *A Short History of Irish Literature,* Deane writes that Stephen Dedalus 'begins by receiving the language of his world ... [and] ends by supplanting these forms of language with his own' (p. 182). In Joyce's book, Deane continues, 'we see a young mind coming to grips with his world through an increasing mastery of language'. This description is also an appropriate one for *Reading in the Dark*.

To What End?:
The Tragic Universe of King Lear

BRIAN COSGROVE

Introduction: The Tragic Cosmos

The opening question in the title is intended to bring together
two senses of the word 'end': firstly, the terminal point of death,
and secondly, the idea of cosmic purpose or pattern (as in the
Greek word *telos*). Each of these, of course, is implicated in the
other. Tragedy culminates in death, and sees in death the absolute
extinction of the precious individual life. But what the extinction
of the precious individual further implies—as, famously, in
Milton's 'Lycidas' (e.g., lines 50–1, 92, 107)—is an inquiry into the
ordering of the cosmos, ultimately an indictment of that cosmos
for its lack of justice or of any pattern that is comprehensible in
human terms.

To speak in this way is to undertake to understand the philosophical (or indeed theological) dimensions of the tragic vision.
Tragedy as a literary genre, like the tragic hero at its centre, is
drawn towards questions of an absolute nature, which concern the
ultimate meaning or purpose of the world. Lear himself in Shakespeare's play voices the kind of absolute question that the text as a

whole provokes: 'What is the cause of thunder?' (III.iv.146), or again, with reference to Regan, 'Is there any cause in nature that makes these hard hearts?' (III.vi.75–6). The first of these in effect raises the larger question: What purpose or meaning is to be found in the cosmic event, or in the cosmos itself? What is the nature of Nature? Is thunder merely a manifestation of weather, a simple matter of meteorology; or has it some alternative, symbolic meaning that would allow us to infer a high, cosmic pattern?[1]

The symbolic force and mystery of thunder in *King Lear*, and of nature generally in Shakespeare, is one marker of the historical gap between his (pre-scientific) culture and ours. In that remarkable survey of the history of realist representation in the Western tradition, Erich Auerbach's *Mimesis*, there is a telling summary of the kind of highly-charged cosmos that was available to Shakespeare's imagination:

The dissolution of medieval Christianity ... brings about the dynamic need for self-orientation, a will to trace the secret forces of life. Through this need and will, magic and science, the elemental sphere and the moral and human sphere, become mutually related. An immense system of sympathy seems to pervade the universe [as, notably, in *Macbeth*] ...

Thus Shakespeare's ethical and intellectual world is much more agitated, multilayered ... There is no stable world as background, but a world which is perpetually reengendering itself out of the most varied forces.[2]

The Shakespearean universe, though post-medieval, is still pre-scientific: as such it is more 'multilayered' and charged with a manifold significance than the world delivered to modernity by what Max Weber called the 'disenchantment' (*entzauberung*) brought about by the rise of science. And because the world has not been stabilized by the imposition on it of rational scientific laws, the cosmos is in a sense untamed—'a world reengendering itself out of the most varied forces'. That in turn implies that the cosmos, not yet safely held behind the grid of rationalistic science, will insistently challenge and invade the human imagination.

It follows, too, that for both Shakespeare and his audience the kind of intense focus on personal interaction and socio-economic relations found much later in the realistic or 'bourgeois' novel (such as Flaubert's *Madame Bovary* or George Eliot's *Middlemarch* or Tolstoy's *Anna Karenina*) will, in a sense, not be enough. The individual, the domestic and the familial will, in a play like *King Lear*, extend into the larger context of the cosmos; and the cosmos itself will function, not just as (neutral or non-reactive) backdrop, but as a kind of vast echo-chamber adding its reverberations to the human actions.

There is one point in George Eliot's *Middlemarch* where the author quite consciously and deliberately refuses to engage with what she terms 'that tempting range of relevancies called the universe', preferring, as she says, to unravel 'certain human lots' *without* recourse to the cosmic.[3] For the Elizabethan author of *King Lear*, however, the separation of the 'human' from the 'universe' would have seemed a highly artificial distinction, a cultural aberration. Lear, then, suffers against a cosmic background; and while we may see him as Everyman, a representative of *homo patiens* (or suffering mankind), his royal magnitude is necessary to enable him to encounter the full (and savage) force of the cosmos, while the magnitude of the cosmos in turn confirms or adds to the stature of the protagonist.

Tragedy and the Question of the Origin of Evil

Lear's question, then, 'What is the cause of thunder?', is one that in a play like *Lear* can be raised naturally, without, as it were, forcing the issue, and without self-consciousness or ironic self-deprecation.[4] The other absolute question from Lear which was cited earlier is: 'Is there any cause in nature that makes these hard hearts?' What is posed here is that most insoluble of problems: what is the source of evil?

There is eloquent testimony to the obsessive human interest in this question in the many myths of the origin of evil (including the story of Adam and Eve). One of the most astute and informed commentators on both the symbolism and the mythology of evil is the French philosopher Paul Ricoeur, and what his analysis in effect confirms is, first of all, the insolubility of the problem, and secondly, its profound relevance to the genre of tragedy.

In an essay on the hermeneutics (or interpretation) of symbols, Ricoeur distinguishes between two different myths on the origin of evil. The first kind attributes evil to 'a primordial conflict prior to man' (wars between the forces of light and darkness before man was created); the second kind refers the source of evil 'back to man' himself (i.e., some lapse or sin of disobedience in early human existence).[5] But having made this distinction, and having noted that the Adam and Eve story belongs to the second category, Ricoeur is then obliged to take note of a major inconsistency or even contradiction. This inconsistency is apparent in the way in which the Adam story includes 'the highly mythical figure of the serpent' which symbolizes 'evil already there, pre-given evil'[6]; which means that the Adam story, besides attributing the origin of evil to human disobedience, at the same time includes the contrary view that evil arises from a source that pre-exists or antedates man.

What this inconsistency lays bare is, in fact, the insolubility of the problem that the myth sets out to address in the first place (the symbol of the fall, Ricoeur suggests at one point, may be 'impenetrable'[7]). Moreover, it is part of Ricoeur's argument to highlight the direct connection between the problem of evil and the genre of tragedy. According to this argument, the 'tragic' arises when the human being confronts 'a "mystery of iniquity" that man cannot entirely handle', the tragedy in fact disclosing 'a *divine* mystery of evil'.[8] But if it is a 'divine' (which is to say, 'non-human') mystery, then the implication must be that it is not man, but the forces which rule the cosmos, which are the source of evil.

Ricoeur further proposes that it is this 'invincible' or ineradicable sense of an evil *exterior* to man which in large part accounts for the persistence of tragedy wherein the tragic hero is both responsible moral agent (the source of the evil that destroys him) and at the same time an innocent victim (destroyed by an evil which is external to himself and which is attributable to the non-human forces that govern the cosmos).[9] In accordance with this view of the tragic experience, then, Lear is quite justified in his self-assessment that he is 'a man/ More sinned against than sinning' (III.ii.59–60).

The final point of Ricoeur's that I wish to emphasize is that the human imagination is recurrently haunted by the possibility that evil emerges, not from human beings themselves, but from some inscrutable exterior force (which we habitually shorthand as 'Fate') at work in the universe. Hence it is, as Ricoeur suggests, that tragedy has a persistent relevance, living on even 'after its double destruction' by Greek philosophy (with its emphasis on an ordered cosmos, the very word 'cosmos' originally meaning 'order', the opposite of chaos), and by Christianity (with its faith in a benign and all-powerful Providence, ruling all things for the ultimate benefit of mankind).[10] It is precisely because neither of these belief-systems dispels the dire cosmic possibilities which continue to haunt our imaginations that we can still respond to the harrowing negativity of the famous summary in *King Lear.*

> As flies to wanton boys, are we to th' gods;
> They kill us for their sport.
>
> (Gloucester, IV.i.36–7)

The Search for (Authentic) Meaning

Now if it be true that the tragic sense persists after its *apparent* destruction by Christianity, and is in reality a primal feeling that Christianity is unable to dispel, then Shakespeare may be said to have revealed a sound instinct in setting his play, as notoriously he does, in a primitive, pre-Christian society. For that primitive setting, in which the characters will generally speak of 'the gods' rather than (the Christian) 'God', allows for a much freer, less censored exploration of that radical tragic sense which, strictly speaking, Christianity can never fully endorse.[11]

There is, however, a further thematic gain in setting the action of the play in a primitive society. In such a society we are all the more conscious of the primal realities that lie beneath the surface; civilization is thereby all the more readily shown to be a thin veneer on a disturbingly feral base. A number of thinkers have prepared our modern and post-modern sensibilities to respond with a particular kind of intensity to the idea of civilization as a mere veneer on darker, more 'authentic' realities—among them the ruthlessly anti-sentimental Nietzsche, the rigorous dismantler of illusory societal structures, Marx, and that sternest of demystifiers, Freud.

King Lear seems to anticipate such demystifying procedures in its imagery of divestment, of stripping off one's clothes ('Off, off, you lendings!': III.iv.103). And it is precisely in this context that the radical question can be posed: 'Is man no more than this? Consider him well' (III.iv.97–8). In that consideration, 'unaccommodated man', meaning not only man unhoused but man as no longer concealed by the thin accoutrements of civilization, 'is no more but such a poor, bare forked animal' as we see in Poor Tom (III.iv.101–2).

This brings us close to *King Lear*'s desperate attempt to affirm some minimally human value. Ineluctably faced with the rock-bottom possibility that 'Man's life is cheap as beast's' (II.iv.262), the play struggles to affirm some kind of irreducible human value against an overwhelming weight of negative evidence; rather as if one who had survived the Holocaust, while still perforce register-ing the real horror of what happened, might seek, without senti-mental regression, to re-discover an authentic human value. In *King Lear*, then, the stripping of man down to the bare essentials is relentlessly maintained, but with the unyielding if muted hope of finding, deep down, a stratum of value or meaning by which we may live (or, perhaps, simply go on living).[12]

It is an obvious point to describe this search for meaning as a humanist one; but it is further necessary to stress that this wish to affirm human value is undertaken not just with a limited focus on the human animal's primal, naked self, but with that wider awareness of a highly problematic cosmos we touched on earlier. The world inhabited by tragic man affords no reliable solace or support: in the case of Lear himself, the buffetings and the expo-sure he undergoes in the pitiless storm suggest a universe that is casually punitive (if not, indeed, vindictive[13]). In *King Lear*, it seems, all we can hope for is a universe that is, at best, neutral, and gods who are not actively vindictive, but just totally indiffer-ent in the face of our trials and traumas. For in spite of the fre-quency with which the gods (or other supernal powers) are invoked in the play, it is clear that (unlike the governing powers found in the subsequent romances, such as *Cymbeline* or *The Winter's Tale*) they have absolutely no input into the human action.

The most telling illustration of this concerns Gloucester's failed suicide attempt in act 4, scene 6. Guided by his disguised son, Edgar, the blind Gloucester throws himself forward over what he takes to be the edge of a cliff. All the time, of course, he is actually on level ground, and thus no harm befalls him. Edgar, at this point assuming a different role and voice, tries to sustain Gloucester with an appropriate piece of theological orthodoxy:

> Think that the clearest gods, who make them honors
> Of men's impossibilities, have preserved thee.
>
> (IV.vi.73–4)

But while Gloucester, locked in his subjective darkness, can, with an equally subjective faith, accept this statement as true, the seeing spectators (or readers) of the play know, objectively and undeniably, that the 'gods' have *not* been instrumental in Gloucester's preservation. Gloucester has here been saved, not by divine agency, but by the fully human agency of his son, who astutely practises deceit in order to bring about the desired consequence.

The Scandal of Cordelia's Death

In *King Lear*, then, there can be no meaningful recourse to a supernatural agency: man is exposed and vulnerable in a universe that is, at best, indifferent to his fate, at worst, hostile to his well-being. The category 'man', however, is too abstract in dealing with tragedy: it is above all the vulnerable *individual* who bears the brunt of tragic experience—vulnerable not only in body (the blinding of Gloucester) but in mind (the madness of Lear). Yet the supreme vulnerability is one that is rather closer to all of us than the somewhat extreme and melodramatic sufferings of Gloucester and Lear (sufferings which we may hold, to some extent, at a fictive distance). The supreme vulnerability arises from that individual finitude known to every human existent, the fact that any of us can, at any time and without forewarning, be struck down by death.

In his book *The Sense of an Ending*, Frank Kermode notes how, in early Christianity, as the apocalypse failed to materialize, attention switched to the much more inevitable End of the individual's death. The general terror of the apocalyptic ending of the world (*Dies irae, dies illa*—'The day of wrath, that [terrible] day'—as the opening of the great medieval hymn on the Day of Judgement has it) was thus transferred to the prospect of the mortality of the individual. Kermode further observes that of all the great religions Christianity has been regarded as 'the most anxious', the one 'which has laid the most emphasis on the terror of death'. Following the Middle Ages, the Renaissance, Kermode adds, constitutes 'the moment when the terrors of apocalypse were absorbed by tragedy'; and he goes on to refer specifically to *King Lear.*[14]

Whatever we fear, however, we may come also to resent: thus our fear of death may include a resentment of death. To begin with, what we consciously resent is unjust or undeserved death, which we may find dramatized in tragedy. The great tragic moment in *Lear*, in this regard, is the death of Cordelia. Yet our conscious resentment of the *unjust* death 'acts out', and provides a 'safe' way of expressing, our less conscious resentment against the very idea of death. The provocation to resentment is very clearly present in *King Lear*; the sequence in the final scene is that Edgar hurries offstage to save Cordelia, while Albany utters a spontaneous prayer: 'The gods defend her!' (V.iii.257). Notoriously, Albany's plea is almost immediately followed by the harrowing stage direction, '*Enter Lear, with Cordelia [dead] in his arms ...*'. The gods do not defend Cordelia; and in our acknowledgement of that there lurks more obscurely the recognition that the gods will not defend any of us, either, from the penalty of death.

So we return, though this time via our own psychological reactions rather than on a philosophical level, to the cosmic question. What kind of world-system is it (we wish to ask, and not without resentment) that calls us into the dubious pleasures of existence ('When we are born, we cry that we are come /To this great stage of fools', IV.vi.179–80), and then compounds the absurdity by despatching us, even more randomly, to the darkness of death? What kind of gods or 'system-devisers' are they who raise us to consciousness (the consciousness, sometimes, of a Hamlet), only to afflict that consciousness with a sense of its own vulnerability and ultimate dissolution in death? And—perhaps cruellest of all—what kind of presiding power would fashion us in such a way that, even as we recognize our own mortality and the mortality of others, we insist on finding an absolute or quasi-absolute value (through love) in another human being, as vulnerable and as subject to contingency as ourselves? It is that question which may bring us closest to the deeper meaning of *Othello*, but is central also to Lear's final awareness: Cordelia in her loving-kindness has become the absolute core of Lear's existence, but her mortality and vulnerability plunge him, irretrievably, into an experience of absolute loss: 'Thou'lt come no more,/ Never, never, never, never, never!' (V.iii.308–9).

Cordelia's death here threatens to unhinge, once more, Lear's mind, but it also threatens to subvert his capacity for expression, or, indeed, to undo language and grammatical control altogether; to rob him, in other words, of that capacity of language to sustain a logical or narrative pattern. It is part of the central argument of Kermode's *The Sense of an Ending* that the possibility of a pattern in literature (including narrative continuity) is dependent on the philosophical availability of a belief in a pattern or order in the cosmos or in history. In order to have a sense of an ending we require a belief in an end or *telos*; as Kermode puts it, we 'make considerable imaginative investments in coherent patterns which, by the provision of an end, make possible a satisfying consonance with the origins and with the middle'.[15] Without that 'satisfying consonance', we drift towards absurdity, as *King Lear* in fact tends to do. The conclusion of the play relates not to *telos* but to mere extinction—which, if it has all the finality of apocalypse, has but little of the apocalyptic sense of climactic revelation. 'Is this the promised end?' asks Kent; but a little later he evaluates that end not as striking apocalypse, but as a world expiring in a state of exhaustion: 'All's cheerless, dark and deadly' (V.iii.264, 291).

Kermode, referring specifically to modern fiction, further dwells upon the tension between pattern and fact, 'the dissonance between paradigmatic form and contingent reality'[16]: that is, the way reality fails to live up to our desire for order and sequence. Such a discrepancy between our expectations and the true nature of things is especially pronounced for our own sceptical age; and, as Kermode notes, in the twentieth century 'our changed principles of reality' compel us 'to discard the fictions that are too fully explanatory, too consoling'.[17] In traditional tragedy, too, we are prepared to acknowledge, even as we hunger for the 'paradigm', that brute 'reality' will always threaten to overwhelm all sense of pattern. The perspective of the Augustan eighteenth century (for which *Lear* was radically revised) was strikingly different: they preferred, we might now say, the pattern to the reality (which is what we might expect in a culture so committed to a belief in rational order).

One of the most famous pronouncements of Leibniz, a leading figure of the German Enlightenment, was quite simply: *Nihil est sine ratione* ('There is nothing without reason').[18] Divorced as we are today from any secure sense of pattern, we find instability everywhere (including our texts); whereas Leibniz, on the contrary, could affirm pattern, system and rational causation. One source for the popularity of Nahum Tate's adaptation of *King Lear* in the eighteenth century (and for the related popularity of the notion of poetic justice, which lies behind that adaptation) is this: that the happy ending introduced by Tate (whereby Cordelia survives to marry Edgar, and Lear to reassume his kingship) affirmed a proper moral pattern according to which the wicked were punished and the virtuous rewarded. Tate's happy ending version of *Lear* (to us a 'too consoling' fiction) satisfied the eighteenth century because it erected rational order as a bulwark against the threatened seepage of the unacceptably irrational into an orderly system.

As is well known, Dr Johnson, as a firm believer in poetic justice, for that reason endorsed Tate's version of the play.[19] In addition, however, Johnson had his own temperamental reasons for being 'so shocked by Cordelia's death' that he found the original ending of the play unendurable.[20] The available evidence suggests not only that, as amply recorded in Boswell's *Life*, Johnson himself had an acute apprehension of his own death, but that he strove, where possible, to repress such terrors.[21] The problem for Johnson, however—as Freud recognized—is that whatever is repressed does not disappear: we may attempt to ignore those aspects of our experience or our situation which generate most anxiety, but out of sight will never truly mean out of mind.[22] And it is in the light of that recognition that we may begin to discern a justification for the raw and unbearable realities in tragedy (such as the horrific blinding of Gloucester: 'Out, vile jelly' [III.vii.83]). Our submission (as trapped spectators) to the harrowing experiences of tragedy, it might be said, is an antidote to nightmare; tragedy projects—ideally (as in the theatre) in a shared, communal ritual—our worst fears about our own vulnerability and mortality. Merely to articulate such fears is a minimal source of comfort; and tragedy, in acting out our nightmare in a communal setting, affords, for all its shocking challenge, an acceptable alternative to the onset of nightmare proper in the individual psyche. Aristotle's notion of catharsis may be relevant to the argument at this point: in *ex-pressing* secret or repressed anxieties, tragedy acts as a purgation—a (temporary) exorcism of those irrational terrors which so plagued the sturdy mind of Dr Johnson.

'A Full Look at the Worst'

From this point of view (tragedy as therapeutic release) the modernist need to know the worst may well be healthier than the wilfully maintained rational optimism of the eighteenth century. In a famous essay on modernism in *Beyond Culture*, Lionel Trilling, taking his cue from Joseph Conrad's *Heart of Darkness*, defined the heroic modern artist as one who prefers the authentic reality of the hell in the depths of the psyche to 'the bland lies of the civilization that has overlaid it …'.[23] If we make the most of the figurative possibilities in that statement, we can return anew to *King Lear* with its metaphors of stripping and denudation, its concern to expose 'the thing itself' (III.iv.101), the bleak actuality that exists beyond the superficial trappings of civilization.

The American critic Geoffrey Hartman has indicted Freudian psychoanalysis because of what he calls 'its *kakangelic* rather than *evangelic* nature'. Where the New Testament is 'evangelical'—literally, bringing us 'good news'—Freud is determinedly the opposite—'kakangelical'—in bringing us 'bad news' about our psyche, our complex and dark and furtive interior selves.[24] Yet it is, after all, not only Freud but much of the history or collective experience of the human race that has made inevitable an honest confrontation of the sinister in human affairs. Those who suffered in Auschwitz may be regarded as extreme instances, but they may still possess a representative quality. What they experienced in an extreme and substantive way, Graham Greene experienced in a related if less extreme and more abstract form: the remoteness of heaven, the immediacy of hell. 'I began', Greene tells us in a memoir of his acutely painful schooldays, 'to believe in heaven because I believed in hell.'[25]

It is from this modernist perspective that we may choose initially to respond to *King Lear*: we want to be led beyond false comforts to authentic knowledge, even if the authentic presents itself in the blackest colours. Like the patient in a state of uncertainty who visits the doctor, we insist on knowing the worst—even if, at the same time, there is a limited consolation of the kind expressed in one of Thomas Hardy's most quoted lines:

if way to the Better there be, it exacts a full look at the Worst ...

('In Tenebris II', l.14)

The Paradoxical Possibilities of Tragic Consolation

Given its emphasis on 'the worst', what positive consolation can we derive from *King Lear*? In an essay on Keats, F.R. Leavis commented on the wasted visage of the goddess Moneta (who, in Keats's *The Fall of Hyperion*, symbolizes the relentless assaults of tragic experience), attempting to do justice to the curious sense of 'comfort' which the poet claims to discover in that tragic icon. The comfort, says Leavis, is to be found in 'that paradoxical strengthening—sense of ability to endure—which rewards the full recognition of necessity'.[26] This is well said, but the consolation it offers is perhaps too limited. In looking upon tragic necessity, in confronting the recognition that 'All's cheerless, dark and deadly', is the only value we can win the reactive virtue of stoic strength and resignation?

What we seemed to discover earlier is that the theological questions raised by tragedy are so problematic that they remain forever unresolved; which may be another way of saying that the world of tragedy is essentially an agnostic one, offering no assured basis for belief. Given, then, that suffering and exposed mankind cannot rely on the 'gods', can we still look for the affirmation of some more purely humanist value? If, in all honesty, we consult the deep emotions aroused in us by the play, in particular by that wonderful reconciliation scene between Lear and Cordelia (IV.vii.44–84), then we must acknowledge that something rare and precious and singularly moving has been affirmed, or (a more risky term) revealed (though much depends, here, on our willingness to distinguish such a depth of feeling from mere sentiment).

Yet whatever affirmation is indeed present is conveyed in the harsh terms of tragic paradox. In the extremity of loss felt in the death of Cordelia, we recognize, in an overwhelming instant of retrospection, the extraordinary preciousness of what has been lost. But the almost insupportable irony is that this knowing (*anagnorisis*) of the absolute appeal of Cordelia occurs at the very moment of the extinction of that value—so that the moment constitutes a nexus of simultaneous pain and affirmation, of loss-in-recognition, and of recognition-in-loss:

> Do you see this? Look on her, look, her lips,
> Look there, look there!
>
> (V.iii.311–12)

A.C. Bradley commented that 'any actor is false to the text who does not attempt to express, in Lear's last accents and gestures and look, an unbearable *joy*'.[27] It may be that such an evaluation will prove acceptable only if due emphasis is given to the word 'unbearable'. What Lear experiences in his final moments (as indeed what Gloucester similarly feels at the point of death) lies beyond the reach of the text; if we are tied to an agnosticism on the theological level, then a scepticism that remains truly sceptical and open to possibilities operates also at the level of textual interpretation. We can enter into that extra-textual dimension only insofar as we can respond ('feelingly', to adopt Gloucester's word, IV.vi.147) to the text's invitation to transcend its own limitations.

And yet, once we speak of transcendence, we risk the loss of authentic self-grounding in what we know in immediate terms.

Our own emotionally charged desire for the affirmation of some 'higher' truth may hurry us into a spontaneous act of faith or commitment which, in retrospect, may appear to have been a mere escape from an intolerable actuality, or a false transcendence. As Keats piercingly discovers at the end of the 'Ode to a Nightingale', if we surrender to the imperative claims of feeling, we may subsequently feel deluded by the high, emotional moment; and, exiled from that intensity of feeling, we turn sceptical and begin to question the validity of the experience, seeking a more substantial, more trustworthy truth. The most certain value we seem to have at the end of *King Lear* is the intensity of our own longing for certain value. It is, alas, our own persistent and low-key tragedy that rarely if ever does any absolute (or even assured) value emerge with sufficient cogency or permanence to validate the intensity of our longing, or to appease what Cleopatra in a later play will call 'Immortal longings' (*Antony and Cleopatra*, V.ii.280).

Bibliography

Erich Auerbach, *Mimesis: the Representation of Reality in Western Literature*, transl. from the German by Willard R. Trask ([1946]; Princeton, New Jersey: Princeton University Press, 1953).

James Boswell, *The Life of Samuel Johnson, LL.D* (new ed., 1953; Oxford: Oxford University Press, 1957).

A.C. Bradley, *Shakespearean Tragedy* ([1904]; London and Basingstoke: Macmillan Education Ltd, 1992).

Stuart Brown, *Leibniz* (Brighton: The Harvester Press, 1984).

George Eliot, *Middlemarch* ([1871-2]; New York and London: Norton, 1977).

Sigmund Freud, 'Repression' (1915), in *The Freud Reader*, ed. Peter Gay ([1989]; London: Vintage, 1995).

Graham Greene, *The Lawless Roads* ([1939]; London: William Heinemann and The Bodley Head, 1978).

Thomas Hardy, *The Variorum Edition of the Poems of Thomas Hardy*, ed. James Gibson (London and Basingstoke: Macmillan, 1979).

Geoffrey Hartman, 'The interpreter's Freud', in *Easy Pieces* (New York: Columbia University Press, 1985), pp. 137-154.

Samuel Johnson, *Samuel Johnson on Shakespeare*, ed. H. R. Woudhuysen (Harmondsworth: Penguin Books, 1989).

Frank Kermode, *The Sense of an Ending: Studies in the Theory of Fiction* (New York: Oxford University Press, 1967).

F.R. Leavis, *Revaluation: Tradition and Development in English Poetry* ([1936]; Harmondsworth: Penguin, 1964).

Paul Ricoeur, 'The hermeneutics of symbols and philosophical reflection', in *The Philosophy of Paul Ricoeur: an Anthology of His Work*, ed. Charles E. Reagan and David Stewart (Boston: Beacon Press, 1978), pp. 36-58.

William Shakespeare, *Antony and Cleopatra* and *King Lear*, in *The Complete Pelican Shakespeare*, general editor Alfred Harbage (Baltimore, Maryland: Penguin Books, 1969).

Lionel Trilling, *Beyond Culture* ([1955]; Oxford: Oxford University Press, 1980).

Notes

1. The modern bias is towards accepting such elemental disturbance in merely meteorological terms, yet interesting atavisms persist. Agnostic, modernist Joyce, for example, remained irrationally afraid of thunder.

2. Erich Auerbach, *Mimesis: The Representation of Reality in Western Literature*, p. 324.

3. George Eliot, *Middlemarch*, p. 96 (opening of ch. XV).

4. When, in a modern drama such as O'Casey's *Juno and the Paycock*, 'Captain' Boyle and, subsequently, Joxer ask what appears to be a similar question—'What is the stars?' (Act One)—they can do so only as part of a comic charade.

5. Paul Ricoeur, 'The hermeneutics of symbols and philosophical reflection', p. 42.

6. Ibid., p. 43.

7. Ibid., p. 56.

8. Ibid.

9. Ibid., p. 43.

10. Ibid.

11. There was, of course, a very real and immediate *official* censorship at work, that of the Lord Chamberlain. In the interests of avoiding what might be construed as blasphemy, it made practical sense to avoid liberal references (in the singular) to 'God', i.e. the Christian deity. In spite of this, a crucial and especially meaningful use of the singular form is possibly to be found at V.iii.16–17: 'And take upon's the mystery of things,/ As if we were God's spies'—though even here some editors insist on printing the plural possessive, Gods'.

12. It is perhaps relevant to recall that one of the most striking records of survival in the concentration camps, Victor Frankl's, bears the title *Man's Search for Meaning.*

13. To accept that the world is positively vindictive in its dealings with us is a step along the path of what might be called 'cosmic paranoia', by which we are all, perhaps, more often tempted than we readily admit (waiting in the rain, for instance, for that bus that refuses to come). The most notorious comic version of such paranoia is Basil Fawlty; but the condition is more memorably manifest in such major tragic figures as Herman Melville's Captain Ahab, or Thomas Hardy's Henchard, mayor of Casterbridge.

14. Frank Kermode, *The Sense of an Ending: Studies in the Theory of Fiction,* p. 27.

15. Ibid., p. 17.

16. Ibid., p. 133.

17. Ibid., p. 161.

18. This was 'stated by Leibniz as a "fundamental principle" in a paper of 1671': Stuart Brown, *Leibniz,* p. 33.

19. Regretting the fact that Shakespeare 'has suffered the virtue of Cordelia to perish in a just cause, contrary to the natural ideas of justice', Johnson preferred to see Cordelia, as in Tate's version, crowned with 'victory and felicity'; see *Samuel Johnson on Shakespeare,* p. 222.

20. *Samuel Johnson on Shakespeare,* pp. 222-3.

21. Boswell, recalling a memorable exchange on 27 October, 1769, in which Johnson's 'dismal apprehensions' regarding death became all too apparent, adds his own vivid image of Johnson at bay:

His mind resembled the vast amphitheatre, the Colisaeum at Rome. In the centre stood his judgement, which, like a mighty gladiator, combated those apprehensions that, like the wild beasts of the *Arena*, were all around in cells, ready to be let out upon him. After a conflict, he drove them back into their dens; but not killing them, they were still assaulting him. To my question, whether we might not fortify our minds for the approach of death, he answered, in a passion, 'No, Sir, let it alone ...' (Boswell, *The Life of Samuel Johnson*, p. 427)

The reactions here of the Christian Johnson, incidentally, substantiate Kermode's contention, cited earlier, that of all the great religions Christianity has laid most emphasis on the terror of death.

22. In his paper on 'Repression' (1915), Freud notes that the results of repression are never 'permanent', as when 'some living thing has been killed, and from that time onward is dead ... we may suppose that the repressed exercises a continuous pressure in the direction of the conscious, so that the pressure must be balanced by an unceasing counter-pressure'; see *The Freud Reader*, p. 572.

23. Lionel Trilling, *Beyond Culture*, p. 18.

24. Geoffrey Hartman, 'The interpreter's Freud', pp. 142-3.

25. Graham Greene, *The Lawless Roads*, p. 3.

26. F.R. Leavis, *Revaluation*, p. 222.

27. A.C. Bradley, *Shakespearean Tragedy*, p. 253.

The Sphinx of Literature: Shakespeare's Hamlet

PAUL HOLLYWOOD

Questions of Interpretation

Hamlet has sometimes been called the sphinx of modern literature, a play which confounds and eventually destroys those who
try to find an answer to the riddles that it poses. That is, no
doubt, a great exaggeration, but certainly *Hamlet* is a peculiarly
complex play and has continually presented its interpreters with
a number of perplexing questions. To begin with, Hamlet is
probably the only one of the 'big' Shakespearean tragic heroes
whom it is impossible to advise. We can say with some confidence what Othello, Macbeth and Lear should have done, or
should not have done, if only for their own sanity or for the sake
of those around them. Antony is a more complex case, perhaps,
but nevertheless he makes a number of clear errors. Hamlet, however, is the most complex of all: we can blame him for his abuse
of Ophelia, and find his prurient interest in his mother's sexuality very strange, but they are the only clear judgments we can
make of him. We cannot say whether he should take action
against the King, with all the moral and political dangers that

involves, or whether he should just forget about the whole thing and learn to live with his suffering as a good patient Christian. We cannot say whether he should listen to what he is told by the Ghost, who is so convincing alone with Hamlet but strikes everybody else who sees him as highly suspect indeed. As T.S. Eliot pointed out many years ago, to some extent Hamlet seems just thrown into the world of this play, presented with a set of horribly pressing and urgent difficulties and then deprived of any implied solution or any authoritative code of action which would allow him to either kill or be at peace in his passivity. Then, to add to the difficulty, *Hamlet* itself presents us with an unusually wide range of interpretative choices with regard to key issues and moments in the play; again, without suggesting any clear answers.

Is Hamlet really mad, or only pretending to be (or as Oscar Wilde famously put it, bemused by the fascination the question held for critics, 'Are the commentators on *Hamlet* really mad, or only pretending to be')? Hamlet himself provides contradictory answers to the question (see, I.v.170–2, III.iv.141–7 and V.ii.220–37) and since we never see his rather ridiculous-sounding 'knees knocking' (II.i.81) antics actually on the stage, we cannot know where the acting ends and the real madness begins. Consequently the play has suggested many possible theories of Hamlet's behaviour to commentators over the years. Why does he spend all of his time talking and delay in taking his revenge? Is the reason simply that he is a moral coward and can kill only through a screen or at a distance, in the way that he despatches Polonius or Rosencrantz and Guildenstern, without a glimmer of conscience? Some critics have found more complex religious or political reasons for his delay: reasons to do with Hamlet's awareness of his public responsibility to set the 'times' right, and his need for both an external sanction and an understanding audience to support his deed of violence—a deed which is, after all, an act of religious and political rebellion against what seems, to others, legitimate authority.

External confirmation is clearly part of what Hamlet seeks in staging 'The Mousetrap' for the court in act III scene 2 and simultaneously, in a sense, staging the King for his and Horatio's special observation. On that occasion, however, sanction does not come unambiguously, since the play does not have quite the desired clear-cut effect and the audience is divided—Horatio is disappointingly noncommittal and says nothing to confirm Hamlet's excited interpretation of Claudius's response (III.ii.295–9). Yet the play within the play helps us to understand why Hamlet is so obsessed with the theatre and the idea of acting—the challenge of getting matters of style and timing right, to create the right impression, to control the meaning of his own actions. We see him repeatedly transform the world into a drama and his own experience into a role (V.ii.29–32). Clearly, theatre is acting as a metaphor within the play: in the view of some critics, it is a metaphor for power, for the ability to display authority and control appearances that we see Claudius so effectively employ and which Hamlet so desires.

The ending of the play offers us a number of particularly complex interpretative choices. What, for example, do we understand by Hamlet's free delivery of himself to his enemies for the fencing match in the final scene, another piece of deceptive theatre into which Hamlet enters against both his own better sense and the advice of Horatio (V.ii.203–18)—is it Christ-like surrender or stoical suicide? Again the play suggests different answers and seems to dramatize the tension between these rival models of surrender as ways of understanding the closing action. The final scene also seems to provide the authorization for action long sought by Hamlet, when a rapid and convenient series of accidents finally exposes Claudius publicly as 'a murderer and a villain' (III.iv.97) and deprives him of the wife who was the source of his power. Thus Hamlet is momentarily promoted to power and can proceed with what appears to be an unambiguously just and necessary public killing, an execution rather than a murder. Are we to understand this as the hand of God or of the author seeing justice done at last, in either case bringing the play to a neat moral resolution? Or do we respond instead to the awful arbitrariness of it all: to the sheer blind chance, to the fact that the stage is littered with the corpses of innocent and guilty alike (even Horatio wishes to join the numbers of the dead), and to the fact that the final words of the play are spoken by Fortinbras, a man prepared to risk the lives of 'twenty thousand men ... for a fantasy and trick of fame' (IV.iv.61–2) and signally unconcerned with justice?

The question of what to make of the Ghost also remains unresolved as the play ends. How do we reconcile the contradiction between his claim to be a Christian soul in purgatory and his demand that Hamlet commit what would be considered a great sin in Christian terms? Why is it that Hamlet, amid all his meditations on the afterlife and complaints against the Christian prohibition of suicide, never fully or explicitly formulates the most glaringly obvious issue of this and all other revenge plays of the period: the Christian God's prohibition of revenge and the Christian state's monopoly on violence, both of which the avenger must violate? Acknowledgement of these issues is suggested in Hamlet's speeches, but it is left to the lesser character of Laertes to make the point explicit for us, with his determination to 'dare damnation' and his sacrilegious preparedness to 'cut [a] throat I'th'church' (IV.v.134–5).

Traditions of Interpretation

One could multiply these questions until one did indeed become like one of the victims of the sphinx: unable to see the obvious and simple answers because one gets lost in the questions. However, it is also true that the role of the student of *Hamlet* has generally been precisely to supply answers to these types of question: to come up with a reading of the play that resolves its difficulties, that renders it coherent and defines its subject matter in terms that are rational and internally consistent. In productions of the play this has often involved altering it materially, sometimes cutting out 'inconvenient' elements like Fortinbras, who did not appear in the most commonly accepted version for over one hundred and fifty years, because it was felt he added nothing of real significance and his intrusion at the end merely distracted us from the tragic effect. We can see this continued in some modern film versions, both Laurence Olivier (1948) and Tony Richardson (1969) ending the play on Hamlet's death. On the other hand, Kenneth Branagh's 1997 film of *Hamlet* moves in the opposite direction and develops Fortinbras and the military subtext significantly, frequently cutting to scenes showing the relentless advance of his army as a backdrop to the power struggles at Elsinore. More generally, however, this rationalization of the text has been simply a matter of emphasizing certain elements of the play as opposed to others, closing it down to some extent in order to make it manageable and to resolve the questions it leaves unresolved. As an example of this, consider the way that interpretations of *Hamlet* can be seen to fall into two related but nevertheless quite distinct traditions, both of which offer us dramatically effective plays or films perhaps, but only partial constructions of the written text as we have it and study it.

The first is a predominantly western tradition, running right back to the romantics, in which *Hamlet* has been what critics call, in the fashionable terminology of our age, 'privatized': that is, interpreted as a play about the mind and character of Hamlet himself, who in most versions is subjected to a test of strength and morality and found wanting in some vital respect. This *Hamlet* is a play about a man suffering from an excess of imagination and intellect (Samuel Taylor Coleridge), a melancholic disposition (A.C. Bradley), an unhealthy sexual obsession with his mother (Sigmund Freud), or infinite variations or combinations of those things.[1] At their most extreme, these types of reading have reduced the play to a kind of psychological case study, claiming to know details of Hamlet's childhood and his life outside of Elsinore. Alternatively they have led to what has been called 'Hamletism': a fashion for idealizing Hamlet as the pale young man of the romantic imagination, seeing him as a symbol of a vague kind of aesthetic alienation from the world of power and politics, compounded out of equal measures of the feelings of frustration, futility and personal impotence he so eloquently expresses in his soliloquies. 'I have a smack of Hamlet myself, if I may say so,' Coleridge is famously reported to have observed, obviously thinking of Hamlet's reputation as a dreamy scholar, and then projecting his own romantically intellectual and yet impractical temperament onto the fictional character—as if Hamlet, as David Daniell has remarked, is a character just too intelligent and sensitive to do the washing up.[2] In turn this romanticization had led to the tendency to abstract Hamlet and his soliloquies out of the play: to seeing them as the most important, the most 'true' part of it, where Hamlet most poetically bears his soul to the world and where the values and issues of the play come through most clearly. To test that proposition, it is always worth comparing what Hamlet actually says in his soliloquies with what we learn elsewhere: his construction of Fortinbras at IV.iv.32–66, for example, is obviously designed to work in tension with what we have just heard of Fortinbras from the Norwegian captain and dramatizes Hamlet's by this time well established tendency to simplify and idealize whenever he is left alone.

The second tradition, stemming predominantly from societies other than those of the liberal West, has tended to interpret *Hamlet* as more of a political drama. Naturally enough, people who have had direct experience of overtly tyrannical governments and supervision by a secret police are likely to seize upon elements of *Hamlet* that reflect that experience. They will look to the nature of Claudius's regime and his establishment of something like a spy network through his use of the secondary characters to 'glean' (II.ii.16) and 'sift' (II.ii.58) the inner thoughts of Hamlet and others (thus, for example, the otherwise superfluous and frequently cut scene where Polonius sends Reynaldo to spy on his son); they will look to the fact that Hamlet feels himself in a difficult political position, displaced from power and silenced at Elsinore (I.ii.159 and III.ii.347). They might also look to the play's repeated evocation of political instability and fear of war: to its images of a population labouring under 'The oppressor's wrong' (III.i.71) and the fact that in Act IV the mob come knocking on the door demanding a change of government. In Russia, Stalin placed performances of the play under an unspoken ban for thirty years, aware of a special and highly politicized tradition of 'Russian Hamletism' that stretched back to the time of the Tsars and in which Hamlet had again been idealized, but this time as a symbol of an oppressed intelligentsia debating the question of 'taking arms' against oppression. As the Russian Shakespeare scholar Alexei Bartoshevich has noted in a recent interview, the interpretation of *Hamlet* has never been 'about Shakespeare, but about Russia and its relationship to itself, [and] today it's much easier to understand the logic of Claudius than that of Hamlet: the political cynicism, the vulgarity, the tendency to violence'. According to Bartoshevich, these aspects of Claudius's character make new sense and suggest new understandings of *Hamlet* within the context of the Yeltsin regime.[3] Similarly, in South

Africa interpreters have been more explicit about their political stance on *Hamlet* and the play has almost openly become a site of ideological struggle in a society where it has been used 'by English-speaking whites to maintain the position of cultural superiority, by Afrikaners to challenge this position and to validate Afrikaner culture, and by Coloureds, Indians and Blacks to establish their bid for inclusion in the rights and privileges of an equal society'.[4]

While it is interesting and useful to compare these different traditions of reading and production, as a way of exploring the range of interpretative possibilities offered by the text of *Hamlet,* the issue, of course, is never which of them is right. We find in *Hamlet* what we want to find, or what we can find, and the real point is that *Hamlet* is one of those texts by which we define, not it, but ourselves: through the things in which we take an interest, the angle of vision we employ, the values we discover, we are always talking about our own worldview and ideas as much as of the play itself. Thus Coleridge finds a romantic, Freud a neurotic, and Stalin a threat to his power.

And it is here, with this recognition, that much of the more recent theoretical criticism of *Hamlet* has originated and begun to develop new ways of reading the play which respond to its ambiguity more directly. Modern theory has established that the relationships of a text to its author, audience and world are more intricate than had been supposed, particularly in the case of a text like *Hamlet* which patently does not offer us a 'closed' meaning determined by Shakespeare himself. The connections between what a text represents and what it 'means' are often indirect, involving a displacement of and negotiation with the inherited meanings of the conventions within which it works. On the other hand, part of the meaning resides in the responses it elicits from its audience and these, as we have seen, are extremely variable in the case of *Hamlet*. Awareness of these issues has led to many new perspectives on *Hamlet*, some of which are my subject in the rest of this piece.

Firstly, then, I look at *Hamlet*'s relationship to the conventions of revenge tragedy as they operated in Shakespeare's time. These form an important context for understanding the play's postponed or incomplete action, since Shakespeare seems to be playing with his contemporary audience's expectations of the form and questioning the values on which it is based. Secondly, I look at some ways in which the play has been related to its historical and cultural context. Many recent critics have seen *Hamlet* as a play that displays some of the most fundamental social and cultural tensions of its time: its ambiguity and contradiction implicitly articulating a profound sense of crisis in both individual and social life in late Elizabethan England.

Theme and Genre

Based upon the ancient Nordic story of Amleth, the clever avenger whose name means stupid, *Hamlet* is firstly a revenge tragedy which explores the ethics of taking the law into one's own hands and returning to the primitive but emotionally satisfying justice of 'an eye for an eye, a tooth for a tooth'. As such, it is an example of an extremely popular and sensational genre of Elizabethan drama that played upon and exploited the well-established tragic and dramatic power of revenge as a theme. With precedents running right back to the heroes and heroines of ancient Greek drama, there has always been something inherently exciting, and yet also tragic, in the figure of the avenger forced to seek private satisfaction for public wrongs. The very nature of the task imposed necessarily drives the hero into isolation from the community; it renders him or her paranoid and suspicious, even insane, as like Hamlet they come to learn that the world is not at it seems, that 'One may smile and smile, and be a villain' (I.v.98). Furthermore, it introduces an element of theatricality into their thought and behaviour as they are forced to plot and dissemble, to descend into villainy themselves, in order to encompass their revenge. In Sophocles' *Electra* (about 410 BC), for example, the heroine feels duty-bound to avenge the murder of her father by her mother and her mother's lover. In achieving that revenge, however, she is driven to such wild and near psychotic extremes of speech and behaviour as to call into question the justice and sanity of her mission. Thomas Kyd's hero Hieronymo in *The Spanish Tragedy* (1589), the most prominent Elizabethan precedent for *Hamlet*, is himself a lawmaker, but cannot obtain justice for the murder of his son. Disillusioned by the corruption of the public world, he withdraws into a bout of introspection bordering on madness, before re-emerging into the world with a series of maniacally vengeful murders topped off with his own suicide.

Hamlet conforms to this general pattern and contains many of its conventional elements (ghosts and scenes of madness were often featured), but it is a peculiarly complex and self-conscious example of the genre, full of contradictions and unusual silences. To begin with, it offers us a famously reticent hero, someone who cannot quite be the highly theatrical avenger the plot requires and who often mocks or despairs at the melodramatic situation in which he finds himself. (Thus moments like I.v.143–63, where Hamlet draws our attention to the transparent theatricality of the stage business that we have just seen; or II.ii.446–563, where he provides an almost comic description of the mien of the typical stage avenger he needs to be.) At the same time, however, he cannot simply forget about the duty of revenge since he is mysteriously haunted by it: literally, in the form of his father's ghost (suited in armour and appearing somewhat anachronistic in the midst of a modern political court where disputes are settled by

diplomacy); metaphorically, in the form of the play's series of parallel avengers, Laertes, Fortinbras, and the doubly fictional figure
of Pyrrhus in the player's speech, all of whom offer Hamlet possible models of conduct for a son whose father has been murdered
and all of whom, like the ghost, seem to urge him to action. For
Hamlet, however, none of those models answers to his need. Neither the fortuitous fact of revenge which Fortinbras achieves, as he
simply walks in at the end of the play to find all his enemies dead,
nor the simple skulduggery into which Laertes descends, can offer
the ideal spectacle of 'the enginer/ Hoist with his own petard'
(III.iv.206–7): that symmetry of 'an eye for an eye', of action and
justice, that is both an aesthetic requirement of the revenge drama
and Hamlet's stated aim. Revenge must occur at the right time, in
the right place and manner, and the difficulty of managing all of
those factors without political power is what finally seems to
defeat him. Significantly, then, it is only ever in theatre that
Hamlet achieves that aim: in the figure of Lucianus in 'The
Mousetrap', whose speech beginning 'Thoughts black, hands apt,
drugs fit, and time agreeing/ Confederate season' (III.ii.264) offers
a model of a conjoining of word, deed and opportunity that
Hamlet often speaks about but never achieves. Indeed, to underline the point, it is shortly followed by Hamlet's failure to seize
his chance in the very next scene.

Hamlet, then, while unable to assume the particular role of
avenger, is also strangely theatrical and cognizant of the conventions of the genre in which he finds himself even as he fails to
observe them fully. He does many of the things an audience well
acquainted with the tradition would have expected of the hero:
he acts out an 'antic disposition' (I.v.172), plunges into moral confusion, violently rails against the world and its corruption, and
even throws himself into swashbuckling action during his adventures at sea (significantly, outside of Elsinore where he is always

ineffective). He even stages a play and speaks as a judge and critic of the theatre in almost the same terms that he uses to criticize the world. Thus his advice to the players, 'suit the action to the word, the word to the action ... to hold, as 'twere, the mirror up to nature' (III.ii.17–22), clearly informs his own principle of conduct as announced in his first speech in the play, where he declares himself to 'know not "seems"' (I.ii.76) even as, paradoxically, he himself is being intensely histrionic. In that very abstract little speech he uses terms like 'forms' and 'denote' (I.ii.82, 83), the language of metaphysics and criticism, which is very little to the immediate purpose unless we apply it to the remarkably smooth performance we have just seen from Claudius. This sets up Hamlet as a critic of signs in the world as well as the theatre: sceptical of all representations and ambitious of being an anti-Machiavellian exposer of the Danish court as merely a sinister theatre presided over by a 'vice of kings' (III.iv.99).

There are, therefore, a number of reasons why *Hamlet* should deal so openly and self-consciously with images of the theatre in treating this revenge theme. Firstly, and most simply, there is the play's presentation of Hamlet as a Renaissance scholar and man of the arts: in a realization of one of the great themes of literature, Hamlet is a kind of dramatist *manqué* using his theatrical experience to understand what is happening to him, trying to expose illusions by counter-illusions, defeat deception by fiction. Secondly, there is also, of course, a political dimension to this. Upon learning of his father's assassination, Hamlet immediately acknowledges that part of his duty is to set 'the time' aright: that he is no ordinary avenger but someone who acts upon the public stage and whose actions have an audience and need to be understood by them. This explains his particular need for Horatio as an ideal audience and interpreter of his actions at the end. Thirdly, there is the fact that the play seems designed to make its audience aware of the conflicts of belief and value on which revenge tragedy is based. *Hamlet* employs the convention of the genre by peopling the stage with an apparent madman and a ghost crying revenge, but then at least partly flouts it, by giving us a hero who can not act out the required role. In this way, the play brings into particularly close focus some of the social and cultural tensions that this type of theatre addressed and seemed to resolve.

Again this can best be understood in relation to the usual pattern of the Elizabethan revenge tragedy, which typically exploited the tension between the direct emotional and imaginative appeal of the simple quest for blood vengeance and the passive Christian ethic of patience and suffering that formed the basis of law— 'Vengeance is mine; I will repay, saith the Lord' (*Romans*, 12:19). But as Blake famously said of Milton, 'he was a true poet and of the devil's party without knowing it,' and we often see something quite similar here: the sympathy these plays generate for their heroes is largely premised upon a challenge to that Christian ethic as inadequate, not just to the demands of natural justice, but to the very feeling and energy of life itself, which these plays insist will not be restricted within such narrow boundaries. It was this tension between the hero's life and the ethic of society that gave these plays such fascination and effect, and kept Elizabethan audiences watching until the final act, when the avenging hero is conventionally and often unconvincingly brought to justice in order for that challenge to be contained or framed within a coherent and safe Christian moral.

Hamlet plays upon these same tensions of value but again varies them, as it does not by any means obviously or unambiguously re-affirm a Christian moral framework at the end. On the one hand, it is true that Hamlet seems to learn a kind of fatalism, described in terms that echo Christ's words in Matthew ('There is special providence in the fall of a sparrow,' V.ii.213–14). This would suggest that we understand his passive abandonment of himself in the final scene as a deliberate act of Christian resignation: as a way of waiting for God's judgment on events, which seems to come soon in the rapid series of accidents that bring the action to a close. On the other hand, to describe the ending in this way hardly seems adequate to its complexity and there is much in the play to contradict it. For example, that explanation is directly balanced by another way of understanding Hamlet's behaviour suggested by his moves into the language of stoicism in his soliloquies and his repeated praise of Horatio: 'more an antique Roman than a Dane' (V.ii.335), and a more realistic role model. The classical stoic philosophy that Horatio espouses requires fortitude and a strong sense of personal justice from its adherents; even to the point, it was believed at that time, of recommending suicide rather letting oneself be compromised by living under the dominion of enemies. And, of course, in most productions and editions of the play Hamlet finally speeds his own death at the end by drinking off the poison: a gesture towards suicide that is a problem for those who would interpret *Hamlet*, and what Hamlet learns, in consistently Christian terms.

Perhaps, then, the message of Hamlet's fate is not religious but political, and the play is using him to conduct a critique of contemporary theories of political absolutism, which employed the Christian doctrine of patience and suffering as protection for itself and left the citizen with no legitimate recourse against even extreme tyranny.[5] According to Tudor ideas of monarchy, and as the language of the play repeatedly reminds us, the monarch was a natural being 'born to greatness' (*Henry V*, IV.i.234), a private individual and yet also an integral part of the political body of the state appointed by God, and to act against him was therefore a rebellion against both the state and God. This is a notion that Claudius and his flatterers repeatedly invoke to bolster his authority (see, for example I.ii., III.iii.1–23, and IV.v.125–8) and that Hamlet seems to question in his riddling lines to Rosencrantz and Guildenstern: 'The body is with the King, but the King is not with the body' (IV.ii.27–8). Claudius, as a usurper of the throne by force and by possession of Gertrude's body, is at once both the violator and the possessor of the political body of Denmark: both the living negation of the doctrine and its figurehead. As Leonard Tennenhouse has pointed out, this gives Hamlet's strange interest in his mother's sexuality a political dimension.[6]

Alternatively, however, we can also take a historical approach to the play and see the very reaching back to classical models for standards of action and explanation as an articulation of contemporary social tensions and developments: partly of a typical Renaissance sense of distance from the absolute world of medieval Christianity, and partly of the crisis in personal identity and subjectivity which that distance brought about.

Historical Context

Recently one of the most frequently quoted maxims on tragedy has been Albert Camus's observation that it is the characteristic expression of periods of rapid historical change or transition between social and cultural systems: 'Tragedy is born in the west each time that the pendulum of civilization is halfway between a sacred society and a society built around man.'[7] Tragedy occurs at a juncture between worldviews, between ways of defining the self, ways of understanding what is personal and what is political; and the tragic hero or heroine is the individual who is caught in the contradiction between them.

Take Sophocles' *Antigone*, for example—a play which, like *Hamlet*, deals with intra-familial violence in a political cause and has been used to express resistance to totalitarian power all over the world.[8] Antigone remains true to the 'laws of Heaven/ unwritten and unchanging', which prescribe her duties within the family and demand respect towards the dead, but in a time of political and social instability, on the very first day after a cataclysmic civil war, this leads her into conflict with the immediate political needs of society. Her adversary, Creon, is true to the antagonistic principle of civic law, which places the safety of the state at the centre of value and demands that social stability be preserved at all costs; but this principle destroys him by transforming him into a tyrant responsible for the destruction of his own family and the denial of the bonds of blood and history. Antigone dies and Creon survives, but only at the cost of feeling that 'My life now is death.'[9] The personal becomes political and the political personal, as the oppositions by which life is organized collapse and merge. Read as a political statement, *Antigone* can be seen as a warning that a society which does not incorporate that part of an individual's identity which is constructed by familial ties and ancestral tradition is inevitably prone to disaster and violence. Read historically, in the way that Camus suggests, *Antigone* can be seen as the story of the contradictions of a period of transition between a primitive society, organized around blood kinship and its valorization in notions of the eternally sacred, and the democratic city state, organized around civic codes and more relative secular values.

Hamlet is often read in this way by critics who relate it back to the confused social and political conditions of England in 1601. This was a time when England was in the middle of a rapid change in the basic structures of its social, economic and intellectual life. Feudalism, with its traditional social order and discourse of social bondedness, was giving way to capitalism, a new social order with a new notion of freedom and self-determination: the idea that people were not limited by birth, but were able to create themselves and establish their own rights through their deeds. Inevitably this process propelled questions of selfhood, of the individual's rights and responsibilities, into the foreground of contemporary ideological debate and made them a political matter. And there is a long tradition of reading *Hamlet* against this background by seeing Hamlet as a transitional character on the brink of modern ideas of selfhood: caught between the old feudal traditions and that new capitalist discourse of self-creation.

Hegel understood Hamlet in something like this way and connected him to Edmund in *King Lear* as an example of a new type of figure in literature, embodying a principle of self-consciousness or self-creativity not seen before. Many years later Bertolt Brecht described Hamlet as a 'new type, fully developed, standing out as totally estranged in a medieval setting'[10]: Hamlet is caught between two worlds, the bourgeois man bemused in a medieval society where ghosts can still cry revenge. More recently critics have picked up on this self-reflexiveness of *Hamlet* but have tended to explain it in terms of the specific political and ideological contradictions of the play's historical background. Hamlet is not so much bourgeois, as a character for whom no coherent model of subjectivity and action is available. Terry Eagleton, for instance, has written of Hamlet as 'a radically transitional figure, strung out between a traditional social order to which he is marginal, and a future epoch of achieved bourgeois individualism'.[11] This is also an important part of Catherine Belsey's influential reading of *Hamlet* in relation to the revenge genre. Like Brecht and Eagleton, Belsey is a Marxist critic for whom Hamlet's problems are not problems of morality but problems of power, concerning not his moral right to do what he wants to do, but his ability to do it in a world which does not yet allow the individual the legal sanction to act for him or herself, even on behalf of the law. For Belsey, the duty of revenge imposed on Hamlet demands from him both aggression and restraint, both action and inaction, according to the contradictory codes of his transitionary world.

As such it exposes one of the ideological fracture points of Eliza-bethan England and, as she says, it 'deconstructs the antithesis which fixes the meaning of good and evil, right and wrong.'[12]

Conclusion

Finally, then, what can *we* make of *Hamlet?* Certainly it is a play that offers a particular challenge to its interpreter and a rich sub-ject for development. As the sheer variety of interpretation demonstrates, traditionally we have made of it what we can or what we will, filled in the gaps or silences or resolved the contra-dictions according to our own worldview and taste, and perhaps that is all we can do: make it relevant to ourselves. Modern criti-cism, however, has recognized this possibility more clearly and has consequently grown increasingly sceptical of the project of defin-ing a single meaning for *Hamlet,* since any attempt to do so inevitably reduces the play and reveals a desire to universalize a subjective and historically relative response. In order to guard against this stultifying tendency, recent criticism has therefore sent us back to the text, not to resolve the contradictions but to read them for what they can tell us: about the conflicts of ideology and power among which *Hamlet* was written, as well as the conflicts of ideology and power within which it continues to be received.

Bibliography

Martin Coyle (ed.), *New Casebooks: 'Hamlet'* (London: Macmillan, 1992).

David Daniell, '*Hamlet*', in Stanley Wells (ed.), *Shakespeare: A Biblio-graphical Guide* (Oxford: Clarendon Press, 1990), pp. 201-21.

Jonathan Dollimore and Alan Sinfield (eds), *Political Shakespeare: New Essays in Materialism and Culture* ([1985]; Manchester: Manchester University Press, 1992).

Terry Eagleton, *William Shakespeare* (Oxford: Blackwell, 1986).

T.S. Eliot, 'Hamlet and his problems', in *Selected Essays* (London: Faber and Faber, 1951), pp. 143-6.

R.A. Foakes, *'Hamlet'* versus *'Lear'* (Cambridge: Cambridge University Press, 1993).

Hugh Grady, *The Modernist Shakespeare* (Oxford: Clarendon, 1991).

Andrew Gurr, *The Shakespearean Stage, 1574-1642* (Cambridge: Cambridge University Press, 1980).

Edward Hubler (ed.), *Hamlet*, The Signet Shakespeare (New York: New American Library, 1987).

Harold Jenkins (ed.), *Hamlet*, The Arden Shakespeare (London: Methuen, 1982).

W.R. Quince, '*Hamlet* on the South African stage', *Hamlet Studies* 10 (1988), pp. 144-51.

Kiernan Ryan, *Shakespeare* (London: Harvester Wheatsheaf, 1989).

Leonard Tennenhouse, 'Violence done to women on the Renaissance stage', in Nancy Armstrong and Leonard Tennenhouse (eds), *The Violence of Representation* (London: Methuen, 1989), pp. 77-97.

Susanne Wofford, *Case Studies in Contemporary Criticism: 'Hamlet'* (New York: Bedford, 1994).

Notes

1. For a brief but useful summary of the Western critical tradition see David Daniell's '*Hamlet*' in Stanley Wells (ed.), *Shakespeare: A Bibliographical Guide*, pp. 201-21. Fuller accounts of the positions of these three commentators can be found in Edward Hubler (ed.), *Hamlet*, The Signet Shakespeare, and Harold Jenkins (ed.), *Hamlet*, The Arden Shakespeare.

2. Daniell, '*Hamlet*', p. 204.

3. *The Guardian*, 17 October 1998.

4. W.R. Quince, '*Hamlet* on the South African Stage', p. 144.

5. That Shakespeare was particularly concerned with this issue in the years running up to the writing of *Hamlet* is confirmed by the fact that both *Richard II* and *Julius Caesar*, written shortly before *Hamlet*, deal with almost identical themes. Brutus in *Julius Caesar* is another clever man whose name means stupid, and who is called upon to kill against his own temperamental leanings. He reproduces Hamlet's

experience in his almost phantasmagoric fall into what he calls a 'hideous dream' (I.ii.68): a feeling of unreality and divided consciousness in the run-up to the assassination.

6. Leonard Tennenhouse, 'Violence done to women on the Renaissance stage'.

7. Albert Camus, *Selected Essays and Notebooks*, trans. P. Thody (Harmondsworth: Penguin, 1970), p. 199.

8. See George Steiner, *Antigones* (Oxford: Oxford University Press, 1984).

9. Edith Hall (ed.), Sophocles, *Antigone, Oedipus The King, Electra*, trans. H.D.F. Kitto (Oxford: Oxford University Press, 1994), pp. 17, 44.

10. Bertholt Brecht, cited in Dollimore and Sinfield (eds), *Political Shakespeare: New Essays in Materialism and Culture*, p. 241.

11. Terry Eagleton, *William Shakespeare*, p. 69.

12. Catherine Belsey, 'Revenge in *Hamlet*', in Martin Coyle (ed.), *New Casebooks: 'Hamlet'*, p. 157.

Exile at Home:
The Drama of Brian Friel

PATRICK BURKE

Preface

When I was a child in the Ireland of the fifties, a favourite song at popular concerts and variety shows was 'Noreen Bawn'. Sad, if sentimental, it outlines the plight of its title character, an emigrant from Donegal who, in the final verse, returns home, dying of tuberculosis. The final lines of the song warn us, ''Twas the curse of emigration that destroyed our Noreen Bawn'. Such a view of emigration, stemming undoubtedly from the horrendous experiences of the many Irish who were forced to emigrate to America in the wake of the devastating potato famines of the 1840s, and extending into the economically-driven searches for employment in Britain during the 1940s and 1950s and in the U.S. in the 1980s, has essentially persisted down to the present day. A much more recent ballad, 'Flight of the Earls' by Liam Reilly—a title which reflects the defining pattern of Irish emigration in the early 1600s—sums that up, with bitter irony: 'Our best asset [i.e. our young people] is our biggest export too!'

Language and Community

Emigration is what confronts the twenty-five-year-old Gar O'Donnell (like Noreen Bawn, a native of Donegal) in the play that brought Brian Friel to prominence, *Philadelphia, Here I Come!*, first staged, with great success, at the Dublin Theatre Festival in 1964. It would appear, at least on the surface, that Gar's decision to emigrate is the result of failure in a number of significant contexts: he has failed his first-year examinations at University College, Dublin; his ardent relationship with Kate Doogan has failed, partly through the manoeuvrings of her upper-middle-class parents, partly through Gar's own ineptitude; he fails, critically, to communicate with his elderly father, though it is movingly inferable from the play that each man loves the other. The small general-purpose shop, owned by his father, in which Gar works for a very low wage (another motive for his emigrating) is beginning, because of changing social patterns, to experience commercial failure. In a very moving double sense, life itself has failed for Gar's late mother: marrying a husband more than twenty years older than herself, she could not resign herself to the failure of her girlhood dreams and dies three days after giving birth to Gar.

For many audiences and readers of *Philadelphia, Here I Come!*, especially when it first became famous as a play, the overarching failure was that of lack of communication. Gar and his father can't talk to each other; Gar can't talk to Kate after she has married; beyond the macho masks of easy sexual conquest, Gar and his friends (the ironically and revealingly titled 'boys') can't talk directly to each other; Gar's father and his nightly visitor, Canon O'Byrne, can only communicate obliquely and through cliché. But as an explanation of the play, 'lack of communication' has only limited validity: Gar *can* talk to Madge, the housekeeper and a mother figure to him, as can his father; Gar can talk to Kate, when their love is direct and uncomplicated; he can talk to the alcoholic schoolteacher, Master Boyle, who loved Gar's mother in the past and, in the words of the play, 'might have been [Gar's] father'. It might be more instructive to speak of *language* itself as the central issue in the play. The characters of *Philadelphia, Here I Come!* are not always in possession of, or (perhaps more philosophically exact) possessed of, a language adequate to their life situations. Friel built the question of language into the structure of the play, through the character of Private Gar. In the words of Friel's introductory note to the play, 'Public Gar is the Gar that people see, talk to, talk about. Private Gar is the unseen man, the man within, the conscience, the *alter ego*, the secret thoughts. Private Gar, the spirit, is invisible to everybody always…'[1] Private is the mechanism in the play by which, in the sole instance of Gar, the discrepancy between what is actually said and what needs to be said, is overcome, though, as the final lines reveal, he is not made, existentially, to *know* more than Public does:

PRIVATE: … God, Boy, why do you have to leave? Why? Why?
PUBLIC: … I don't know. I-I-I don't know.[2]

In so far as it highlights the moral plight of its protagonist in the face of an often intractable, sometimes mysterious external reality, *Philadelphia, Here I Come!* anticipates such later plays of Friel as *The Loves of Cass McGuire* (1966), *Lovers* (1967), *Living Quarters* (1977), and, in particular, *Crystal and Fox* (1968) and *Faith Healer* (1979), the last of which I discuss below. But it is also thematically anticipatory in other ways, having to do both with language (a recurring concern across Friel's work) and with ritual, religious and secular. Moreover, in such plays as *Aristocrats* (1979) and *Making History* (1988), such themes are framed within a distinctive historical context.

It is implicit in *Philadelphia, Here I Come!* that, as an essential framework for being in the world, a community needs an adequate language. This insight becomes explicit in what for some readers and audiences is Friel's greatest play, *Translations* (1980). Set in 1833, in the Donegal townland of Ballybeg (literally, 'small place'), *Translations* gives prominence to its linguistic concerns essentially by means of its focus on the process of naming, the naming of persons and places. The play opens with a striking example of that focus: Sarah, who 'could be any age from seventeen to thirty-five', is trying, under the tutelage of Manus, to pronounce her name, notwithstanding a severe speech defect. Manus is the elder son of Hugh Mor O'Donnell, the master of the old-type Irish 'hedge school', i.e. a form of education resorted to by Catholics, on a small fee-paying basis, mainly during the eighteenth century, when more orthodox forms of schooling were denied them. During Hugh's absences on drinking bouts the school is run by Manus. On the occasion represented in the opening of the play, however, Hugh's absence is thematically significant: he has gone to attend the christening, a naming into the community, of the baby of one Nellie Ruadh ('red-haired'). Both of those indices of the communal significance of naming in turn illuminate and are illuminated by the recurring naming formulation presented in *Translations*, whereby characters, especially when introducing themselves, offer a triple combination of their personal or 'fore' name, their fathers' names and the name of the geographical area to which they belong. This is illustrated most clearly in the first act, just after the return of Manus's younger brother, Owen, to his home place after a lengthy absence:

OWEN: That's a new face. Who are you?
(A very brief hesitation. Then:—)
SARAH: My name is Sarah.
OWEN: Sarah who?
SARAH: Sarah Johnny Sally [i.e. her father's name].
OWEN: Of course! From Bun na hAbhann! I'm Owen—Owen Hugh Mor. From Baile Beag. (p. 403)

It would seem to follow logically, then, that disturbance of one part of that triple mode of self-identification will have consequences for the other two. This is precisely what happens in the play, and indeed historically, in that the place names are about to be anglicized at the behest of the British government; the work involved in the consequent map-making, cataloguing, measurements, etc.—the Ordnance Survey—was to be undertaken by British soldiers. One of those soldiers, Yolland, soon to fall in love with Maire, a local girl, is uneasy about the work of which he is a rather reluctant part, describing it to Owen (who is working with the soldiers as 'a civilian interpreter') as 'an eviction of sorts', because, that is, of its ontological consequences.

If the survey is a threat to the Ballybeg community's naming processes, the advent of the new English-sponsored national school system (which commenced in Ireland in 1831) is an even greater threat to that community's whole linguistic heritage. As one of the adult hedge-school pupils, Bridget, puts it: '... from the very first day you go, you'll not hear one word of Irish spoken. You'll be taught to speak English and every subject will be taught through English ...' (p. 396). In addition, there is the view, voiced principally through Maire, that English is the language of what a later era would call 'upward social mobility' and of self-enhancement; moreover, in her challenging articulation of that view, in the first act, Maire invokes for cultural support one of the great political figures of nineteenth-century Ireland, Daniel O'Connell:

We should all be learning to speak English. That's what my mother says. That's what I say. That's what Dan O'Connell said last month in Ennis. He said the sooner we all learn to speak English the better ... And what he said was this: 'The old language is a barrier to modern progress.'

(pp. 399–400)

Friel never confines the scope for his audiences' reflections on matters linguistic to the analytical or discursive: in an engrossing plot, Maire and Yolland become lovers (or believe they do); Yolland is abducted, as a consequence, by the Donnelly twins (paramilitaries, in today's terms); and the formerly amicable relationship of British soldiers and local community breaks down. Symbolism here is quiet but telling; in parallel with the breakdown just referred to, Nellie Ruadh's baby, an image of new beginnings, dies—'It didn't last long, did it?', says Maire—and, under the pressure of the British commanding officer's bullying, Sarah regresses to dumbness.

Translations is an extremely subtle play. Failure to perceive this subtlety can result in a kind of critical commentary which not only undervalues its density but, because it is in many ways a 'public play', can cause almost dangerous incomprehension at the political level. I refer in particular to the kind of viewpoint which sees the defining action of *Translations* in terms of a conflict between, on the one hand, an unspoilt, idyllic organic community and, on the other, the colonizing oppressor. (Friel himself was to be so exercised by such a reductive view of the play that he made its successor, *The Communication Cord* [1982], an 'antidote' [his own word] to it.) In any close examination of the play, however, it becomes clear that the culture of Ballybeg is one of crisis, even prior to the British presence. So much is signalled both by image—the setting is ramshackle, the stairs lacking a banister, and the clothes of the Irish characters (except for the newly-wealthy Owen) simple, even shabby—and by characterization: Manus is lame, Sarah almost dumb, Hugh alcoholic. These features constitute, in Friel's words, 'a public representation of their spiritual deprivation',[3] reinforced imagistically by the local pub's name, 'Anna na nBreag', 'Anna of the Lies', and the connection thereby established between alcohol and the absence or denial of self-knowledge. Such a culture stands in need of renewal. In resonant speeches, towards the end of the play, Hugh, thumbing through the book which contains the new forms of the local place names, outlines the terms of that renewal:

We must learn where we live. We must learn to make them our own. We must make them our new home ... it is not the literal past, the 'facts' of history, that shape us, but images of the past embodied in language ... we must never cease renewing these images; because once we do, we fossilize.

(pp. 444-5)

Such renewal, however, cannot, in this play, entail collective amnesia or severance from the past; *Translations*, crucially, does not advocate absorption of a smaller by a dominant culture. In reply to a comment of Maire's as to the importance of learning English, Hugh sagely remarks:

I will provide you with the available words and the available grammar. But will that help you to interpret between privacies? I have no idea ...

(p. 446)

The Importance of Ritual
In the second act of *Philadelphia, Here I Come!* one of the 'boys', Tom, observes: 'Bit of life about the place next week, lads, —the Carnival'. While in more recent manifestations of popular culture in Ireland (i.e. from about the 1940s to the 1970s) 'carnival' would have been a general term connoting musical events, dancing, longer opening hours in public houses, fairground amusement, spectacle and so on, it would, however residually, have retained its overtones of the communally religious in the sense of the Latin American 'carnivale', the Shrovetide festivities prior to the asceticism of the Catholic Lent. Tom's remark, then, serves to bring to prominence the question of ritual, religious and secular, in the plays of Friel, and its relationship to a 'bit of life'.

While priests and ministers of religion figure quite prominently in the plays of Friel (and he was himself, for a short while, a Catholic seminarian), Catholic ritual *per se* receives rather less attention. Thus there are priest characters in *The Enemy Within* (1962), *The Blind Mice* (1963), *Philadelphia, Here I Come!*, *The Freedom of the City* (1973), *Living Quarters, Making History* and *Dancing at Lughnasa* (1990). Catholic rituals, however, such as Mass (except as a background to the very moving ending of *The Freedom of the City*), the Rosary (except for the opening section of the final act in *Philadelphia, Here I Come!* and for satirical purposes in *Lovers*) or Benediction (except for a jocose reference in *The Freedom of the City*), do not impinge on the central action of such plays. This, I believe, is because of the frequent suggestion in the work of Friel, recurring as recently as the much underrated *Wonderful Tennessee* (1993), that established, orthodox ritual is not informed by a sufficiently dynamic authentic religious sensibility and, conversely, that such existing sensibility lacks a meaningful ritualistic expression. Similar ideas are suggested in scenes of secular ritual, such as the putative civic receptions in *The Blind Mice* and *Dancing at Lughnasa*, the song-and-dance routines of Lily and Skinner in *The Freedom of the City*, the game of cards in *The Gentle Island* (1971), the story-telling in *Volunteers* (1975) and *Wonderful Tennessee*, and the children's bedtime routines in *Aristocrats*.

Friel's most impressive presentation of the need for, and adequate expressions of, ritual is in *Dancing at Lughnasa*, a factor which undoubtedly bore on the phenomenal success of that play, particularly on Broadway in 1992. By setting it in the family home of the Mundys, in Donegal, in 1936, and by having the eldest and only male member of the family, Father Jack, rejoin his five sisters after twenty-five years' priestly service in Uganda, Friel makes possible a compelling alignment of the ritual practices of Africa with those of an Ireland that was still, in many respects, pre-modern. Theatrically, that alignment is both verbal and physical. Its most celebrated, if sometimes misunderstood, manifestation is the dance of the five sisters in the first act. Beginning with Maggie, the most 'light-hearted' of the sisters, and passing rapidly to Rose, an engaging character who is slightly simple-minded, to Agnes, the most graceful and sensuous dancer, to Chris, the youngest sister (and the mother of the play's narrator, Michael), it is finally taken up, initially with reluctance, then with total concentration, by Kate, the oldest sister, who is a very 'proper' national-school teacher. They dance with abandon to an Irish dance coming over the radio, a reel played by a céilí band; Friel refers to its 'very heavy beat' and its 'raucous sound'. In many productions the dance has received a prolonged round of applause and by the time the play was filmed (1999) the dance had become so celebrated that the film holds it until much later in the action, for the sake, presumably, of audience impact. The risk in all of that is that the dance becomes categorized as unambiguously celebratory, a release of energy, a direct expression of the erotic and the animal in the female make-up of the five sisters. Such a view, whether by director or by audience, is reductive of the effect Friel wishes to see attained, as is clear from the stage directions:

AGNES and ROSE, CHRIS and MAGGIE, are now all doing a dance that is almost recognizable. They meet—they retreat. They form a circle and wheel round and round. But the movements seem caricatured; and the sound is too loud; and the beat is too fast; and the almost recognizable dance is made grotesque ... With this too loud music, this pounding beat, this shouting—calling—singing, this parodic reel, there is a sense of order being consciously subverted, of the women consciously and crudely caricaturing themselves, indeed of near-hysteria being induced ... (pp. 21–2)

Thus the dance is less a celebration in itself then powerfully indicative of a need, a hunger, *to* celebrate, as a later piece of dialogue between Agnes and Gerry, Michael's father, suggests:

GERRY: You should be a professional dancer.
AGNES: Too late for that.

GERRY: You could teach dancing in Ballybeg.
AGNES: That's all they need.
GERRY: Maybe it is! (p. 65)

The Lughnasa (i.e. harvest-time) rituals of the people in 'the back hills', to which extended reference is twice made in the play, might appear to constitute the valid expression of deep-rooted energies and hungers which the Mundy sisters are trying to find. Those rituals (well evoked in the film version of *Dancing at Lughnasa*) involving fire, dancing and drinking, are limited, however, in two respects: the people who practise them are presented as ignorant and backward ('savages', Kate calls them), and some of what is practised during them is dangerous, as indicated by the near-burning of a young boy. It is from Father Jack and his experiences in Uganda (experiences which, presumably, because of their heterodoxy *vis-à-vis* Catholic norms, have got him into trouble with his superiors) that the play offers the clearest outline of what constitutes adequate rituals for persons and the society they live in. In a lyrical passage in the second act he describes the harvest-time festivals of the people of Ryanga, among whom he had worked, and the non-distinction between the religious and the secular, inherent in what they do:

… when the [religious] thanksgiving is over, the dance continues. And the interesting thing is that it grows naturally into a secular celebration; so that almost imperceptibly the religious ceremony ends and the community celebration takes over … the Ryangans are a remarkable people: there is no distinction between the religious and the secular in their culture. And of course their capacity for fun, for laughing, for practical jokes–they've such open hearts! In some respects they're not unlike us …
(p. 48)

In so far, then, as *Dancing at Lughnasa* has a thesis (always a risky presumption in relation to Friel), it might be argued that it is the importance of contemporary Western civilization—post-Christian, secular, rational, economically focused—finding ritual forms equivalent in impact to those of Ryanga. In this respect, *Dancing at Lughnasa* forms a diptych with Friel's next play, *Wonderful Tennessee*, in which characters from contemporary middle-class Ireland create their own religious rituals.

Gender and History

Despite occasional suggestions to the contrary, Friel has consistently shown awareness in his drama of the feminine and its vulnerability in male-dominated worlds. Gar O'Donnell's mother, as I have suggested, died from loneliness, and a character such as Sarah in *The Gentle Island* becomes dangerous, even murderous, when her female sexuality is not properly valued. Friel's most explicit emphasis on the importance of women and feminine values occurs in *Making History* and the insistence by Hugh O'Neill (the famous Gaelic leader of the sixteenth century) on what he calls 'the overall thing'. The phrase relates to the putative writing by Peter Lombard, Bishop of Armagh, of a history of Hugh O'Neill and his time, a history which O'Neill will regard as severely inadequate if it fails to give centrality to his late wife, Mabel, and, by extension, to the importance of human love in the life of a major political figure. 'The overall thing' requires that, in the projected account, the personal, the emotional, the sexual, be honoured at least as much as the political. A similar balancing of thematic elements obtains in relation to much of Friel's other work, notably *The Mundy Scheme* (1969), *The Freedom of the City, Volunteers* and *The Communication Cord*. In these and other plays, we encounter the Brechtian paradox, namely that a healthy society relies on individual loving hearts but individual loving hearts need sustaining by society.

The play in which it seems to me Friel most adroitly integrates a concern with femininity with broader historical concerns is *Aristocrats* (1979). The play revolves around the declining fortunes

of a Big House, in this instance—and unusually in Irish literature—a Catholic Big House, owned for generations by the
O'Donnells, the 'aristocrats' of the title. The present generation
of the family comprises—as in Chekhov's *Three Sisters*, by which
Friel's play is influenced—three sisters and a brother: Judith, aged
forty, Alice, in her mid-thirties, Claire, in her twenties, and
Casimir, in his thirties. The occasion of the play's action is the
forthcoming wedding of Claire to Jerry McLoughlin, a local busi-
nessman, and more than twice Claire's age. Claire, a potentially
fine concert pianist, is manic-depressive; Alice is alcoholic and
having difficulties in her childless marriage to Eamon, a local
man; and Casimir, whom Friel emphasizes is not 'disturbed',
makes a rather boring life more bearable by the creation of
charming fantasies about the past of the house and of the writers
who frequented it (Yeats, Chesterton, O'Casey). Of the O'Donnell parents Mother has been dead, probably through suicide, for
about twenty years; Father (whose voice we hear through the first
two acts while he is being nursed by Judith, but whom we see
only once), a former court judge, is infirm from a stroke and dies
at the end of the second act. Each parent has a well defined and
mutually opposed set of associations. With Mother we associate
nurture, delicacy, music, the social graces of the House, and
fragility; with Father, social conformity, law, paternal power,
sexual aggressiveness, insensitivity to art, aloofness. Their defec-
tive marriage may also be seen as figuring a failure in Irish history,
the failure of Big House Catholics to adequately defend and support their impoverished and colonized co-religionists.

The Search for Meaning
The play in which the various elements I have examined above
come most powerfully together is probably Friel's greatest, *Faith
Healer* (1979). It revolves around Frank Hardy, the faith healer (or
should it be 'would-be faith healer'?) of the title, Grace, his wife

(or should it be 'mistress'?) and Teddy, his road manager. The emphasis on the personal has to do with all three characters, but in particular with Frank and his search for a meaning to his life as a man and as a faith healer:

Faith healer–faith healing. A craft without an apprenticeship, a ministry without responsibility, a vocation without a ministry. How did I get involved? ... let's say I did it ... because I could do it. That's accurate enough. And occasionally it worked—oh, yes, occasionally it *did* work. Oh, yes. And when it did, when I stood before a man and placed my hands on him and watched him become whole in my presence, there were nights of exultation, of consummation—no, not that I was doing good, giving relief, spreading joy—good God, no, nothing at all to do with that; but because the questions that undermined my life then became mean-ingless and because I knew that for those few hours I had become whole in myself, and perfect in myself ... (p. 333)

The intensity of that search can drive Frank to drinking, espe-cially when his faith healing gift fails him; it can also make him callous and indifferent to Grace and Teddy, most painfully when, according to both of them, Frank abandoned Grace when she was giving birth to a child who, sadly, was stillborn. Nonetheless, they recognize in their own terms something of the meaning of Frank's 'ministry', as the very ending of Grace's monologue in particular serves to show:

O my God I'm in such a mess ... how I want that man to come across that floor and put his white hands on my face and still this tumult inside me—O my God I'm one of his fictions too, but I need him to sustain me in that existence—O my God I don't know if I can go on without his sus-tenance. (p. 353)

Behind both the emotional distress that we witness in Grace and the Cockney comedy of Teddy is the clear recognition that both of them love Frank. Thus, the value of love is asserted by a play which might otherwise be seen as a powerful but rather chilly endorsement of artistic mission. (One thinks immediately of

Ibsen's John Gabriel Borkman or Thomas Mann's Doctor Faust.)

Ritual in *Faith Healer* is either a memory or an aspiration. A memory as reflected, for example, in the following observation by Frank on the kind of venue in which, usually to very small audiences, he would practise his faith healing:

The kirks or meeting-house or schools—all identical, all derelict. Maybe in a corner a withered sheaf of wheat from a harvest thanksgiving of years ago or a fragment of a Christmas decoration across a window—relics of abandoned rituals. Because the people we moved among were beyond that kind of celebration. (p. 332)

Elsewhere, as with the back-hills people in *Dancing at Lughnasa*, ritual is evoked (again by Frank) as vibrant but maimed; here he is referring to the pub in Ballybeg to which he has arrived from Britain with Grace and Teddy, and the drunken aftermath of a wedding celebration:

A Dionysian night. A Bacchanalian night. A frenzied, excessive Irish night when ritual was consciously and relentlessly debauched. (p. 340)

It is in the pub in Ballybeg that Frank confronts his greatest challenge to date, the healing of a cripple named McGarvey, a friend of some of the wedding guests. The meeting of the two men at dawn is made to carry cosmic overtones—Frank, a Christ-like figure, however flawed, versus McGarvey and the wedding guests, maimed spiritually as well as physically:

... as I walked I became possessed of a strange and trembling intimation: that the whole corporeal world—the cobbles, the trees, the sky, those four malign implements—somehow they had shed their physical reality and had become mere imaginings, and that in all existence there was only myself and the wedding guests. And that intimation in turn gave way to a stronger sense: that even we had ceased to be physical and existed only in spirit, only in the need we had for each other ... (pp. 375–6)

From the daring dramatic action of *Faith Healer* we infer that the healing powers of Frank, the flawed Christ, fail in face of an obdurate world: McGarvey is not cured and Frank is savagely killed by the wedding guests. The ritual available to Frank *within* the play does not work, unlike the ritual of the play *itself.*

While *Faith Healer* is full of the idiom of 'watching', 'looking' and 'seeing'—most tellingly conveyed in the use of, and references to, the Fred Astaire song, 'The Way You Look Tonight'— it nonetheless intimates something of the importance of language, pursued in its successor play *Translations.* Frank is troubled most acutely by what he calls 'the nagging, tormenting, maddening questions' (p. 334). On other occasions, solace or, at least, a basis for meaning is provided by, in Grace's word, 'fictions':

... it was some compulsion he had to adjust, to refashion, to re-create everything around him. Even the people who came to him ... yes, they were real enough, but not real as persons, real as fictions, his fictions, extensions of himself that came into being only because of him ... (p. 345)

The play makes powerfully clear how cruel the consequences of such a search for 'perfection', for 'excellence', can be, involving not merely intolerance of human imperfection (Frank's father's rotten teeth are referred to, for example) but callous disregard for those one is supposed to love—Grace and their stillborn child.

Conclusion

Friel's *oeuvre* consistently implies both the importance and difficulty of individual fulfilment in societies which themselves continue to require sustenance by means of language adequate to human experience and of authentic ritual. But Friel's achievement has to do with dramatic power, with utterance in all its forms reaching to the deepest recesses of the audience's awareness, with a kind of grace. This is most apparent, as hinted above, in relation to *Faith Healer*: what is in many respects a terrible story does not leave its audience downcast or depressed but rather affirmed, if not elated. Such is the power of Friel's theatre, power in evidence as early as *Philadelphia, Here I Come!* and a delicate deployment in that play of comedy, memory, sub-text and language, so that in the midst of disappointment, loss and hurt, the dignity of being human is cherished.

Bibliography

Brian Friel, *Selected Plays* (London: Faber and Faber, 1984).
Brian Friel, *Dancing at Lughnasa* (London: Faber and Faber, 1990).

Elmer Andrews, *The Art of Brian Friel: Neither Reality nor Dreams* (London: Macmillan, 1995).
Ulf Dantanus, *Brian Friel: A Study* (London: Faber and Faber, 1988).
William Kerwin (ed.), *Brian Friel: A Casebook* (New York and London: Garland Publishing, 1997).
Irish University Review 29, 1 (Spring/Summer 1999), ed. Anthony Roche. A special issue dedicated to Friel's work.
George O'Brien, *Brian Friel* (Dublin: Gill and Macmillan, 1989).
Alan Peacock (ed.), *The Achievement of Brian Friel* (Gerrards Cross: Colin Smythe, 1993).

Notes

1. Brian Friel, *Selected Plays*, p. 27.
2. Friel, *Selected Plays*, p. 99. Of the plays discussed in detail in this essay, *Selected Plays* includes *Philadelphia, Here I Come!*, *Translations* and *Faith Healer*. *Dancing at Lughnasa* was published by Faber and Faber in 1990. All further page references to Friel's plays will be given in the text.
3. Fintan O'Toole, 'The Man from God Knows Where: An Interview with Brian Friel', *In Dublin* 165 (28 October 1982), p. 21.

Narrative and Genre in
Jim Sheridan's My Left Foot

SARAH SMITH

Introduction

The aim of this essay is to offer an introduction to two fundamental concepts in the study of film, indicating their literary
roots and outlining their specificity to film. Once introduced,
each concept provides a focus for an analysis of *My Left Foot*
(1989), through a detailed reading of two short sections from the
film. The definitions of each concept provided here are quite
basic and are intended to act as a starting point from which to
begin studying film.

Narrative concerns the way that stories are told and the order
in which the events of a story are presented. It is a central and
perhaps the most important concept in film studies, as all other
aspects of film work to support this basic component. Formal elements of film such as framing, set design, editing, music, type of
shot, etc., all function primarily to tell the story or to advance the
narrative. An understanding of narrative and its operations is
therefore essential for an understanding of all other aspects of
film. Although our investigation focuses on fiction film, the basic
concept of narrative is equally relevant to the study of non-fiction

(i.e. documentary) film. In fact, a knowledge of the principles of narrative in relation to film is necessary even when discussing the 'non-narrative' film of some avant-garde movements[1] as it is usually the dominant narrative model against which avant-garde cinema reacts.

Genre is a French term that means type or kind and, in relation to cinema, refers to different modifications or variations of what has become the standard narrative pattern. Generic conventions provide us with a very useful framework when considering a film in terms of issues such as prominent themes or character types. The following discussion of *My Left Foot* employs the concepts and terminology introduced here, demonstrating one possible reading or interpretation of the film using the tools supplied by both concepts.

The Development of Classical Narrative Cinema

Since its inception over a hundred years ago, cinema has developed a unified system of conventions that have come to convey particular meanings to its audience. Although a number of possibilities were open to film when the technology was first developed, it quickly became appropriated for the purpose of storytelling and it did this by utilizing established cultural forms. Early filmmakers borrowed a great deal from the traditions and forms of the theatre and of the nineteenth-century novel. The novel provided many plots while the visual presentation of the narrative was influenced by the theatre, and is particularly evident, for example, in an early style of filmmaking known as *tableau*. For this method, a stationary camera was positioned in front of and at a distance from the action being filmed, as if occupying the best seat in the theatre, while the sides of the frame served as wings through which the actors entered and exited. Although cinematic forms and techniques have changed and advanced a great deal over the decades, literature and cinema still share many common features today, and these features shall be pointed out throughout this discussion.

Mainstream fictional cinema, as we now know it, can largely be attributed to the style of filmmaking developed and practised by the Hollywood studio system between the early 1930s and the late 1950s. At this time a small number of film studios dominated the American film industry from production through to exhibition. The studios continually attempted to ensure box-office returns by repeating what had proven to be successful formulae in previous films. A desire to capitalize on established successes and the assembly-line nature of the studio-based process of filmmaking resulted in a uniformity in film production during this period. Soon, a recognizable style emerged from this formulaic approach and established itself as the dominant model.

Realism and Classical Narrative Cinema

Despite its seeming obviousness, the notion of realism is a rather complex one and takes on different meanings depending on the context of its usage. Quite different 'realisms' were proposed by, for example, the schools of Italian neo-realism, Soviet cinema of the 1920s, British social realism and classical Hollywood cinema.

Realism in classical filmmaking does not imply a reflection of reality but, rather like the nineteenth-century realist novel, concerns the presentation of what can be described as a self-contained, logical and ordered fictional world. This fictional world appears plausible to the spectator because of its spatial and temporal coherence. In other words, the story takes place in a clearly delineated location or series of locations, and the events of the story are presented to the spectator in a linear, logical manner. Every effort is made to depict a credible world that can be easily understood. So, while classical cinema does not reflect reality, it does aim at verisimilitude, at appearing or seeming real and this is achieved by numerous formal conventions. For example, the film attempts to hide its own construction, to draw attention away from the fact that it is working to create and present a fiction. There are no sudden cuts within the film that are not relevant to the narrative and the camera's presence is never acknowledged by the characters on screen. The illusion that we are looking in on another world is maintained throughout.

Like the novel and the play, the classic realist cinema is a narrative form of representation, which usually implies the telling of a story. Like these other narrative forms, classical cinema contains a four-act structure revolving around a central (usually male) protagonist. It is a goal-orientated narrative, driven by the motivations of a central protagonist, in which problems are presented but only with the promise of their inevitable solution.

The dramatic structure of classical narrative can be plotted in four acts as follows: a) a state of equilibrium or balance; b) the disruption of this equilibrium; c) a struggle to overcome the disruption; and d) the restoration of equilibrium. The first act in this structure does not necessarily involve a state of happiness and the reintroduction of equilibrium in stage four does not always return us to the same state as at the beginning of the film. Situations and characters have changed through the disruption and struggle within the narrative and instead this final stage denotes a new, different equilibrium. A high degree of closure is also achieved by the last stage of this narrative structure. All questions raised within the narrative have been answered by this point, all puzzles solved.

The Narrative Structure of *My Left Foot*

The narrative structure outlined above is found to a greater or lesser degree in most mainstream films. Although it emerged from the classical cinema of the Hollywood studio system, it has influenced all filmmaking in the west, particularly the national cinemas of Britain and Ireland, and has impacted on filmmaking worldwide. An examination of *My Left Foot* in the light of this traditional structure reveals evidence of each of the four acts. The film's opening sequence, which describes the preparations for the benefit at Lord Castlewelland's house, marks the first act. The disruption that defines act two is created when Paddy Brown is informed that there have been some complications with the birth of his son Christy. Christy's ongoing battle with his father and his struggle to express himself through speech, painting and writing provide us with the third act of the structure. Finally, act four establishes a new equilibrium with the success of Christy's book and the beginning of his life with Mary Carr.

My Left Foot offers us a circular narrative—another common feature of the classical model—both beginning and ending on the day of the fundraising benefit at Lord Castlewelland's house. The essential villain or antagonist, who places obstacles in the path of the heroic protagonist, thus preventing the attainment of the goal and prolonging the quest, is here played by the father. Another important ingredient of this format is the love interest, a role that is shared by both Mary Carr and Eileen Cole. The drive of the classical model towards resolution, which usually takes the form of the 'happy ending' and involves the securing of romantic love, is also demonstrated by this film.

A system of cause and effect governs the development of the narrative. It progresses in a sort of chain reaction, with each shot directly related to that which precedes it and that which follows. This system is known as causal narrative. For instance, in a scene towards the end of *My Left Foot*, Christy asks his mother to buy some ice cream for the children for dessert. Eventually giving in to their demands, she goes to the kitchen to get some money from her hiding place, where she discovers eight hundred pounds. This scene is preceded by Christy hiding the money that he has earned from his book as a surprise for his mother and is followed by the scene where Eileen asks him to attend the fundraising benefit as guest of honour. This status is offered to him because of the success of his book. Thus, when the money is hidden, we anticipate its being found, and its appearance marks the start of a sequence devoted to informing us of Christy's success.

Cinema as a Unique Mode of Representation

As we have already established, cinema has always borrowed from other narrative forms, most notably the theatre and the novel, and still displays many of these borrowed features today. However, its potential as a unique mode of representation was eventually realized and new ways of telling a story were developed which were specific to film. For example, problems were encountered with the use of the tableau style of filmmaking mentioned earlier; it was difficult to discern individual characters as the camera was positioned quite far away from the action and identification with a particular character was almost impossible. The solution to this problem was discovered by moving the camera closer to the actors (i.e. the close-up shot) and cutting between different types of shots instead of shooting a scene in its entirety from one stationary position. In relation to editing, numerous linking devices between shots were developed, each signifying something different; a dissolve came to connote a brief passage of time, while a fade-in or fade-out implies that a longer period of time has passed. We 'read' a film based on our familiarity with these formal conventions, our understanding of this language. When we watch a film, we expect the events of the story to be presented in a particular way, and if our expectations are not satisfied we feel confused and annoyed. Without these conventions, we cannot make sense of the film.

Camera movement, angle and distance from that which is being filmed all work to convey meaning, as do editing, lighting, props, music, sound-effects and the movement and behaviour of actors. Endless possibilities exist within each of these elements.

The first scene in the Brown house in *My Left Foot* offers us a shot of Paddy Brown from Christy's point of view as he sits propped up against the wall under the stairs. In this shot the camera is positioned close to the ground, and shakes slightly as if it is hand-held. This effectively echoes the movement of Christy's body and suggests the unease he feels in the presence of his father, who appears threatening and powerful from this angle. It is an interesting exercise to look for other technical and stylistic devices that work to convey meaning in a specifically cinematic way.

In the classic realist cinema, decisions concerning form (e.g., whether to use a medium close-up or a close-up shot) are always made in order to serve the basic requirement of telling the story. In other words, the formal aspects of the film serve to support and further the narrative. They are agents of the narrative. Consequently everything we see on the screen and hear on the soundtrack and the ways in which these are presented are all relevant to the narrative and no superfluous information is offered. This practice is known as narrative economy.

Narrative Economy in the Opening Shot of *My Left Foot*

The opening shot or scene of any film provides us with a great deal of information, all of which is relevant to the story we are about to be told. It usually introduces us to the main character/s and themes, and positions the story in a particular time and place. In *My Left Foot* the opening shot begins with a shot of a typewriter keyboard and ends just as Christy turns his face towards the window.

The possessive adjective 'my' in the film's title suggests that it is an autobiography, and the appearance of a man's left foot into the frame of this first shot suggests that the character on screen is both the film's narrator and its main protagonist. When he looks momentarily into the camera lens towards the end of this shot, he acknowledges both the presence of the audience and his role as narrator. The film is quite self-consciously presenting itself as autobiography.

A close-up of a typewriter keyboard is the very first image that we see in the film. A man's foot enters the frame from the bottom right-hand corner and moves up to a vertical stack of records positioned to the left of the typewriter. As he proceeds to select a record, remove it from its sleeve and place it on the turntable of the record player, it becomes apparent that the typewriter is also his. All of these objects are positioned at this low level because he uses his left foot to operate them. So far we know that this character writes, that he enjoys listening to music and that he performs everyday actions with his foot. By introducing Christy in this way, an emphasis has already been placed on his ability and creativity. We are not immediately shown his wheelchair, the symbol of disability beyond which we usually fail to see; instead our first view of him focuses on his *ability*. It is with his foot, through writing and painting, that Christy first communicates with people and expresses his thoughts and desires, so this shot is a fitting introduction to his character.

A certain amount of information is offered to us through the use of light and dark in this shot. The set is lit quite harshly from within, creating a series of high contrasts. These contrasts are further emphasized by Christy's clothing—dark trousers and a bright white shirt—and other props (e.g., the black record emerging from its white paper sleeve). When he turns to the camera in the last moments of the shot, strong shadows are cast over one side of his face and the whites of his eyes exaggerated. These purely formal contrasts serve to underline the film's thematic contrasts, which are set up in this shot and continue throughout the film. Christy sits dressed in formal clothing in a small dark room with one tiny window, listening to Italian opera. In this setting he simply looks out of place. We may conclude from this that Christy is at odds with this environment, but because he occupies

it, he somehow belongs here too. In this shot, Christy simultaneously occupies two very different worlds, something that he struggles to come to terms with in the rest of the film.

As we can see from this single shot, all of the objects and
actions on screen, their formal arrangement (through lighting,
camera movement and framing) and the ordering of this information support or further the narrative. It is a perfect illustration
of the classical cinema's insistence on narrative economy.

Genre

The term genre is used in relation to literature and cinema to
describe a system of classification. We use the notion of genre as a
way to analyse, interpret and discuss films critically, but it is a relatively recent addition to the study of film. While genre is by no
means a new approach to studying a text (it has been employed by
literary criticism since Aristotle), it was not until the mid-1960s
that it was introduced into English-language film criticism.

Despite the fact that genre criticism took so long to develop
within film studies, generic forms have always been used by the
film industry to organize the production and marketing of films.
As certain narratives prove successful, patterns are repeated and
soon become familiar and identifiable across a number of films.
The industry continues to produce hundreds of films based on
the formulae of a few successful ones. Genres develop due to the
popularity of particular kinds of film at any time, and often we
discover reasons for their popularity by investigating the socio-
political climate of the country in which they are produced. Film
noir, for example, a popular genre emerging from Hollywood in
the 1940s and 1950s, is believed to have expressed the insecurity
felt by the public in post-war American society. Similarly the anti-
heroic action-crime films of 1970s American filmmaking tapped
into the public's growing distrust of government following the
events of the Vietnam War and the Watergate scandal.

Established genres borrowed from literature provided the early cinema with a framework to operate within and provided the audience with a familiar, recognizable aspect to this very new medium. Also, placing a film within a particular generic category creates a very marketable product. The advertising campaign of a genre film is generally quite unproblematic; posters, trailers and reviews all indicate its generic make-up. In fact, genre has become the main tool with which to market films. Audience members base their decisions to attend particular films on past experience, and enjoyment of a film belonging to a certain genre is likely to prompt a visit to see another similar film.

Each genre is defined by the combination of a number of stylistic and thematic features. As we have already seen, classical narrative cinema is a *type* of cinema, governed by particular rules and conventions, and so in ways may be classified as a genre in itself. Certainly we may apply the same approach to the identification of genre in film as we did to the identification of this form of narrative by locating and describing its dominant characteristics and structure. Yet within this standard narrative model there are many other distinctive types to be found and it is these that are commonly referred to as film genres. Examples of these are the western, the melodrama, film noir, the horror film, the musical, the gangster film, the detective film, costume drama and the action-adventure film.

Problems with Genre Study

With many films, genre is quite easily discerned. *The Searchers* (John Ford, US, 1956), for example, is indisputably a western film while *Singing in the Rain* (Gene Kelly, Stanley Donen, US, 1952) is a musical. Such clearly categorized films are known as classic genre films. But what of those films that do not fall into a generic category quite so neatly? Attempts to categorize films according to strictly defined notions of genre can cause problems. Where does one genre end and another begin? The boundaries of genre are in fact very fluid and therefore difficult to define. A film such as *Calamity Jane* (David Butler, US, 1953), for example, displays characteristics of a number of genres: the western, the musical and the romantic-comedy. Other film genres, such as the gangster film, the melodrama and film noir, often coincide in individual films. In other words, a single film can contain elements of many genres. A more recent and frequently cited example of this hybridity is provided by *Blade Runner* (Ridley Scott, US, 1982), which combines science fiction and film noir—it is what we might call a sci-fi noir. It is important to adopt a flexible approach to genre identification in order to permit a productive study of either a single film or a number of films.

Genre and *My Left Foot*

My Left Foot has proven difficult to define in generic terms. The film adapts Christy Brown's autobiography of the same name and can therefore be classified as a biography. By featuring the book in the narrative, the film leads us to believe that we are being offered an authentic account of the life of Christy Brown, yet many omissions, additions and alterations have been made to the original text in adapting it to the screen. All of these changes heighten the dramatic impact of the film. The lives of real people are only subject to this sort of attention and representation if they have been remarkable in some respect. Typically, *My Left Foot* tells a very admirable 'true' story of one man's struggle in the face of adversity. While it is possible to look at the specific way that Jim Sheridan chooses to represent Christy's life, it becomes difficult to discuss the work in terms of the generic category known as biography because there are very few defining characteristics of this genre.

There is, however, another genre into which the film more readily fits, and that is social realism, a genre that is more usually associated with a tendency in British cinema of recent years and particularly with the work of two filmmakers, Ken Loach and

Mike Leigh. Films such as *Kes* (Loach, 1969), *My Name is Joe* (Loach, 1998), *Naked* (Leigh, 1993) and *Secrets and Lies* (Leigh, 1996) offer a social commentary by presenting stories of the lives of working-class people who struggle within a system of economic inequality and oppressive social hierarchies. Generally, these stories take place in an impoverished urban environment. All of these features are present in *My Left Foot* and many of them are revealed in the opening scene.

Opening Scene

Beginning with the first shot already described, the opening scene includes the build-up to the Brown family's arrival at Lord Castlewelland's home and ends when Mary begins to read Christy's book. Immediately we are presented with images of two very different worlds. A picture of wealth and excess develops as two large white cars drive through the impressive streets of Dublin city and pass such magnificent buildings as Trinity College and Christchurch Cathedral. The long shot used to present these images contrasts sharply with the tight framing in the close-up shots of the interior with which they are intercut. The close-up shots suggest a small, cluttered and enclosed space while the long shots of the cars imply breadth and expansiveness.

The difference between the two environments depicted is marked even more clearly by their fusion in the shot of the cars driving into the narrow streets of the inner-city neighbourhood. In the previous shots, the cars had seemed to fit in perfectly with their surroundings; now they appear huge and strange. Two men standing with a horse and cart stare in amazement as they drive past and the juxtaposition of the two modes of transport in this shot underlines the cultural and economic divide.

A series of close-up and medium close-up shots follows as the Brown family prepare to leave in the cars that have pulled up outside their house—a small grey two-storey terraced house with a plain black door and two windows at the front. The tight framing of these shots invites us into this world and encourages identification with the characters who inhabit it. We return to the long shot again moments later with an establishing shot of the other location in this scene: a large white house surrounded by a neatly trimmed lawn and what appears to be a small lake. Not only are the two houses remarkably different in appearance, but by presenting one through close-up and the other through long shot, the camera also treats them quite differently.

Extravagant objects and furnishings, such as stained-glass windows and life-sized statues, fill the interior of the large house. A shot of the library from Christy's point of view reveals paintings with ornate frames, books and period furniture. Lord Castlewelland himself embodies the traditional, if somewhat antiquated, notion of the landed gentry. The ordered, polite society to which he belongs could not be more removed from the realm of the Brown family. Apart from the opulent surroundings, the presence of servants and the dismissive manner in which Castlewelland treats them clearly point out his position at the pinnacle of a social hierarchy.

While the film may seem to present these two environments without offering any commentary on their relationship, one shot draws a very strong parallel between two of the Brown sons and the two chauffeurs who take them to Castlewelland's house. The two young men stand in the doorway of their house and talk quite casually with the chauffeurs. All four of them are dressed in black and white: the Browns in formal wear, the chauffeurs in uniforms. Placing both pairs within the frame and showing them communicating as equals throws Castlewelland's later treatment of his domestic staff into sharp relief. Given the parallel that has been set up between the servants and the Brown family, it becomes hugely ironic that Christy should be guest of honour at the fundraising benefit held that day. In this case, irony works to emphasize social inequality.

The use of long shot and medium long shot also works to keep this world at a distance, where it can be observed critically. In the establishing shot of Lord Castlewelland's house we can just about make out a group of children playing on some sort of climbing frame. Separated from the adults and assigned a specific recreation space, their 'play' is very organized and controlled. Placing them to one side of the frame comments on their positioning within this society; they are not a central aspect of life here, but are instead unobtrusive, peripheral. This contrasts greatly with the positioning of children within the Browns' neighbourhood. Earlier in this scene we witnessed a noisy group of children playing on the streets in a very uncontrolled way. They mix freely with the adults and their presence is certainly both seen and heard.

We are drawn into the world of the Brown family, and invited to identify with Christy through the use of the point of view shot, and at the same time we are offered quite a critical portrait of Lord Castlewelland's home. Locations, accents and speech all indicate cultural difference. Like the opening shot, this scene is full of contrasts and these contrasts serve to point out the social, cultural and economic discrepancy between the two worlds depicted. In keeping with the thematic concerns of social realism, the film goes on to highlight other oppressive social hierarchies in the dominance of the aggressive father within the family and the social power of the Catholic Church.

Conclusion

The overview of narrative and genre provided here is intended to further an understanding of narrative cinema at a number of levels. An analysis of these concepts enables students of film to describe sections of film text—narrative *and* visual content—using specifically filmic terminology. At a more advanced level, it aids an understanding of the operation of cinematic devices and their significance. This understanding is a pre-requisite to performing independent 'readings' or interpretations of a film.

The sections of *My Left Foot* that were analysed above illustrate the narrative economy of classical cinema and demonstrate some of the features of social realism. Many other aspects of narrative and genre could become the focus for a study of *My Left Foot* (or any other narrative film) and many other sections of the film provide suitable material to interpret. For instance, one investigation might centre on the role that the camera, editing, music and mise-en-scène play in conveying story information and the various ways that films employ these formal devices. Another interesting area for further consideration might be the historical and cultural specificity of particular film genres, or the co-existence of a number of different genres in one film. While film has been introduced onto the Leaving Certificate syllabus for comparative study with literary texts, it is important to understand and study it as a distinctive medium, with its own unique ways of expressing different narrative concerns—theme, character, etc. The formal differences between literary and filmic texts provide both teacher and student with a wealth of new possibilities for studying narrative genres and must therefore be considered a very welcome and exciting addition to the revised course.

Recommended Reading
Jill Nelmes (ed.), *An Introduction to Film Studies* (London: Routledge, 1996).

Note
1. Examples of non-narrative film are found in the work of Dadaist and Surrealist filmmakers and, more recently, the American avant-gardists of the 1960s and 1970s, of whom filmmaker Stan Brakhage is one.

'To One Thing Constant Never': Kenneth Branagh's Much Ado About Nothing

CHRIS MORASH

Sigh No More, Ladies ...
The words scroll slowly across the screen, as if from the hand of an invisible typist. As they unfold, white letters against a black screen, we hear them recited by a woman's voice, apparently reading to herself:

> Sigh no more, ladies,
> Sigh no more,
> Men were deceivers ever,
> One foot in sea and one on shore,
> To one thing constant never.
>
> Then sigh not so,
> But let them go,
> And be you blithe and bonny,
> Converting all your sounds of woe,
> Into Hey nonny, nonny!

This, the opening of Kenneth Branagh's 1993 film *Much Ado About Nothing*, is a moment of unease for the viewer: we are presented not with images, but with words in all their stark abstraction. Indeed, for a brief, terrifying moment we might even expect the entire film to continue in this way, an avant-garde experiment with the film as endless teleprompter. At the same time, we know that the written word began appearing on movie screens almost with the advent of film itself, and is still so much a part of cinema that every time a *Star Wars* film opens, for instance, we expect words to scroll up out of interstellar darkness to bring us the latest developments from 'a galaxy long, long ago and far, far away'. However, whether we are watching a silent film or *Star Wars*, we know that those words were written specifically for a particular movie, whereas with *Much Ado*—as with any Shakespeare adaptation—we are always aware that the words have been seen and heard elsewhere, in other contexts. This should remind us that audiences who go to see a Shakespeare film are hoping to be able to juggle two very different cultural experiences: they watch a Shakespeare film partly because they enjoy knowing that somewhere in the background looms a body of theatrical writing venerated like no other—writing originally intended not for a film, but for a particular stage long, long ago and (London audiences excepted) far, far away. At the same time, the audiences watching a Shakespeare film want to see a *film*.

The problem, of course, is that the pleasures we associate with Shakespeare are not necessarily those we associate with film. This is partly because Shakespeare's plays were not (and could not have been) written for the screen, but also because Shakespeare is often (although by no means exclusively) encountered in the context of high culture, and film is often (although, once again, by no means exclusively) considered in terms of popular culture. Even in recent decades, when the borderlines between high and popular culture have become increasingly difficult to distinguish, few people would consider a Royal Shakespeare Company production of *Hamlet* anything other than high culture, just as most people would think of the *Star Wars* films as part of popular culture. In short, the challenge for the film-maker who would adapt Shakespeare for the screen is to balance the cultural expectations that audiences bring to Shakespeare with the expectation of being entertained that audiences bring to the mainstream cinema.

One Foot in Sea and One on Shore ...
When he set out to film *Much Ado About Nothing*, Branagh was very clear that he wanted to make a film audiences would enjoy; he was equally clear that this involved thwarting the expectation that Shakespeare could only be acted in a style of 'incomprehensible booming and fruity-voiced declamation' (Branagh, p. ii). In this respect, Branagh's film is part of a long line of Shakespeare adaptations that use casting as a device to offer their audiences the prospect of Shakespeare without the Shakespeareanisms. Whenever an actor takes on a role, there is always a tension between the character being played that moment, and the actor's past roles; when these spectral past roles are non-Shakespearean, it allows the production to keep, as it were, 'one foot in sea and one on shore'. Consequently, from Max Reinhardt's *A Midsummer Night's Dream* (1935), which cast James Cagney as Bottom, through to Michael Hoffman's version of the same play (1999), with Kevin Kline as Bottom, casting actors with strong screen personae in Shakespearean roles offers one way of balancing the competing pleasures of 'film' and 'Shakespeare'.

While most of the roles in *Much Ado* are played by actors from the Renaissance Theatre Company who are, Branagh writes, relatively young and 'free of actory mannerisms and the baggage of strutting and bellowing that accompanies the least effective

Shakespearean performances' (ix), he also cast a number of Hollywood actors, including Keanu Reeves, Denzel Washington, and Michael Keaton. In the case of each of these American actors, Branagh made use of echoes of their earlier screen appearances to flesh out parts that are undeveloped to begin with, and which Branagh was to cut further in order to speed up the pace of the film. Hence, anyone who had seen Reeves play alienated loners in films such as *River's Edge* (1986), *Point Break* (1991) and *My Own Private Idaho* (1991), could easily accept that he was the sullen outcast Don John in *Much Ado* (although viewers would have to erase the memory of *Bill and Ted's Bogus Journey* [1990]). Similarly, no one would dare doubt that Denzel Washington as Don Pedro was a man of the utmost integrity. After all, audiences had already seen him die for his beliefs at least three times before *Much Ado* opened: as the title character in Spike Lee's *Malcolm X* (1992), as a black Civil War soldier in *Glory* (1989), and earlier as the South African activist Stephen Biko in *Cry Freedom* (1987). Finally, Michael Keaton as Dogberry revives the twitching, manic decrepitude of his supernatural 'exorcist of the living' in Tim Burton's *Beetlejuice* (1988), giving the bumbling Shakespearean clown a dark edge of sadism (and producing the *frisson*-inducing expectation that he will swallow a cockroach, as he does in Burton's film).

Branagh casts American actors with strong screen personae both to differentiate his work from an 'actorly' English tradition and to emphasize that *Much Ado* is as much a film in its own right as it is an adaptation of a Shakespeare play. In this regard, *Much Ado* resembles Branagh's previous Shakespeare film (and his own directorial début), *Henry V* (1989). Branagh's *Henry V* opens with a prologue delivered in an empty film studio, cluttered with cameras, lights, reflectors and miscellaneous paraphernalia of filmmaking. The sequence both sweeps away an earlier stage tradition attached to the play, and acts as a riposte to the film with which it was inevitably compared, Sir Laurence Olivier's *Henry V*, made in 1945. Olivier's film, in contrast, opens with an aerial shot that swoops over a model of Shakespeare's London, before zooming in on the Globe theatre, its flags waving merrily in the breeze from a miniature Thames. For Olivier, the authentic *Henry V* originates on a particular stage at a particular moment in history; the film is, at best, a simulation. For Branagh, on the other hand, the film is not the copy of a distant stage version; it is a work in its own right, created from the materials lying around a film studio. Its original audience is the one watching it in the cinema at the moment of its projection.

To One Thing Constant Never ...

This spectre of an imagined stage original has haunted film versions of Shakespeare since the earliest days of the cinema. The first Shakespeare film, *King John* (1899), shows Sir Herbert Beer-bohm Tree sitting on a throne, waving his arms valiantly in an attempt to convey the sense of an impassioned monologue which, of course, we are unable to hear, since the 'talkies' were still thirty years away. Even where they move beyond this level of futility, however, most early Shakespeare films (and, indeed, many films in general prior to 1915) look like plays because of the way in which they are filmed. In the early days of cinema, this was partly because directors often turned to theatre for their material, and partly because early film equipment was not very flexible. Consequently, the usual way to shoot a film was to set up a camera in front of a scene, so that all of the actors were visible at the same time in either a medium shot or a full shot, and then simply roll the film while the actors did their stuff. From the audience's point of view, watching such a film was not dissimilar from watching a play, in that the apparent distance from the actors remained the same throughout an entire scene.

By about 1915 film-makers such as D.W. Griffith began to realize that they could do things with movie cameras that were impossible in a theatre. For instance, it was possible to place the movie camera either extremely close to a subject (or else use a lens on the camera that made the subject appear close), in what became known as a close-up; or, conversely, move the camera very far away from the subject (or use a lens that made the subject seem farther away), in what became known as a long shot. This meant that an object as small as an eye could fill the screen as fully as the Plains of Montana. Once they began cutting from shot to shot within a scene, film-makers made another discovery. When we watch a play in a theatre, we can only watch the action from one position. In the cinema, however, the camera can be placed anywhere in the action. More importantly, it need not stay in one place; it can be, as it were, 'to one thing constant never', moving around from subject to subject, sometimes up close, sometimes keeping its distance.

Following from this, early film-makers soon found that if you shot an actor looking at a subject, and then set up your camera where the actor had been standing, this second shot will be read by an audience as the actor's (or, more precisely, the character's) view. This means that in the cinema we look through the eyes of another person every time the camera cuts to what is known as a point of view (or P.O.V.) shot. There is something extremely tempting—and extremely coercive—about looking through another's eyes. At the most basic level, if a film-maker wants us to empathize with a character, the film can put us in her position and create a powerful feeling of identification. In a sense, the P.O.V. shot is perhaps closer to a first-person narration (using the pronoun 'I') in prose fiction than to any technique of the stage. We also need to keep in mind, however, that it is not the audience who chooses the eyes through which they are to see the world in a film; it is the film-maker (and to a certain extent the editor). This means that when those eyes happen to belong to Freddy Krueger in *A Nightmare on Elm Street* (1984), or to Norman Bates in *Psycho* (1960), for instance, a number of questions about the ways in which the cinema can manipulate us are brought into focus. Indeed, some of Alfred Hitchcock's films, such as *Vertigo* (1958) and *Rear Window* (1954), are primarily about the strange pleasures associated with watching other people through someone else's eyes, and for this reason many film theorists point to them as purely 'cinematic' films.

Early film-makers were very quick to learn that audiences took pleasure from looking through other people's eyes, and before long the reverse-angle scene, made up primarily of point of view shots, had become a central part of the vocabulary of film-making. In the reverse-angle scene, the camera begins by showing what is known as an establishing shot, which shows two (or more) people talking to each other, usually in a medium shot. The camera then cuts back and forth 180° between shots seen alternately through the eyes of each of the two people who are holding the conversation, so that we see person A through the eyes of person B, and then cut to a view of person B through the eyes of person A, and so on back and forth. The reverse angle scene quickly became so pervasive that it was not confined to fiction films; it remains, for instance, the basic technique used in the television interview and on talk shows.

Even though the reverse-angle scene and the P.O.V. shot are 'unnatural', in that they provide an experience we cannot have outside of the cinema, they are so much a part of the vocabulary of cinema that they have become, in a sense, transparent. We no longer see them; we see through them. This should tell us something very important about the way in which we read a film. When we watch a film that uses these invisible techniques exclusively, our focus is not on the way the film is made (and hence, not on the film itself, as such), but on the film's narrative.

By contrast, when a film like Carol Reed's *The Third Man* (1949) uses frequent Dutch angles and unexpected P.O.V. shots, we become as conscious of the film itself—and hence, in this case, of cinematographer Robert Krasker's camera—as we are of its narrative or subject matter. In other words, if we see an image of a building that we assume to be level, but the building is shot so that it appears to be leaning at a 45° angle, we must conclude that it is the camera which is off-centre. Hence, even though the camera is not visible, we are forced to become aware of it. The same is true of the jump cut, bird's-eye view shot, or other techniques of film-making which either deviate considerably from the way in which we usually perceive the world, or which are used so seldom in cinema that we sit up and take notice when we see them.

Then Sigh Not So …
'Sigh no more, ladies,/ Sigh no more …' When those words scroll across the screen at the beginning of *Much Ado About Nothing*, it might seem that Kenneth Branagh is primarily reminding us that the film originates with Shakespeare's printed word, from which the images spring. However, the passage does something else as well. The words are in fact titles, which are a uniquely cinematic convention. For film-goers of the silent period in the first three decades of the twentieth century, they were so common that they were an invisible convention. For cinema audiences today, however, after more than seven decades of sound film, they remind us with a jolt that we are watching a film.

This impression is reinforced in *Much Ado* by the highly cinematic (and complex) sequence shot, lasting one minute and twenty seconds, immediately following the opening 'Sigh no more' titles.

The shot begins with a full-frame close-up of a painting of a villa, linking it to the titles which have just preceded it. The camera then pulls back to reveal the painting on its easel, and the painter, Leonato (Richard Briers), tracking slowly left to show his subject, the real villa, in the background. Without cutting, the camera then tilts down, before reversing to track right and tilt up, showing us more and more of a leisurely Tuscan picnic, complete with grazing donkey. Throughout these camera movements, we continue to hear Beatrice (Emma Thompson) reading 'Sigh no more', and at this point a number of the actors in shot begin to look in the direction of her voice. The camera follows their gaze, tracking left again, tilting first down, and then up, at which point it 'sees' her sitting in a tree, and begins to zoom from a medium long shot to a moderate close-up. 'This move', wrote Branagh, 'involved the perfect co-ordination of sun, actors, camera track and zoom, cleavage, bare chests, bread slicing, song lyrics and donkey. It took a while' (Branagh, p. 119)—in the end, twenty-nine takes, more than for any other shot in the entire film.

In many ways, this sequence shot encapsulates the relationship to Shakespeare's text for which *Much Ado* is striving. Branagh has often claimed that in his film versions of Shakespeare he has looked for 'spontaneity, freshness and naturalism', so that two characters speaking to one another appear to be really speaking, not simply reciting great speeches. At the same time, he writes in the introduction to the published screenplay of *Much Ado*, 'we must remember that at all times we are speaking the words of a great dramatic poet' (Branagh, p. iv), and it is this quality which can easily be lost, either by casting actors without a background in verse-speaking, or by cutting the text in the interests of pacing. By first showing us the words of 'Sigh no more', and then showing us a shot in which we hear them spoken, but are unable to identify the speaker until the end of the shot, the words themselves appear more important than their content. To put it more simply, we read (and hear) them as poetry, not as dialogue. As soon as we see Beatrice reciting the poem, her delivery becomes increasingly self-conscious and ironic, so that by the end of the shot we are concentrating less on the words themselves and more on her character, on her motivations for speaking the words, and on her possible relationships with the other characters who are listening to her. The sequence thus draws our attention to the language *as language* (and more importantly, as Shakespearean language with its rich metaphorical conceits), before it allows us to think about things like character and plot development, which are the most important values in the classic Hollywood film. In short, the opening few minutes of *Much Ado About Nothing* attempt to find a balance between the competing values of 'Shakespeare' and 'film'.

Of course, Branagh did not need to use twenty-nine takes of a single moving camera shot simply to show us a picnic. He could have cut much more simply from an establishing shot of the group as a whole to a series of medium shots of the more important figures in the group (say, Leonato and Beatrice), with the odd close-up (of the bread or the painting) for detail. Such unobtrusive piecing together of different shots, known as cutting to continuity, is so widely used in film-making that it is one of the most invisible techniques of the classic Hollywood film. In such sequences, the establishing shot shows the viewer the entire *mise-en-scène*, complete with all the characters, their physical relationships to one another, and their environment. This style of editing gives the viewer a feeling of quiet omniscience (much like that conveyed by a third-person narration in prose fiction). We are given the impression that we can see everything we need to see, and consequently we do not worry about who or what is controlling our view. By contrast, at the beginning of *Much Ado*, when Branagh fails to provide us with an establishing shot, instead choosing to reveal one character at a time and withholding the speaker from our sight, he forces his audience to admit that their vision is limited. In other words, he gives us a shot that looks like a point of view shot; but we are not told through whose eyes we are seeing.

Denied a point of identification from within the film, we are forced to identify (at least provisionally) with the one thing we know to be looking at the picnic: the camera (and, of course, the director). This means that the opening sequence shot of *Much Ado* makes us aware of the film *as film*. The opening of his *Henry V* tries to remind us of the same thing, although in a very different way. In *Henry V*, we are shown the tools of film-making, but we see them from a slight distance, as the camera tracks smoothly and unobtrusively through reflectors and unpainted props. In *Much Ado*, by contrast, the movements of the camera—gently tracking back and forth and tilting—mimic the motions of a human eye (in a way that would not happen, for instance, had the camera swooped down through the olive trees). It roves lazily (as befits a shot of a lazy, mid-afternoon picnic) from one person to another, lingering for a moment on a face or a piece of bread, before wandering across the frame to locate the voice just out of view to the left. In other words, because the shot works like a point of view shot, our provisional identification with the camera must be balanced with another provisional hypothesis: that there is an as-yet unseen character watching the picnic, and it is through his/her eyes that we are seeing. With no other information available concerning the character's identity, we as viewers become this missing character, not sitting in a cinema, but watching from a hillside somewhere in Tuscany. We become, for a moment, guests at the picnic, even though we will never see ourselves on the screen.

Converting All Your Sounds of Woe ...

When it was first performed, probably at the Curtain Theatre late in 1598, *Much Ado About Nothing* did not begin with Beatrice reading 'Sigh no more'. Indeed, for most of the play's four-hundred-year production history, 'Sigh no more' has been sung by a solo male tenor (with occasional choral support, particularly in the nineteenth century) at the point where it appears in the script: near the middle of the play, in act II, scene iii. The First Folio edition of the play (1623) opens not with a song, but with Leonato's far more functional announcement, 'I learn in this letter, that Don Pedro of Arragon comes this night to Messina'—thereby both setting up the events that kick the plot into action, and telling the audience that the bare stage they are watching is supposed to be somewhere in Italy. Branagh's reshaping of the script to open with the song owes a hidden debt, in part, to a stage tradition of beginning the play with a scene of languor preceding the arrival of the letter. John Gielgud's productions of the play, for instance, in the late 1940s and 1950s, began with Beatrice and Hero playing the lute; similarly, in a 1956 Old Vic production, the curtain opened on Leonato and Hero playing backgammon, while Beatrice lay on a chaise-longue, her face covered with a straw hat (Cox, p. 87). In other words, for all its assertion of its own cinematic qualities, Branagh's film is not entirely divorced from the play's stage history.

At the same time, just as Branagh uses the song in the film's opening sequence to signal an unabashedly cinematic moment, he repeats it twice more for the same purpose, once in the middle of the film, and again just before the closing credits. The second time the song is used, it is sung, again on a leisurely afternoon, as a group of characters lounge around a large fountain. And, once again, Branagh uses a virtuoso sequence shot both to remind us that we are watching a film, and to suggest that we are a character in the film, seeing events as if they were happening around us. In this case, he uses a steadicam shot, and as the song is sung by a visible group of musicians, we complete a full circuit of the fountain, beginning with a seated Don Pedro, leisurely panning left and right as we move, before we wind up back where we started. The importance of this shot in the film as a whole does not become apparent until the film's final moments, when the song strikes up again, this time with a full, extradiegetic orchestral and choral accompaniment. Branagh again shoots the sequence with a steadicam, which this time weaves and winds its way through a dancing group of wedding guests, who cross left and right in front of the moving camera; the camera then backs onto a hidden crane, and floats up ninety feet into the sky, transforming an eye-level shot into a bird's-eye view shot, so that the film ends with an aerial shot of ordered gardens and swirling dancers. Like the opening shot, this 'took a while'—more than eight hours of shooting and nineteen takes to produce two and a half minutes of film.

In this complex final sequence shot, we finally see the reasons for introducing 'Sigh no more' sequence shots in the beginning and middle of the film. Shakespearean comedy characteristically begins with a world whose order is about to be disrupted ('I learn in this letter that Don Pedro of Arragon comes this night to Messina'); there then follows a period of chaos (when Branagh's character, Benedick, hears the song sung around the fountain, he snaps: 'An' he had been a dog that should have howled thus, they would have hanged him! [Branagh, p. 41]'). Finally, at the end of the comedy, there is the establishment of a new, more stable order, usually signalled by at least one marriage. Moving from a world at peace with itself (as in the film's opening shot), to a point of break-down (witness the strange camera angles and dark shadows which accompany almost all of Michael Keaton's appearances as Dogberry), Branagh's *Much Ado About Nothing* concludes with a utopian cinematic image of a new order in which all wrongs are resolved in harmony. As we move further and further away from the smiles and confetti, the image on the screen becomes a series of perfect geometric patterns, the straight lines of the hedges containing the swirling circles of the dancers. As in the opening shot, we are reminded of the camera, whose movement gives us a form of aesthetic distance from the film so that we regard it as an art object in its own right. At the same time, this is balanced once again by the fantasy that we are in the film, watching the wedding as if through the eyes of an unseen guest. This time, however, our character has wings, for we have the ability to transcend the setting—'transcend' in both the literal sense ('to pass over or go beyond an obstacle') and in the theological and aesthetic senses ('to be above and independent of'). The final shot of *Much Ado About Nothing* thus makes us feel, at least for that moment, that it is possible to do precisely as the song promised us at the beginning of the film: 'Convert all your sounds of woe,/ Into Hey nonny, nonny'.

Bibliography

Kenneth Branagh, *Much Ado About Nothing by William Shakespeare: Screenplay, Introduction and Notes on the Making of the Movie* (London: W.W. Norton, 1993).

John F. Cox (ed.), *Much Ado About Nothing* by William Shakespeare. Shakespeare in Production Series (Cambridge: Cambridge University Press, 1997).

Recommended Reading

The key text for studying Branagh's *Much Ado About Nothing* is his edition of the screenplay, which contains a good set of production photos. At the time of writing, there were plans to release the film on DVD, incorporating these and other production stills as part of the package. Cox's book provides a line-by-line stage and film history of the play from the original 1598 production up to, and including, Branagh's, making it possible to compare how any one scene was played over time. There is increasing interest in Shakespeare on film, with books by Anthony Davies (*Filming Shakespeare's Plays* [Cambridge: Cambridge University Press, 1988]), Peter S. Donaldson (*Shakespearean Films/Shakespearean Directors* [Boston: Unwin Hyman, 1990]), and others. As regards the wider issue of studying film, there are many textbooks which explain how to read a film. One of the best is: William H. Phillips, *Film: An Introduction* (Boston: Bedford and St Martin's, 1999). Microsoft's *Cinemania* also contains good explanations of film terms, some of which include illustrative video clips.

Film Form, Narrative and Genre

GERARDINE MEANEY

At its inception at the end of the nineteenth century, film was heavily influenced by existing narrative forms, particularly theatre and the novel. It continues to share with both of these forms a common repertoire of stories and story-telling devices. Film is nonetheless a distinct medium, with a very different relation to reality.[1] Film narrative differs from other narrative modes, in its peculiar plausibility which derives from the mechanical repro-duction of 'real' people, places and actions. The development of film narrative is also much more overtly linked to technological, industrial and economic developments than the development of other art forms.

Reality and Form

The realism of the cinema follows directly from its photographic nature ... The objective nature of photography confers on it a quality of credi-bility absent from all other picture making ... we are forced to accept as real the existence of the object reproduced, actually as re-presented in space and time.[2]

As Bazin points out, film shares with (and indeed developed from) photography a physical relationship with that which it represents which is distinct from both the immediacy of theatre and the linguistic representational mode of the novel. The importance of this relationship has been much debated by filmmakers and film critics throughout the twentieth century. It was crucial to the initial claims made for film as an art form. Some early filmmakers and critics stressed the potential of film to be a truly 'objective' art with a privileged relation of authenticity and urgency in depicting real life. Others strenuously argued that film should move beyond both realism and its own mechanical and physical qualities. Direction and cinematography, in particular, create effects through, for example, the use of camera angles (high, low, level) or framing (e.g. close-up) which show us a picture, but show it from a particular point-of-view. 'Special effects', producing a cinematic world which exceeds or contradicts reality, are not a recent technique, but date from the earliest days of film-making: the pioneer film-maker George Melies produced a whole range of 'trick films', science fiction and fantastic shorts, including *La Lune à un Mètre* (1898, *The Astronomer's Dream*) where the moon descends from the sky and swallows an ageing astronomer.

The Persistent Trick of Vision: Space and Place
Much more fundamental than cinema's ability to create places we know we can never be is its ability to represent space and places in ways to which our eyes respond as they would to real spaces and places. What is the mechanism by which we experience a flat image on a two-dimensional screen as a three-dimensional object in space?

The answer to this is less physical and technical than cultural and historical. Since the Renaissance, Western art forms have relied heavily on perspective as an organizing principle for pictorial composition and as a mode of representing a three dimen-

sional scene in two dimensions in such a way that it is apprehended visually in three dimensions. Such a perspective is crucial
to the emergence of a naturalistic art which renders the three
dimensions of space, height and depth and for which verisimilitude is consequently an attainable aim. Techniques of perspective
self-consciously manipulate the relationship between our position
as spectator and the two-dimensional flat surface we view.
Leonardo Da Vinci described the process thus:

Perspective is nothing else than seeing a place (or objects) behind a pane
of glass, quite transparent, on the surface of which the objects behind that
glass are drawn. These can be traced in pyramids to the point in the eye,
and these pyramids are intersected on the glass pane.[3]

The picture is organized in relation to the eye and the eye orga-
nizes what it sees around its own centrality. In 1981, Stephen
Heath published a very significant account of the relationship
between this 'quattrocento' system and spectatorship in film, in
an article entitled 'Narrative Space'.[4] Heath argued that 'the concept of the quattrocento system is that of scenographic space,
space set out as spectacle for the eye of the spectator. Eye and
knowledge come together … '[5] In effect, the screen becomes an
illusory window frame through which we see the world of the
film. The frame is not neutral, however. We do not see, we are
shown; and the position of the camera, the use of close-up,
medium or long shots and lighting are all narrative devices,
investing what we see with significance.

Time and Narrative
One of the great innovators and theorists of early cinema, Sergei
Eisenstein, argued that in film

each sequential element is arrayed, not *next* to the one it follows, but on
top of it. *For*: the idea (sensation) of movement arises in the process of
superimposing on the retained impression of the object's first position the
object's newly visible second position.[6]

The cinematic technique which he derived to exploit this was *montage*, which creates meaning through the juxtaposition of shots, generating meaning from complex images rather than linear narrative. The most famous and powerful example of montage in Eisenstein's own work is the Odessa steps sequence in *Battleship Potemkin* (1925). Montage in a more muted form has become an important component of mainstream cinematic narrative techniques, offering the opportunity to crosscut simultaneous events or to denote the passage of time.

Film spatializes the temporal. It does so not only through montage, but also through a whole range of commonplace, ordinary and now scarcely noticeable devices. The impression of the passing of time is created by the manner in which images on screen are juxtaposed. The evolution of continuity editing techniques was crucial to the development of feature-length, complex narratives as the primary mode of filmmaking. Technically, film is composed from millions of stills, projected so rapidly that the eye sees movement on the screen, not in the projection. This combination and juxtaposition of images is responsible for more than the impression of movement, however: it is crucial to the cinematic construction of time and place.

Classical Hollywood narrative technique, which remains dominant, depended on continuity editing for verisimilitude and transparency. In other words it perfected a technique of editing that was invisible, reinforcing the sense of the screen as an open window into another world, drawing attention away from the constructedness of that world.

Until the recent advent of digital editing techniques, film editors cut and spliced film stock to compose scenes. Shots taken on location, close-ups shot in studios, and long, panning, establishing shots of cities scarcely visited by the cast were combined in the cutting room to make a coherent whole. Moreover, editing was crucial in effecting the seamless transition whereby days, weeks and even years of 'screen time' or narrative time could be experienced in one hour and forty-five minutes of 'real time'.

In contrast to straightforward continuity editing, montage sequences often juxtapose locations, characters and plot developments for symbolic purposes. For example in the closing minutes of *Michael Collins* (1996), the scene of the ambush at Béal na Bláth is intercut with Kitty Kiernan shopping and trying on wedding dresses in Dublin. The use of continuity on the soundtrack is often used in this context to emphasize that the events shown are simultaneous; this function is fulfilled in this instance by Sinead O'Connor singing 'She Moves Through the Fair'. The conjunction of elements in this specific example also invokes an older tradition of representing Ireland in allegorical terms as a bride whose rightful lover never comes to claim her.

Film Genre and Social Change

Film genre was not really studied seriously until the last two decades. Previously genre films were considered as the opposite of good films, with those genre movies which were undeniably classics, like *The Big Sleep* (1946) or *Stagecoach* (1939), praised for the extent to which they managed to transcend genre conventions. A less value-laden analysis of genre is a more recent phenomenon. It owes a considerable debt to anthropology, to the study of mythic and narrative paradigms in culture and to structuralism. The most influential current film theorists, like Thomas Schatz, argue that genre is a narrative system that can be analyzed according to its fundamental structural components. These components vary, but the fundamental ones are:

- plot
- character
- setting
- thematics
- style

Not all films in a genre will have every one of these elements in common, but they will share some. For example, Westerns vary enormously in style and the themes have changed considerably over the years, but all have a basic setting and related plot elements in common; action movies share a particular visual style; and romances have the most consistent plot structure of all genres.

According to Schatz, a genre is a contract of expectations between filmmakers and the audience.[7] Genres work by satisfying their audiences' appetite for recognizable and consistent stories, but they must also have the ability to renew themselves. Without surprise, suspense and adaptation to changing social mores, genre films become either anachronistic or boring. They therefore walk a tightrope between static and dynamic components. They depend upon a relatively unchanging formula of interrelated narrative and cinematic components and often re-examine a basic cultural conflict (for example, the relationship between the individual and society in the Western). However, genres survive only if they are also flexible, adapting to changes in cultural attitudes as well as being responsive to the economics of the film industry.

Genre Example 1: Science Fiction
Science fiction is an excellent example for the purposes of introducing concepts of genre to a young audience, because they are familiar with it and because it is one of the most clearly marked and easily defined of genres. Many contemporary films are genre hybrids, combining, for example, elements of the romantic comedy and the thriller, as in *Out of Sight* (1998). Science fiction is unusually dominant in such combinations, however. Even if a film is concerned with a romance or a mystery set on another planet, on a spaceship or in the future, the film will be classified and understood as science fiction.

Science fiction narratives are structured by the relationship

between two basic narrative devices that define the genre, alienation and cognition. Alienation (sometimes rendered as estrange-
ment) is a critical term derived from Brecht's theories of drama
and describes a technique which actively seeks to prevent identification with characters and situations and places its emphasis on
analysis and criticism. Cognition is the process by which audiences orient themselves in the alien environment of the science
fiction narrative by identifying familiar situations and recognizable characters. It gives the audience a frame of reference to work
with and a point of identification within the narrative. Usually,
but not always, these familiar elements, characters or forms are
there in order to be put into question.

Alienation provides a quasi-scientific or futuristic context in
which the unexpected is plausible, part of the film's 'reality' which
may cast light on our own reality. For example, the central narrative concern in Ridley Scott's *Blade Runner* (1982) is the instability of the boundary between human and android (this is
reinforced in the 'Director's Cut', which is now the version most
widely available on video). This strange problem allows the film
to pose questions about the appropriate relationship between the
artificial and the natural, the commercial and the social. It further
allows it to ask more fundamental questions about what it means
to be human without becoming alarmingly metaphysical. This
process is facilitated by the presence of a recognizable hero, complete with a raincoat and attitude inherited from the Marlowe of
Chandler's novels and of *The Big Sleep*, who acts as point of identification and guarantor that the narrative will, ultimately, make
some kind of sense.

Cognition is not simply a device of reassurance, however.
Familiar elements are there to be made strange, for example, the
noir romance in *Blade Runner*, maternity in *Aliens* (1986), sibling
rivalry in *Gattaca* (1997). Alienation in science fiction is therefore
the unfamiliar or exotic context which allows the recognizable,

familiar 'cognitive' element to be presented and seen in a new light and so made available for questioning.

Darko Suvin and Robert Scholes were key figures in developing this form of analysis of science fiction (both preferred the term 'speculative fiction'). The interaction of alienation and cognition that characterizes science fiction constitutes a speculative mode. It elaborates an hypothesis from a given premise, asking 'what if this were so?' For example, *Gattaca* asks 'What if genetic analysis were taken to one particular and extreme, but logical conclusion?' A work of speculative fiction calls into question some aspect of our commonly held assumptions; thus it could be argued that the category would exclude *Star Wars*, which conforms quite deliberately to previously established mythic and narrative paradigms.

The originary text for the genre of speculative fiction is Mary Shelley's *Frankenstein* (1818). Working partly within the established narrative conventions of Gothic fiction, it also established a new genre where the narrative adopts a speculative relation to science, asking 'What if' contemporary scientific developments were to proceed to an extreme or unexpected conclusion. *Frankenstein* also laid the foundations for this new genre as a forum of social and philosophical analysis, questioning as it did the Enlightenment emphasis on rationality and progress. In the process, Shelley's novel generated a metaphor for the monsters created by science which would powerfully seize the popular imagination for two centuries.

Though the novel has been adapted, misappropriated, reinterpreted and exploited in a myriad of twentieth-century adaptations, *Blade Runner* is its most influential contemporary offshoot. Both *Frankenstein* and *Blade Runner* are centrally concerned with what it means to be human in the context of the denigration of the natural, physical and maternal and the valorization of the technical, metaphysical and patriarchal. Both were produced at times of great ecological anxiety. Both are said to epitomize the fundamental uncertainty of their time about human identity.

Genre Example 2: Film Noir

Unlike science fiction, which is defined by a clearly identifiable narrative structure, film noir has often been described not as a genre, but as a style. It too has novelistic origins, in the 'hard-boiled' detective fiction of Chandler and Hammett. As its name insists, however, film noir is a fundamentally cinematic mutation, which draws plots from detective fiction and melodrama, but is defined by visual effect, not necessarily by plot devices. The look of film noir is unmistakable. The 'chiaroscuro' effect, in which shadows are used to depict the dark side of human experiences, is characteristic (see the still from *The Third Man*, overleaf). Low-key lighting effects, use of claustrophobic interiors and rainy, dark, menacing exteriors, extreme close-up and high angled shots juxtaposed to maintain a sense of unease and tension—all of the above give to this group of B movies a visual style that has had a powerful influence on contemporary cinema.

The term 'film noir' was coined by French film critics who were the first to argue that, far from being a perverse and decadent deviation from cinematic standards, these films constituted a powerful artistic achievement. The genre is usually defined as beginning with *The Maltese Falcon* in 1941 and ending on a high note with *Touch of Evil* in 1958, but noir elements continued to surface in films like *Klute* (1971), and the 1980s and '90s have seen a wholesale revival of the genre, notably in *Body Heat* (1981), *The Last Seduction* (1993), and *The Usual Suspects* (1995). *Payback* (1999), the recent remake of *Point Blank*, achieved an effective reproduction of the visual effects of film noir, which are usually diluted by the use of colour. John Boorman's *The General* (1998) uses black and white to extraordinary effect, adapting noir conventions to a

Chiaroscuro in The Third Man *(courtesy British Film Institute)*

portrayal of Dublin in the 1980s. In the last instance, the use of film noir's visual techniques is very much part of the narrative strategy, suggesting as it does a social context of corruption and moral ambiguity.

Critics have extensively debated the historical context in which film noir developed its distinctive style and thematics. A

range of factors has been identified as contributing to its emergence: post-war disillusion and cynicism; the influence of existentialist and psychoanalytic thinking during this period; a crisis
in gender identity with men returning to civilian roles and
women pushed back out of the work force; the onset of the Cold
War; and the influence of immigrant directors, particularly given
the genre's undoubted debt to the German Expressionist movement. Like most Hollywood genres, film noir had both an
international origin and an international influence.

The Third Man

In *The Third Man* (1949), the British director Carol Reed combined many of the stylistic and thematic features outlined above
in the untypical setting of post-war Vienna. In many respects the
film itself offers an account of the historical triggers for film noir's
dark aesthetics. The American author Holly, in seeking to resolve
the mystery of his friend Harry Lime's disappearance, must confront a world in direct contradiction to the optimistic fantasies
from which he makes a living. Holly writes popular Westerns.
The dark interiors of film noir have often been contrasted with
the open spaces of the traditional Western. *The Third Man* in
effect inverts both the geography and philosophy of the Western.
At the outset, Holly has journeyed east from the open frontier of
the imaginary West, to the new frontier against which America
will define itself. He encounters there a ruined urban claustro-
phobia where even the lives of sick children are commodities and
the manoeuvring of the erstwhile allies for strategic dominance
moves people from 'zone' to zone, like chess pieces on a board. In
this environment, the cowboy is only a nuisance and, while his
journey has educated him, he has learned not only that the world
is darker than he knew, but that evil may be more attractive than
good (Harry's former lover, Anna, rejects Holly and persists in her
grief for the morally worthless but charismatic Harry). The film

concludes, not with the hero riding off into the western sunset, but with his gazing wistfully after her indifferent retreat to the east.

Unusually, however, the central enigma, the puzzle to be solved which is always at the heart of film noir, is not a *femme fatale*, a fatally attractive and dangerous woman, but an attractive and dangerous man, Harry Lime. It is through his investigation into the nature of Harry that Holly develops: the similarity of names implies they are two sides of the same coin, each realizing aspects of himself, in post-war Europe, that were unimaginable when they were old friends 'back home'. Lime's famous 'cuckoo clock' speech about the productive capacity of chaos and destruction is very close to the heart of film noir's fascination with the nature of evil. The setting of *The Third Man* reminds us that the context for that preoccupation was very specifically one of post-war destruction. A ruined domain of ordinariness frames film noir's adventure into the shadows. Harry Lime's ultimate predecessor is Milton's Satan, who gets all of the best lines. Holly, lacking the vitality which goes underground and into the shadows with his friend, can offer no heroic alternative. Powerless and rejected, he typifies film noir's pessimism about the viability of the old narrow codes by which he longs to live.

Classroom exercise 1: *Michael Collins*
- Ask students to identify each shot in the montage discussed above, counting the number of shots in each action sequence at Béal na Bláth and comparing it to the number of shots in the Dublin scene.
- What are the dominant colours in each location? Is colour used to create contrast or continuity? In what way?
- What is the role of the soundtrack in establishing a relation between the two scenes?

Classroom exercise 2: Genre
- Ask students to identify three contemporary popular genres, then three films or television programmes within each genre.
- Identify common elements in each group of three under the headings listed below:

  1. plot
  2. character
  3. setting
  4. thematics
  5. style

Classroom exercise 3: Genre II
- Returning to your examples from exercise 2, ask students to identify the ways in which each of the films in each group conforms to and differs from the norms of its genre.
- Are they satisfied that each honours the genre 'contract'? If so, why? If not, why?
- To what extent is their satisfaction dependent on the films' endings?
- Can they identify ways in which the films reflect the social attitudes of their time?

Classroom exercise 4: Science Fiction Genre
- Ask students to identify elements within a science fiction film or television series with which they are familiar, which are alien or strange, then elements which are recognizable or familiar.
- Ask them to identify the relationship between these two elements.
- Have these films or programmes made them question their usual assumptions about any given topic? How?

Classroom exercise 5: What if … ?
- Ask students to return to the examples they took for exercise 4 and examine whether they are speculative fictions.
- Examine the way in which these examples deal with time and plausibility. Are they set in the future? How is this established? Do they present alien or strange events occurring in the present?
- Classroom debate: is *Star Wars Episode One* speculative or merely science fiction?

Classroom exercise 6: Comparative study of *Frankenstein* and *Blade Runner*

• Compare *Frankenstein*'s monster with *Blade Runner*'s androids.
• To what extent can either the novel or film be read as an ecological parable?
• Consider the significance of a sense of the past and of an origin in both film and novel. How significant is the absence of 'real' mothers for the monster and the androids in this regard?

Classroom exercise 7: *The Third Man*

• Can you identify the following elements in *The Third Man*?
  – low-key lighting effects
  – use of shadows
  – use of claustrophobic interiors
  – menacing exteriors
  – extreme close-up
  – high angled shots
  – ambiguous characterization

Further Reading

Jill Nelmes (ed.), *An Introduction to Film Studies* (1996; second edition London: Routledge, 1999). A very good introduction to film studies, lively, accessible and comprehensive. Originally aimed at A-level and first-year university students, the second edition also operates as a handbook for teachers, with a wide range of case studies and suggestions for further viewing and reading.

John Hill and Pamela Church Gibson (eds), *The Oxford Guide to Film Studies* (Oxford: Oxford University Press, 1998). This provides a more advanced introduction, with a very broad range of essays. While most of these are eminently readable as critical essays, the volume is most useful as a reference work.

Susan Hayward, *Key Concepts in Cinema Studies* (1996; second edition, London: Routledge, 1998). This is more than a glossary of technical and critical terminology. Concepts and approaches to film studies are outlined. A very useful reference work.

Leo Braudy and Marshall Cohen (eds), *Film Theory and Criticism: Introductory Readings* (1974; fifth edition, New York: Oxford University

Press, 1999). Regularly revised since 1974, Braudy and Cohen's anthology offers an overview of thinking about film as a medium, its relation to other cultural forms and its place in society over the course of the twentieth century. Despite the title description as introductory, this material assumes a good deal of knowledge and represents a more advanced level than the other three texts outlined above. It includes material from Bazin, Eisenstein and Schatz, cited above.

Notes

1. I am distinguishing here between 'reality', the world we experience, and 'realism', the aspiration of art to represent that world and that experience as accurately as possible. The relationship between these two is not straightforward: our experiences differ, the reality we know may not be the reality of our neighbour. Narrative realism is ultimately an aesthetic goal bounded by the conventions of plausibility on the one hand and the 'beginning, middle, end' structure which storytelling imposes on the other. Both the concepts of reality and realism have changed over time and it is worth remembering that a narrative which seems the epitome of harsh realism in one context can seem sentimental and artificial in another era (*Oliver Twist* is a classic case in point).

2. André Bazin, 'Theatre and cinema', in Braudy and Cohen (eds), *Film Theory and Criticism: Introductory Readings*, p. 416.

3. Cited in J.P. Richter (ed.), *The Literary Works of Leonardo Da Vinci* (London: Oxford University Press, 1939), vol. I, p. 150.

4. Stephen Heath, 'Narrative space', *Screen* 17, 3 (1976), pp. 19-75; reprinted in Philip Rosen (ed.), *Narrative, Apparatus, Ideology* (New York: Columbia University Press, 1986), pp. 379-420.

5. Heath, 'Narrative Space', in Rosen, *Narrative, Apparatus, Ideology*, p. 387.

6. Sergei Eisenstein, 'The dramaturgy of film form', in Braudy and Cohen (eds), *Film Theory and Criticism: Introductory Readings*, p. 29.

7. Thomas Schatz, 'Film genre and the genre film', in Braudy and Cohen (eds), *Film Theory and Criticism: Introductory Readings*, p. 642-53.

Glossary of Film Terms

aerial shot: A shot taken using an aircraft or crane. Usually an extreme long shot [*q.v.*].

bird's-eye-view shot: A shot taken from a camera that is directly above its subject, and is pointing downward.

classic narrative cinema: A style of film characterized by a concentration on a single character (or small group of characters), a cause-and-effect narrative, relatively transparent cinematography and a resolution in which all of the film's questions are answered. Its conventions were consolidated in Hollywood in the 1930s.

close-up: A shot in which the object (e.g., the human face) is detailed and large in scale; this shot can be achieved by positioning the camera very close to the subject or by using a zoom lens.

cutting: A 'cut' occurs when a shot begins and again when it ends. 'Cutting' is sometimes used as synonym for editing or montage, which is the combining of two or more shots [*q.v.*].

cutting to continuity: also termed 'continuity editing' or 'invisible editing'. A style of editing in which time and space are invisibly condensed by avoiding jump cuts [*q.v.*] or unexpected camera angles. This style ensures that the smooth flow of the narrative is maintained and the mechanical process of editing remains unobtrusive.

diegetic sound: Sound that arises from a visible element in the shot, such as Balthasar's singing of 'Sigh no more' in *Much Ado About Nothing* or Sam's piano playing at Rick's Café in *Casablanca*.

Dutch angle: see 'oblique angle' [*q.v.*]

establishing shot: A shot at the beginning of a scene, showing all of the characters, their physical relationship to each other, and their setting. Usually a long or medium-long shot.

extradiegetic sound: Sound that does not arise from a visible element in the shot (e.g., voiceover, or music on an accompanying soundtrack); compare with 'diegetic' sound [*q.v.*].

film noir: a film genre, or film style, with distinctive visual effects including characters cast in shadows, claustrophobic interiors and dark menacing exteriors. These effects are generated by low key lighting, extreme close-up and high angled shots, juxtaposed to maintain a sense of unease and tension. The plots of film noir are drawn from melodrama and detective fiction, chiefly the fiction of Chandler, Cain and Hammett.

frame: A frame is one distinctive image or picture in a strip of film. Cinematic images are both recorded and projected at a rate of twenty-four frames per second to create the illusion of movement. Frame may also refer to the rectangular shape of the cinema or television screen.

full shot: A shot which shows a full human figure. Often the standard shot in martial arts or dance films, where the actor's feet and face are equally important.

genre: A French term meaning 'type' or 'kind'. Films that share common features, themes, narrative conventions, etc., are grouped together and identified as a distinctive *type* or *genre*. Examples of film genres are the western, the musical, film noir and action-adventure.

jump cut: A transition between two shots where the shots involved are far removed from each other in time and/or space.

The jump cut purposefully calls attention to the artifice of cinema by creating a dislocation in space and/or time.

long shot: A shot in which both the full figure and much of the surrounding setting is visible (more than is the case in a full shot [q.v.]). If the figure is only a small element in the composition (e.g., a landscape), it is called an 'extreme long shot'.

medium shot: A shot beween a long shot and close-up shot; for example, a medium shot may show a human subject from the waist up, or approximately what you would see of a person while having a conversation. A tighter version is the self-explanatory 'head and shoulders' shot.

mise-en-scène: Literally, 'putting in the scene'; the arrangement of the set, the direction of the actors, and camera placement; in short, all of the elements which go towards creating a shot prior to editing.

montage: A cinematic techique which creates meaning through the juxtaposition of shots, most famously exemplified by the work of Sergei Eisenstein, who wrote extensively on the subject, drawing many analogies to literary technique.

narrative: The way in which a story is told. In film, story information is communicated in many ways: through formal elements such as editing, lighting, type of shot, music, etc. These elements become narrative agents.

oblique angle: A shot in which the camera is not level. Sometimes called a 'tilt shot' or 'Dutch angle'. Often used to show disorientation.

panning: A movement of the camera lens horizontally, rather than vertically as in 'tilt' [q.v.].

point of view [P.O.V.] shot: A shot which shows the viewer what a particular character is seeing.

pull back: A shot in which the focal length of the lens decreases, making the subject fill less of the screen, and revealing more of the setting. See 'zoom'.

reverse angle scene: see 'shot-reverse-shot sequence' [*q.v.*].

scene: A group of consecutive shots edited together to form a continuous unit, usually with narrative or thematic unity.

sequence: A group of consecutive scenes edited together to form a continuous unit, usually with narrative or thematic unity.

sequence shot: A single shot which by itself makes up a complete sequence (or scene); usually involves a number of camera moves (or movements by actors within the frame).

shot: The basic compositional unit of film-making. A shot lasts from cut to cut [*q.v.*] and is a continuous length of film.

shot-reverse-shot sequence: also called 'reverse angle scene'. A scene made up of alternating shots involving the points of view of two or more characters. Usually begins with an establishing shot.

steadicam: A camera which is strapped to the operator via a device which dampens shocks caused by movement. Produces a characteristic floating effect which is distinct from the jolting motion of a conventional hand-held camera.

tilt: A movement of the camera lens vertically. Horizontal movement is called 'panning' [*q.v.*]. Only the camera lens moves in panning, tilting or zooming [*q.v.*]. Compare with 'tracking' [*q.v.*].

tracking: A movement of the entire camera along the ground, either parallel to the subject, or away from (or closer to) the subject. In the latter case, the effect is similar to a zoom shot [*q.v.*]. The camera often runs on small rails to make movement smoother (hence the term).

zoom: When a camera 'zooms in', the focal length of the lens increases, making the subject fill more of the frame, even though the camera itself does not move. When the focal length decreases, or 'zooms out', the subject fills less of the frame; see 'pull back' [*q.v.*].

Notes on Contributors

CONRAD BRUNSTRÖM lectures in the English department at NUI Maynooth. He has published on Thomas Sheridan the younger and James Beattie, and is currently preparing a full-length study of William Cowper. In addition to 'the long eighteenth century', research interests include modern British and American poetry.

PATRICK BURKE lectures in the Department of English at St Patrick's College, Drumcondra, where he is also director of its MA in Theatre Studies. He is a member of the National Committee of ATE and has published extensively on Irish drama and Shakespeare on film.

JOE CLEARY lectures in the English department at NUI Maynooth. Recent publications include articles on contemporary film, drama and fiction, as well as the development of postcolonial studies in Ireland. He is currently completing a book on partition and literature in Ireland, Israel and Palestine, to be published in 2001.

LUCY COLLINS lectures in the Department of English at University College Dublin. She has published on twentieth-century Irish poetry, including the work of Austin Clarke, and on contemporary Irish women poets. Research interests also include American poetry of the fifties and sixties.

BRIAN COSGROVE is Professor of English and Head of Department at NUI Maynooth. His published works include *Wordsworth and the Poetry of Self-Sufficiency* (1982) and numerous articles on modern Irish writing, including the work of Yeats, Joyce, Brian Moore and Seamus Heaney.

PETER DENMAN is Senior Lecturer in English at NUI Maynooth. He has published articles on contemporary Irish poetry and nineteenth-century Irish writing, and is a former editor of *Poetry Ireland Review.*

JOHN DEVITT is Head of the English department at Mater Dei Institute of Education, where he also lectures on English methodologies. He is a member of the National Committee of ATE. Recent publications include essays on Yeats and Kavanagh, on Irish drama, and on the teaching of writing in second-level schools.

RICHARD HAYES lectures in the English department at Mater Dei Institute of Education. He is co-editor of *Fearful Realities: New Perspectives on the Irish Famine* (with Chris Morash, 1996) and has also written on Irish occult writing of the nineteenth century and modern Irish poetry.

PAUL HOLLYWOOD lectures in the English department at NUI Maynooth and LSB College, Dublin. Previous publications include articles on Joseph Conrad, Henry James and Shakespeare.

MARGARET KELLEHER lectures in the English Department at NUI Maynooth. She is the author of *The Feminization of Famine* (1997) and has also written on nineteenth-century fiction and on Irish women's writings.

GERARDINE MEANEY is the Director of the Centre for Film Studies at University College Dublin. She is the author of *(Un) Like Subjects: Women, Theory, Fiction* (1993) and an editor of the forthcoming *Field Day Anthology of Irish Women's Writing.*

CHRIS MORASH is Senior Lecturer in English at NUI Maynooth. He is the author of *Writing the Irish Famine* (1995) and numerous articles on various aspects of Irish cultural history. He is currently completing a history of the Irish theatre from the year 1600 to the present, to be published in October 2001.

EMER NOLAN lectures in the English department at NUI Maynooth. She is the author of *Joyce and Nationalism* (1995) and essays on Irish literature and postcolonialism.

SARAH SMITH is currently reading for a PhD in film studies at the Department of Theatre, Film and TV of the University of Glasgow, where she also teaches. She worked for Film Institute Ireland from 1995 to 1997, and is the author of two study guides produced by FII, on *Into the West* (with Sean Conlon) and *Edward Scissorhands.*